The Stock Options Book

Seventh Edition

The Stock Options Book

Seventh Edition

Alisa J. Baker

The National Center for Employee Ownership
Oakland, California

This publication is designed to provide accurate and authoritative information regarding the subject matter covered. It is sold with the understanding that the publisher is not engaged in rendering legal, accounting, or other professional services. If legal advice or other expert assistance is required, the services of a competent professional should be sought.

Legal, accounting, and other rules affecting business often change. Before making decisions based on the information you find here or in any publication from any publisher, you should ascertain what changes might have occurred and what changes might be forthcoming. The NCEO's Web site (including the members-only area) and newsletter for members provide regular updates on these changes. If you have any questions or concerns about a particular issue, check with your professional advisor or, if you are an NCEO member, call or email us.

The Stock Options Book • Seventh Edition
Alisa J. Baker
Edited by Pam Chernoff
Book design by Scott S. Rodrick

The National Center for Employee Ownership
1736 Franklin Street, 8th Floor
Oakland, CA 94612
(510) 208-1300 • (510) 272-9510 (fax)
E-mail: *nceo@nceo.org* • Web: *www.nceo.org*

First printed May 1997
Reprinted with additions and corrections, January 1998, June 1998
Second edition, February 1999
Third edition, July 1999
Third edition, revised, December 1999
Fourth edition, June 2001
Fifth edition, October 2002
Sixth edition, January 2004
Seventh edition, January 2006; reprinted October 2006

ISBN: 1-932924-19-1

Contents

Part II:
Special Issues: The Changing Landscape

Appendixes

Preface

2006 brings the seventh edition of *The Stock Options Book,* which was first put it into its current form in 2002. As with each of the preceding four years, 2005 saw significant changes to the rules affecting executive compensation in general and equity compensation in particular. Under the invaluable editorial guidance of Pam Chernoff, NCEO's director of equity compensation projects, the seventh edition now incorporates all of the updates noted in prior revisions (including the 2005 supplement to the sixth edition) along with this year's updates. It also includes organizational changes that I hope will make the book, if not the subject matter, easier to navigate. For example, in response to reader comments, we have included (in chapter 1) a basic explanation of how the various federal laws and regulations that affect equity compensation interact with one another. Throughout, you will find material segmented into shorter chapters, with endnotes at the end of each chapter, rather than at the end of the book. Finally, this edition includes new, fully updated chapters on stock-related legislation, case law, and accounting (the latter with the assistance of NASPP Executive Director Barbara Baksa).

I hope you will find this seventh edition useful, and as always I look forward to hearing your suggestions for next year. Please continue to let me know which issues concern you the most and how you would like to see them addressed. Readers should feel free to contact me through my Web site, *www.levinebakerlaw.com,* or by email at *abaker@levinebakerlaw.com.*

Alisa J. Baker
San Francisco, California
December 2005

Con abrazos por mis sobrinos queridos, Elijah y Madeleine.

Introduction

This book is intended to give the reader a general overview of how stock options are used in the United States to reward employees for their participation in and commitment to the success of the employer corporation (referred to variously here as the "company" or the "employer"). Stock options are but one of several forms of equity incentives, which may range from outright gifts of stock to specialized restricted stock purchase arrangements. For the sake of keeping this discussion focused, these other forms of equity incentives are not covered here.

There are two basic kinds of stock options: (1) "qualified" or "statutory" stock options, including incentive stock options (ISOs) and employee stock purchase plan (ESPP) options, which are specific creatures of the Internal Revenue Code of 1986, as amended (the Code), and (2) all other stock options, called "nonstatutory" or "nonqualified" stock options (NSOs). This book will carefully examine the tax aspects of employee stock options and cite appropriate authority on tax issues.[1] However, although the primary focus of this text is on taxation and design issues related to taxation, the day has long passed when the equity compensation planner could feel free to review tax aspects of employee stock options in a vacuum. Such options are increasingly subject to a complex web of rules regarding their creation and exercise that are unrelated to the Code, including federal and state securities laws, accounting principles, and local (foreign) country laws governing grants made to employees resident outside of the United States. Therefore, as appropriate, this book gives an overview of how non-tax rules apply and indicates the types of issues raised by the interaction of these rules. Readers should note that the non-tax discussion is intended to provide only general planning guidance; where appropriate, I have provided references to authoritative sources on these subjects.

The main body of this book is divided into two parts. Part I provides an overview of stock option plans and employee stock purchase plans, focusing on the tax and securities aspects of equity compensation (including compliance). Part II explores the related accounting, and international law issues as well as some of the recent developments in plan design and certain ongoing regulatory issues. Where helpful, illustrative tables are included as exhibits to assist in explaining the operation of the law. At the end of the book, there are supporting materials, including an article by NCEO Executive Director Corey Rosen on designing a broad-based plan; primary sources; a glossary; and a bibliography.

As a caveat, it is important to remember that the use of equity incentives is under ever-increasing scrutiny by the Internal Revenue Service (IRS), the accounting profession (as represented by the Financial Accounting Standards Board (FASB)), the Securities and Exchange Commission (SEC), and Congress. When the original form of this text was first published in the early 1990s, stock option planning was a relatively esoteric function of tax and compensation design. Since that time, the rules regarding statutory options have been amended many times, and various proposed tax regulations, securities law legislation, and accounting projects are pending or in the early days of implementation at the time of this writing. Although this book generally describes current areas of ambiguity, the equity compensation professional must be aware that complex issues will continue to arise with respect to individual options and option plans. Each situation should always be reviewed carefully with legal and accounting experts to ensure compliance with the most current rules.

Notes

1. The tax authority cited throughout includes published authority: the Code, Treasury regulations, Internal Revenue Service (IRS) published rulings, notices and advisory memoranda, and unpublished (but publicly available) materials: IRS private letter rulings (PLRs), field service advice, and technical advice memoranda (TAMs). When using these sources, it is important to be

aware that the unpublished materials bind the IRS only as to the taxpayer requesting the ruling (PLRs) or the IRS field agent requesting advice on a specific fact pattern (TAMs). Under Section 6110(k) of the Code, unpublished materials may not be cited as precedent. However, they provide a reliable indication of IRS positions on controversial issues and are valued by tax practitioners for this purpose.

Part I

Overview of Stock Options and Section 423 Plans

CHAPTER 1

The Basics of Stock Options

Contents

1.1 What Is a Stock Option?

Generally, when an individual (the "optionee") is granted a compensatory stock option, that individual receives a contract right to purchase shares in a corporation for a fixed term at a fixed price—in most cases, the fair market value of the stock on the date the option was granted. Companies typically grant options to employees, consultants, or other persons associated with the company to encourage their retention and participation in the success of the company.

This book discusses stock options granted in connection with performance of services only. The tax treatment of stock transferred pursuant to compensatory stock options is governed either by Sections 421–424 (statutory options) or Section 83 (nonstatutory options) of the Internal Revenue Code (the Code). Different rules apply to determine the amount, character, and timing of the optionee's income inclusion as well as the availability of the corporate tax deduction when options are granted or purchased for investment purposes.

Most (although not all) compensatory options are granted pursuant to the employer company's stock option plan.[1] Companies generally adopt stock option plans that permit grants of both incentive stock options (ISOs) and nonstatuory stock options (NSOs).[2] An ISO is a statutory option, subject to the technical requirements prescribed in Section 422 of the Code. ISOs may be granted only to employees of the issuing company (including employees of its parent and subsidiary corporations). Taxation of NSOs is governed by Section 83 of the Code, but they are not subject to special technical requirements for income tax purposes and may be granted to employees, consultants, nonemployee directors, or any other persons associated with the company. However, NSOs do not receive any preferential tax treatment under the Code. Another form of option available to employers, the employee stock purchase plan (ESPP) option, may be either statutory (under Section 423 of the Code) or nonstatutory (under Section 83 of the Code). Because ESPP options are subject to distinct planning and tax considerations, they are discussed separately in chapter 4.

1.2 Legal and Regulatory Framework

As we will see throughout the book, the laws and regulations governing stock options are complex and ever-changing. Options are subject to tax and securities laws and regulations and accounting standards that often diverge in their requirements. In the federal tax and securities arenas, once a bill is signed into law, federal agencies are charged with interpreting and enforcing it.[3] Those agencies then promulgate binding regulations that govern the application of the laws. Proposed regulations generally go through a comment period in which practitioners can review them and make suggestions to the agency that is responsible for them. In addition, a body of case law has developed as various stock-options-related matters have been litigated. Recent developments in case law, as well as current agency rulings, are discussed in detail in chapter 12.

Accounting is somewhat unusual in that the Securities and Exchange Commission (SEC) has delegated its authority to set and interpret financial accounting standards to a private body called the Financial Accounting Standards Board (FASB).

In all three arenas, compliance with complicated laws, regulations, or standards is sometimes made easier by the inclusion of a list of requirements called a "safe harbor." Companies that adopt the safe harbor provisions are considered to have automatically satisfied the rule or law and are shielded from responsibility. In effect, companies using the safe harbor are sheltered from more complex compliance testing. For example, the SEC's Rule 144 is a safe harbor exemption that allows people who are not issuers, dealers, or underwriters to publicly resell stock that is restricted for securities law purposes under Section 4(1) of the Securities Act of 1933. To do so, they must follow all of the rule's requirements.

In designing and administering stock option plans, practitioners must pay equally careful attention to tax, securities, and accounting issues, because they are distinct bodies of law and regulation. For instance, a transaction or plan design feature that is legitimate for tax purposes might not work for securities law purposes. An example of this arises when a company CEO wants to sell shares purchased by exercising an ISO. The CEO may well have satisfied the statutory holding period under the Code, making him eligible for preferential tax treatment on sale. However, he may nonetheless be barred from selling by securities laws that do not allow him to buy or sell shares if he is in possession of "material nonpublic information" that would give him an advantage over other investors.

1.2.1 Tax Law

The Internal Revenue Service (IRS), an agency of the U.S. Department of the Treasury, is authorized to promulgate Treasury regulations that interpret and elaborate upon the Code. Thus, in many cases throughout the book, references to Code sections are interspersed with references to the corresponding Treasury regulations. While a specific section of the Code may be only a few pages long, the corresponding regulations can be much longer as they delve into much more detailed discussions of what the Code does and does not allow and in some cases offer examples of specific applications. For example, the portion of Section 422 of the Internal Revenue Code that describes the maximum value of stock options that may become exercisable in a given year and still be considered to be ISOs is just three short paragraphs, while the corresponding regulations take up four pages of the Code of Federal Regulations.

In addition to the Code itself and Treasury regulations, the IRS occasionally rules on specific circumstances. Its revenue rulings and revenue procedures officially interpret the Code and its related statutes and regulations. Companies and taxpayers can rely on them in determining how to proceed on a specific issue. IRS *notices* are pronouncements that may provide substantive interpretations of the law and may provide guidance on what forthcoming regulations will include. In addition, when a taxpayer has questions about how to handle a specific circumstance, it can request a private letter ruling. These do not set precedent; they apply only to the taxpayer to whom they are addressed. However, they are often studied as an indication of the IRS's thinking on certain issues about which there has been little previous guidance. Other forms of IRS guidance are also available; these are described in more detail in section 12.1 of chapter 12.

1.2.2 Securities Law

The SEC is charged with oversight and enforcement of federal securities laws, which are designed to protect investors by ensuring that adequate information is available to them and by prohibiting fraud in the sale of securities. The primary securities laws that affect stock options are the Securities Act of 1933 and the Securities Exchange Act of 1934, which Congress passed in the hope of restoring investor confidence after the stock market crash of 1929. The 1933 Act requires that securities be registered with the SEC before they are sold unless they qualify for an exemption from registration. The 1934 Act is a far-reaching law that includes requirements for corporate reporting, proxy solicitations, tender offers, and trading by corporate insiders. More recently, the Sarbanes-Oxley Act of 2002 has affected stock option plan design and corporate disclosures—especially as they pertain to company executives.

Like the IRS, the SEC promulgates legally binding regulations that interpret the securities laws. Many regulations have built up around the 1933 and 1934 acts in the 70-plus years since their passage. Those that affect stock options and other forms of equity compensation are discussed in detail in chapter 7.

Regulations aside, the SEC has numerous avenues for making public pronouncements. The commission itself occasionally issues interpretive releases that reflect its views of legal and regulatory issues. Additionally, the commission's staff issues periodic legal bulletins that are not legally binding. In other cases, when a company asks the SEC for a ruling on a specific set of circumstances, the agency will issue a no-action letter saying that as long as the company does exactly what it proposes, the agency will not seek enforcement action for violations of securities laws.

In addition to federal securities laws, most states have their own securities laws that apply to private companies. These are known as "blue sky laws." The term apparently originated with judicial characterizations of "speculative schemes which have no more basis than so many feet of 'blue sky.'"

1.2.3 Accounting Rules

The Securities Exchange Act of 1934 gives the SEC the authority to set accounting standards, but the agency has historically delegated that authority to a private-sector organization. That organization, the FASB, is responsible for both establishing financial accounting standards and offering guidance on implementing those standards. The SEC retains the authority to veto FASB decisions and to punish companies that fail to follow FASB standards.

FASB's primary regulations are issued through statements of financial accounting standards. In the case of stock options, the most notable FASB standard is "Statement of Financial Accounting Standard No. 123 (revised 2003)," generally abbreviated as FAS 123(R). This statement has substantially altered the rules governing accounting for stock options. Chapter 10 discusses it in detail.

The SEC's staff occasionally issues accounting bulletins that interpret accounting rules as they pertain to securities laws. For example, Staff Accounting Bulletin No. 107 (SAB 107) describes the SEC's interpretation of FAS 123(R) as it pertains to stock option valuation.

The staff of FASB itself uses FASB staff positions (FSPs) to correct or make narrow revisions to FASB statements or to offer guidance on applying statements. Proposed FSPs are open for comments for 30 days before they are finalized. FSPs were created in 2003 to ensure more timely and consistent communication about the application of FASB literature than had been possible before.

In 1984 FASB created the Emerging Issues Task Force (EITF), which is charged with addressing new issues that arise before widespread practice develops that complicates rulemaking. In the late 1990s and early 2000s, the EITF addressed many issues related to stock options accounting. However, because the issue has been on FASB's front burner in recent years, the EITF has had little to do in the area.

1.2.4 Miscellaneous Laws

In addition to the rules described above that specifically address equity compensation, many other laws affect the use of stock in exchange for services. Federal and state labor laws, state employment laws, the federal Employee Retirement Income Security Act of 1974 (ERISA), state corporate and choice of law rules, and general common law contract principles all have a bearing on how and when equity can be used in an employment situation. The cases discussed in chapter 12 offer some insight into how these areas of the law interact with technical equity compensation issues.

Notes

1. When used for tax purposes, the term "compensatory option" may have a different meaning than when used for accounting purposes. See chapter 10, "Basic Accounting Issues."

2. These are also sometimes referred to as nonqualified stock options.

3. The legislative history of stock options is discussed in detail in chapter 11.

CHAPTER 2

Tax Treatment of Nonstatutory Stock Options

Contents

Section 83 of the Code governs the tax treatment of property transferred in connection with services (as opposed to cash for services). For these purposes, the NSO transaction is no different than any other form of service-related property transfer: the service recipient (the company) receives services from the service provider (the employee or contractor) in exchange for payment with property (in this case stock, but it also could be any other form of real or personal property). This chapter discusses the ways in which the general rule of Section 83 applies to the specifics of the NSO scenario.

2.1   General Rule

An individual service provider (employee or nonemployee) who has been granted an NSO will be subject to income tax only at the time the option is *exercised*,[1] unless Section 409A of the code applies (see below). The amount taxed will be the spread (if any) between the purchase price and the fair market value of the stock at time of exercise. As a general rule, the employer/service recipient will be entitled to take a tax deduction in an amount equal to that included in income by the optionee.[2] Gain recognized on the sale of shares acquired pursuant to the exercise of an NSO after December 31, 1987, will be treated as long-term capital gain if the shares were held for more than one year.[3] The holding period for tax purposes generally begins at date of exercise (with the narrow exception of stock acquired one-for-one in a stock swap, described in chapter 5).

2.2   Grant and Exercise Price

Who can receive grants? NSOs may be granted to employees, but they may also be granted to outside directors and independent contractors who are not employees of the company. NSOs may be granted under an employee option plan, or as separate contracts outside of the plan. In any case, the grant and exercise of NSOs will be subject to applicable securities laws (including blue sky laws).[4] Federal securities laws, however, may apply to limit the exercise of options by directors who are public company "insiders" under Section 16(b) of the Exchange Act, as further described in section 2.5 of this chapter.

Setting the Exercise Price after 2005. The federal income tax laws impose no statutory limit when it comes to setting the exercise price of an NSO. As always, under current tax law NSOs may be granted at fair market value, at a discount to fair market value, or at a premium over fair market value without triggering a tax event at *grant*.[5] However, as of 2005, Section 409A of the Code provides a serious disincentive to granting NSOs at a discount. Under Section 409A, a grant at less than fair market value will be considered to be a "deferred compensation arrangement" and (1) will be taxed at the time of *vesting, regardless of whether exercised* and (2) will be subject to a 20% penalty tax in addition to ordinary income taxes at that time.[6] The IRS has stated that any technique that serves to provide a discount, including paying dividend equivalent rights upon exercise, will bring the grant into the scope of Section 409A.[7]

The concept of "fair market value" is a tricky one, made even more so by the enactment of Section 409A. For both NSO and ISO purposes, the IRS has traditionally deferred to the public market or, in the case of a private company, to the good-faith valuation of the issuer's board of directors.[8] However, the proposed regulations to Section 409A require that in order to support a fair market value grant, privately held companies must either follow one of three specific safe harbor valuation methods or demonstrate that the valuation method actually used was reasonable.[9] Depending on the stage of a company's life cycle, the safe harbor could include using an independent appraiser, providing an in-house written valuation that satisfies certain specified criteria, or working with a non-lapse restriction based on a formula price. The IRS will respect a valuation based on a safe harbor unless the issuer's reliance is "grossly unreasonable." A company that chooses not to use a safe harbor method must be prepared to show that its valuation made reference to the valuation factors set out in Section 409A, and there is no assurance that the IRS will agree that the method is reasonable for these purposes.[10]

Given the severity of the penalties assessable under Section 409A, it's safe to say that few companies will want to take chances with an unapproved valuation method and even fewer will wish to purposely grant discount NSOs after 2004. The remainder of this chapter 2 describes the tax treatment of NSOs that are granted at or above fair market value only.

2.3 Application of Section 83 of the Code

As described above, the spread on exercise of an NSO represents compensation income to the optionee and accordingly is subject to the special rules of Section 83(a) of the Code that govern the timing of income inclusion for tax purposes. Under Section 83(a), the value of property (in this case, stock) received for services must be included in income in the year the optionee's rights to the property become "vested." Section 83(c) provides that vesting occurs at the first time an optionee's rights in the property are (1) transferable or (2) not subject to a "substantial risk of forfeiture."

For these purposes, a substantial risk of forfeiture exists when the transfer is conditioned on (1) the performance or nonperformance of substantial services in the future, or (2) the occurrence of a condition related to a purpose of the transfer when there is a substantial possibility of forfeiture if such condition is not satisfied. A requirement for repurchase at fair market value, the risk that the value of the property will decline over a period of time, or a nonlapse restriction (without more) do *not* constitute a substantial risk of forfeiture. As a general rule, the determination of whether a condition constitutes a substantial risk of forfeiture is purely factual. However, under the regulations to Section 83(c) of the Code, indications of a substantial risk of forfeiture are: (1) expectation of regular and time-consuming future services; (2) stock transferred to an underwriter conditioned on successful completion of a public offering; and (3) return required if earnings of the company do not meet certain milestones. Examples of conditions that are *not* substantial risks of forfeiture are: (1) a request for services in the future that may be declined by employee; (2) a requirement that property be returned if employee commits a crime; (3) a covenant not to compete when there is little likelihood that it will need to be invoked or it will be enforced; and (4) a requirement of future consulting services by retired employee that is likely not to be enforced or to be fulfilled.[11] Furthermore, "insider trading" restrictions that limit transferability after exercise do not necessarily constitute a substantial risk of forfeiture for these purposes.[12]

In many cases, NSOs are drafted so as to be exercisable for fully vested stock only. This is the simplest form of option and results in the optionee including the spread in income in the year of exercise. The optionee's adjusted basis in the shares acquired under the option then equals the purchase price plus the amount of the spread included in that year. Exhibit 1-4 above gives an example of this type of option.

Some companies, however, prefer to allow optionees to exercise NSOs for restricted stock that vests based on continued employment or on the attainment of performance goals. In such cases, the company retains a right to repurchase the shares at cost over a period of time (sometimes limited by state securities laws). When full vesting does not occur in the year of exercise, tax is deferred until the restrictions lapse. This means that if the value of the stock appreciates between the date of exercise and date of vesting, the optionee will be subject to tax on a much greater spread than the spread at date of exercise. The tax (and in the case of an employee, the provision for withholding) will be due regardless of whether the optionee sells or otherwise disposes of the stock in order to finance the liability.

2.4 Section 83(b) Election

To avoid the adverse result described above, the optionee may wish to file an election under Section 83(b) of the Code. The Section 83(b) election, which must be filed within 30 days of the date of exercise, allows the optionee to "freeze" the compensation element of the spread (if any) on exercise and pay tax in the year of exercise as if the stock were already vested. There will be no further tax consequences as the stock vests, i.e., filing the election avoids ordinary income tax on any appreciation between the date of exercise and the date of vesting but does not avoid ordinary income tax on the excess of fair market value on the date of exercise over the exercise price. Thus, if the stock appreciates, the optionee avoids the adverse tax consequences described in section 2.3 above. The drawback to a Section 83(b) election, however, occurs if the stock is forfeited or depreciates in value after exercise of the option. In that case, the optionee may be in the unenviable position of having paid unnecessary tax on income with no recourse to capital loss treatment.

To make the Section 83(b) election, the taxpayer should file the original form with the IRS office where they file their income tax return. A copy should be retained in the files of the company, and the taxpayer should attach another copy when he or she files the applicable tax return.[13] The role of the company in filing the election should be carefully described in the materials given to the optionee, and it should be limited to administrative assistance only.[14] Optionees must be advised to consult with their own tax advisors at the time of exercise of an NSO to determine whether it is necessary to file an election under Section

83(b). Failure to timely file cannot be corrected once the 30-day period has passed and could result in serious adverse tax consequences to the optionee.[15]

Exhibit 2-1 gives an example of vesting, with and without an 83(b) election.

Exhibit 2-1. Understanding Vesting Restrictions

Assumptions

Stock Price at Grant: $1

Fair market value (FMV) at time of purchase: $1

Number of shares: 1,000

  total purchase price = $1,000

Vesting schedule: 5 years, 20% per year

Tax Consequences:

Without 83(b) election:

Vesting date	FMV	Spread	Income
Year 1	$ 2.50	$ 1.50	$ 300.00
Year 2	5.00	4.00	800.00
Year 3	10.00	9.00	1,800.00
Year 4	20.00	19.00	3,800.00
Year 5	30.00	29.00	5,800.00

Total income taxed as compensation: $12,500

At the time of sale, the tax basis is $13,500, and the rest is capital gain.

With 83(b) election:

Purchase price	FMV	Spread	Income
$1	$1	-0-	-0-

Total income taxed as compensation: 0

At the time of sale, the tax basis is $1,000, and all is capital gain.

2.5 Restrictions on Transfer Under Section 16(b) of the Exchange Act

If employees who exercise options for unvested stock are public company insiders, their stock may be subject to statutory securities law restrictions in addition to contractual vesting restrictions. Under Section 83(c)(3) of the Code, stock is considered to be restricted if the beneficial owner of the stock could be subject to suit upon sale of the stock under Section 16(b) of the Exchange Act. As described in chapter 7, the Exchange Act provides a six-month short-swing profit period, during which time any insider who sells shares at a profit must disgorge such profit to the company. The insider is subject to suit by the company for any profit during the six-month period.[16]

Under the Pre-1996 Rules (and particularly before 1991), public company insiders frequently chose to make a Section 83(b) election because of the securities law-related risk of forfeiture occurring during the six-month period following the option exercise. Under the 1996 Rules, however, most public company insiders will no longer be subject to a substantial risk of forfeiture solely due to the operation of Section 16. Unless the transaction fails to qualify for any Rule 16b-3 exemption, the risk of forfeiture will not attach under Section 83(c)(3) of the Code.

In the event the insider does makes a Section 83(b) election for Section 16(b) purposes, he or she should note that the Section 83(b) election resolves the vesting problem for tax purposes only. It does not remove the Section 16(b) restriction for securities law purposes.

2.6 Accounting Treatment

Under FAS 123(R), NSOs granted to employees at fair market value must be reported as an expense on companies' income statements beginning in 2005 for public companies and 2006 for closely held companies.[17] All NSOs must be valued using an option-pricing model; if the option is granted at a discount, the company must use a valuation model to estimate the value of the option, including the discount, expensed over the expected life of the award.

2.7 Employer Deduction

Section 83(h) of the Code provides that a service recipient is allowed to take a deduction for amounts included in income by a service provider in the taxable year in which or with which ends the taxable year of the service provider's inclusion. Under the regulations to Section 83(h), the amount included in income is generally the amount reported on the service provider's income tax return.[18] However, if the employer timely files a Form W-2 (or, as applicable, a Form 1099), it need not show that the service provider actually included the spread in income in order to take the deduction (the "deemed inclusion" rule).[19] For purposes of stock options, this means that an employer may take a deduction for the spread on exercise so long as it timely reports the amount included by the service provider.[20]

Under the regulations to Section 83(h), the employer deduction is predicated on meeting the reporting requirements and not on withholding (even when withholding is required under Section 3402 of the Code). However, note that compliance with Section 83(h) (including the deemed inclusion rule) will not relieve the employer from any applicable payroll withholding requirements otherwise imposed with respect to the spread (or from penalties or additions to tax associated with failure to properly withhold). For more on NSO reporting and withholding, see chapter 9.

Notes

1.   An exception to the general rule occurs when the NSO has a "readily ascertainable fair market value," as determined under Treas. Reg. § 1.83-7. In such rare cases, the option may be taxed on the date of *grant*. Ordinarily, an NSO will not have a readily ascertainable fair market value unless the option itself is publicly traded on an established securities market.

2.   Section 83(h) of the Code; Treas. Reg. § 1.83-6(a).

3.   Sections 1222–1223 of the Code. For shares acquired after June 22, 1984, and before January 1, 1988, only, the long-term capital gains holding period was six months. In 1997, Congress enacted certain staged capital gains brackets, depending on the length of time (12 or 18 months) stock has been held, but proposals to revise these brackets were adopted in 1998. Optionees

should check with their tax advisors for up-to-date information on the status of capital gains rates at the time they purchase their stock.

4. In particular, note that in a privately held company, NSOs granted outside of a plan will not be eligible to rely on state or federal securities law exemptions for sales made under an employee plan. Separate exemptions will need to be relied upon for such grants. See, e.g., "the accredited investor" exemption in Section 4(6) of the 1933 Act; California Commissioner's Rules 25102(f) (personal knowledge exemption).

5. Note, however, that there may be other limitations: for example, in a private company, state corporate and/or securities laws may place a limit on the NSO discount.

6. Section 409A(1) and Prop. Treas. Reg. § 1.409A-1(b)(5). Companies are required to withhold income and penalty taxes at the time of vesting.

7. Prop. Treas. Reg. § 1.409A-1(b)(5)(i)(D), (E). Such rights can however be offered separately from the stock option award itself.

8. For ISOs, Section 422(c) of the Code addressed this good-faith valuation directly. See chapter 3. For NSOs, valuation (other than as to "reasonably ascertainable fair market value") has had the meaning normally given to it under the Code (i.e., in Sections 61 and 1001).

9. The burden of proving for tax purposes that an otherwise good-faith valuation would *not* be treated as "fair market value" has, until now, fallen on the IRS. The proposed regulations place the burden of proof squarely on the issuer. *See* Prop. Treas. Reg. § 1.409A-1(b)(5)(iv)(B).

10. Please note that the valuation methods in Section 409A are different from— and are used for a different purpose than—the "fair value" models required by FAS 123(R) for accounting purposes. See chapter 10.

11. Treas. Reg. § 1.83-3(c)(2).

12. See Rev. Rul. 2005-48, in which the IRS ruled that a post-exercise lockup period that took effect eight months after grant was not a substantial risk of forfeiture, notwithstanding the optionee's limitations under the company's insider trading policy. The IRS pointed out that the first Section 16(b) short-swing profit period, which does in fact constitute a substantial risk of forfeiture under Section 83(c)(3), began on the date of grant rather than the date of exercise and so was already over at the time of exercise. See section 2.5 below. Note that this decision contradicts a 40-year precedent of the First Circuit Court of Appeals, *Robinson v. Comm'r*, 44 T.C. 20 (1965). The IRS has stated that it will follow *Robinson* only with respect to taxpayers in the First Circuit. For more on this ruling, see chapter 12.

13. Treas. Reg. § 1.83-2.

14. Companies should take care to avoid assuming legal responsibility, and potential liability, for the Section 83(b) filing. The ultimate responsibility for timely filing should remain with the individual taxpayer. Notwithstanding the foregoing, the IRS Chief Counsel's office has approved the use of a consent form giving Power of Attorney to the employer for the purpose of filing the 83(b) election on behalf of an employee. See CCA 200203018 (January 18, 2002).

15. A Section 83(b) filing may be corrected only if it was filed as a result of a genuine mistake of fact regarding the underlying transaction. See IRS Info. Ltr. 2001-0224 (Aug. 20, 2001) (mistake as to tax consequences not a mistake of fact).

16. Treas. Reg. § 1.83-3(j)(1) provides that, for purposes of Section 83(a), the Section 16(b) restriction comes off the stock at the earliest of: (1) the end of the Section 16(b) six-month period, or (2) the first day that sale at a profit will not subject the holder to suit. See also *Tanner v. Comm'r*, 117 T.C. 2001 (construing 16(b) restriction period for purposes of Section 83(c)(3)).

17. See Chapter 10 for further details.

18. Treas. Reg. § 1.83-6 (a)(1).

19. Treas. Reg. § 1.83-6 (a)(2).

20. Note that such reporting will include compliance with the requirements set out in Sections 6041 and 6041A of the Code, as applicable. So long as the employer complies with the requirements of Section 6041 (or 6041A) of the Code and timely files the Form W-2 or Form 1099, as applicable, it may rely upon the "deemed inclusion rule" as the basis for the amount of the deduction.

CHAPTER 3

Tax Treatment of Incentive Stock Options

Contents

Congress created the incentive stock option (ISO) in the Economic Recovery Tax Act of 1981. ISOs were intended to serve as a tax-advantaged investment vehicle for employees, with special benefits if a current employee committed to the investment in his employer for a combined holding period of (1) at least one year from the date of exercise and (2) at least two years from the date of grant (the "statutory holding period"). As a general rule, if an ISO satisfies all of the statutory requirements outlined below, the tax deferral benefit of ISO treatment remains the same today as it was in 1981.[1] However, in the last quarter century the rules governing the tax treatment of ISOs have undergone numerous reviews and revisions, the most recent of which resulted in the final regulations to Sections 421 through 424 of the Code (the "2004 regulations"). The 2004 regulations were generally effective as of August 3, 2004 (with some transitional exceptions) and must be applied in their as entirety of January 1, 2006. The 2004 regulations are incorporated into the following discussion.[2]

3.1 Statutory Requirements for ISOs

ISOs are governed by the specific requirements prescribed in Section 422 of the Code and the general requirements for statutory options set out in Sections 421 and 424 of the Code. As a prerequisite to granting ISOs, the employer must have a written option plan that sets forth the maximum number of shares that may be issued under the plan as well as the class of employees eligible to receive options. The plan must receive shareholder approval within 12 months before or after its adoption by the company's board of directors.

Assuming that the plan satisfies these requirements, the option grant also must conform to a number of statutory prerequisites under Section 422(b), including:

1. The option exercise price must be no less than the fair market value of the shares (as determined by the board of directors in good faith) on the date of grant.[3]

2. The option must be granted within 10 years after the plan is adopted.

3. The option, by its terms, cannot be exercisable for a period longer than 10 years after the date of grant.

4. The option may be granted only to a person who is an employee of the company (or its parent or subsidiary) on the date of grant.

For these purposes, and that of all statutory options, "employee" is defined with reference to the common-law definition of employee as used for purposes of wage withholding under Section 3402 of the Code.[4]

5. The option must be exercised by the employee no later than three months after termination of employment (except in case of Section 22(e) disability, after which an ISO can be exercised for up to one year, or death, for which there are no time limits for exercise by the estate), subject to the above-stated requirement that the option cannot be exercisable for a period longer than 10 years after the date of grant.

6. The option, by its terms, cannot be transferable (other than by will or laws of descent). During the employee's lifetime it can be exercised only by the employee.

7. If an option is granted to a more-than-10% shareholder of the company, its parent, or subsidiary, the exercise price can be no less than 110% of fair market value at the date of grant, and the option cannot be exercised for a period longer than five years after the date of grant.

Section 422(c)(4)(C) states that an option meeting the requirements of Section 422(b) shall be treated as an ISO if it is subject to any additional conditions, so long as such conditions are not inconsistent with the provisions of Section 422(b). Frequently, conditions include a right of the company to repurchase option shares upon voluntary termination, or a right of first refusal to repurchase vested shares if the optionee proposes to transfer the shares to a third party. Other examples of permissible provisions include the right of an employee to receive property (e.g., stock) at the time of exercise and to pay for stock with stock of the granting corporation.

3.2 Analysis of Statutory Requirements

The statutory requirements set out above must be understood in the context of the previously proposed regulations as they existed for 20 years (the "1984 proposed regulations") and tax legislative history related to ISOs, as well as with respect to the IRS positions on their interpretation. As noted above, the 2004 regulations are fully effective for all ISOs as of January 1, 2006.

Generally, the 2004 regulations follow or clarify the 1984 proposed regulations, notices and letter rulings; accordingly, they have not had a significant impact on our understanding of how the rules work. However, where there are important differences (treated, for the most part, as clarifications by the IRS) between the 2004 regulations and the 1984 proposed regulations, they are noted below.[5]

3.2.1 ISO Plan Must Be Properly Adopted

To qualify as an ISO plan, a stock option plan must contain certain terms and conditions prescribed by Section 422 of the Code, and must be adopted by the company's board of directors and approved by the shareholders within 12 months before or after such adoption. The plan must be in writing, which under the 2004 regulations now includes electronic format.[6] The plan must state the maximum number of shares that can be issued under it as ISOs, even if it is a broad omnibus plan that allows for the issuance of several kinds of equity compensation, and must specify which classes of employees are eligible for option grants under it. If the plan is a broad equity compensation plan that allows for grants to nonemployees, then the class or classes of employees eligible for ISOs must be stated separately.[7]

Shareholder approval must be by a method that would be treated as adequate under applicable state law in the case of an action requiring shareholder approval for the issuance of corporate stock or options. If state law does not prescribe a method and degree of shareholder approval for such issuances, then the plan must be approved by either (1) a majority of the votes cast at a duly held shareholder meeting at which a quorum is present either in person or by proxy or (2) a method, and in a degree, that would be treated as adequate under state law for an action requiring shareholder approval (for example, unanimous written consent).[8]

The window for shareholder approval can be longer than 12 months if the board conditions its adoption of the plan upon shareholder approval. In that case, both the shareholder approval and board adoption are considered to have occurred on the same day.[9]

3.2.2 Amendment of ISO Plan Must Be Properly Approved

The company may at some time wish to increase the number of shares authorized for issuance under its ISO plan or to change in some manner the class of employees eligible to receive ISOs under the plan. Such changes to the ISO plan are treated as the equivalent of adopting a new plan, and thus must be approved by the board of directors *and* the shareholders of the company in accordance with Section 422(b)(1) of the Code. Changes to an ISO plan that do not affect the number of shares available for issuance under the plan or the class of employees eligible to participate in the plan may be approved by the board of directors alone.[10]

3.2.3 Options Must Be Granted Properly

ISOs (and all other stock options of the company) can be granted only by the board of directors or by an authorized subcommittee of the board. Options should be granted by formal board resolution, either at meetings or by written consent (pursuant to state law).[11] An option is generally deemed to have been granted on the date on which the board of directors (or an authorized board subcommittee) resolved to grant the option. The regulations provide that the option will be considered to be granted *for tax purposes* in accordance with the intention of the corporation, even if there are "conditions" on the grant. Conditions that do not prevent a grant from being effective for tax purposes on the date of grant include shareholder approval of the plan and government approval or registration requirements.[12] *At the time of grant,* all of the elements prescribed by Section 422 of the Code must be present or the ISO will be treated as an NSO.

3.2.4 ISOs Are Only for Employees

Unlike NSOs, ISOs can be granted only to persons who are employees rendering services to the company or who are employees of a "parent" or "subsidiary" corporation of the company (as such terms are defined in Section 424(f) of the Code). "Employee" is defined by reference to the common-law definition of employee (as it applies for purposes of withholding under Section 3402 of the Code). Thus, ISOs generally cannot be granted to persons who serve as independent contractors, consultants, or outside directors to the company since they are not employees. A question that frequently arises is whether ISOs may be granted to employees of a corporate entity in which the granting corporation has a "joint venture" interest. The Code is clear on this point: unless the corporation's stake is at least 50% (i.e., the joint venture satisfies the statutory definition of subsidiary), the joint venture employees would not be eligible to receive ISOs under the granting corporation's plan.[13]

In addition, to receive ISO tax treatment, the optionee must be an employee of the company at the time of exercise or have terminated employment with the company no more than three months before the date of exercise (or 12 months in the case of a person whose employment was terminated by permanent and total disability within the meaning of Section 22(e) of the Code). In the case of a leave of absence, the regulations provide that the employment relationship will terminate (for purposes of the option) on the 91st day of leave unless the individual has the right to continued employment with the company under either statute or contract. Accordingly, persons whose employment with the company is terminated will be able to exercise ISOs only for a limited period of time, which the company can always shorten by contract.[14] If the employee dies, the Code places no time limit on exercise by the estate other than the option's existing expiration date. Note that these are statutory maximums. The option-granting company is free to set more restrictive limits on post-termination exercise.[15]

3.2.5 Option Exercise Price for ISOs

The concept of "fair market value" is very important for ISO purposes under Section 422, just as it is for NSO purposes under Section 409A.[16] Section 422(b)(4) of the Code provides that to qualify as an ISO, an option cannot be granted at an exercise price lower than the fair market value of the optioned stock on the date the option is granted (without regard to any restrictions on the stock that will expire at some future time). Further, an employee who owns stock possessing more than 10% of the total combined voting power of all classes of stock of the company (or of any parent or subsidiary of the company) cannot be granted an ISO at an exercise price less than 110% of the fair market value of the stock subject to the ISO on the date the option is granted. The regulations to Section 421 of the Code state that "any reasonable valuation" (including the valuation methods permitted under the estate tax regulations) may be used to determine the fair market value of a statutory option, and the 2004 ISO regulations restate this rule.[17] Regardless of the valuation method used, fair market value must be determined without regard to any restriction other than a restriction which, by its terms, will never lapse.[18]

Setting fair market value is the responsibility of the board of directors, and there is no definitive rule as to the proper means of determining the fair market value of non-publicly-traded stock. The stakes are high because a failure to set fair market value correctly could result in an ISO being treated as an NSO, which in turn could mean penalties (both for employer and employee) for failure to withhold and pay over taxes at the time of exercise. Section 422(c)(1) of the Code addresses this problem by providing a safe harbor: if the board makes *a good-faith attempt* to set a valuation at the time of grant that valuation will be treated as fair market value for ISO purposes even if such fair market value is subsequently challenged by the IRS. Regardless of future findings, the optionee's ISO status will be protected.[19]

In this context, what constitutes a good-faith attempt? The 2004 regulations provide that when stock is publicly traded, valuation based on a method using market quotations will be presumed to be in good faith.[20] Shares in privately held companies present a more difficult challenge. In setting the value of such stock, the board of directors should look to the prices at which recent sales of the same or similar classes of stock have been made. An independent appraiser may also provide a good estimate of the stock's value.[21] To this end, Treas. Reg. § 1.422-2(e)(2)(iii) states that a non-public company can successfully establish a good-faith attempt to meet the option price requirements by demonstrating that fair market value was based on an average of the fair market values for a specific grant date as "set forth in the opinions of completely independent and well-qualified experts." However, Treas. Reg. § 1.422-2(e)(2)(iv) further states that regardless of whether an option is publicly traded, there will *not* be a good-faith attempt unless the fair market value of the stock on the date of grant is determined both with regard to nonlapse restrictions and without regard to nonlapse restrictions.

3.2.6 Limitation on Size of Option

An ISO may be first exercisable only as to $100,000 worth of stock (determined as of the date of grant) in any calendar year.[22] However, under Section 422(d) of the Code, an ISO will not fail simply because it exceeds the $100,000 limitation. Instead, the amount of the grant exercisable for stock in excess of $100,000 will be automatically treated as an NSO.[23]

Moreover, there is no limit on the aggregate value of stock that may be subject to an ISO grant. Thus, for example, an employee could receive an ISO for $500,000 worth of stock, as long as the ISO was first exercisable in no more than $100,000 increments annually.[24] Of course, the first exercisable rule does not require that the optionee actually exercise any portion of the ISO in the year it first becomes exercisable. In this example, the employee would be entitled to wait until the entire ISO became exercisable and then exercise for $500,000 worth of stock in one installment. However, note that if the exercise schedule under the option were accelerated at any time during its term, the first exercisable rule would come into play. Continuing the example, assume in year three the option is accelerated to allow exercise of the $100,000 increment originally first exercisable in year four. In year three, $200,000 worth of stock is now first exercisable, of which $100,000 qualifies for ISO treatment and $100,000 is now treated as an NSO. In year five, the remaining $100,000 worth of stock would still qualify for ISO treatment.

Furthermore, if the $100,000 limit is exceeded because multiple grants vest in a year, then for purposes of determining which options retain their ISO status and which are disqualified, the options are taken in the order in which they were granted.[25]

If an option is disqualified from ISO treatment by a modification or cancellation before the year in which it would have become exercisable, then it is not considered when calculating the $100,000 limit. But if the modification or cancellation happens any time in the year the option would have become exercisable, the option is counted for purposes of the limit for that year.[26]

3.2.7 Limitation on Term of Option

Generally, Section 422(b)(3) provides that an ISO may be exercisable for no more than 10 years. However, in the case of an employee who owns stock representing more than 10% of the total voting power of all classes of stock of the company, Section 422(c)(6) provides that the term of an ISO is limited to five years. The company may, of course, grant options with shorter terms than the maximum permitted by the Code.

3.2.8 Payment for Option Shares

Employees may exercise ISOs with cash payments. However, if an employee wants to exercise an ISO with a promissory note, with shares of the company's stock, or with other non-cash consideration, he or she will not be able to do so unless the plan, the original board resolutions granting the ISO, and the option grant itself specifically permit payment by means of the particular non-cash consideration in question. Any addition of financing methods after grant will result in a "modification" of the ISO under Section 424(h) of the Code (discussed further in section 3.6 of this chapter). Thus, when granting an ISO, the board of directors should resolve at that time whether it will permit the employee to pay for his or her option stock with any particular non-cash consideration, and it should provide for such method of payment in the option grant. If the board of directors and applicable state corporate law permit an employee to exercise an ISO by payment of a promissory note, the terms of the promissory note must be carefully structured so as to avoid adverse tax consequences to the employee or the company.[27] Chapter 5 treats the financing issues mentioned above in more detail.

3.3 Tax Consequences of ISO Exercise

The principal federal income tax benefit of an ISO to an optionee is that there will be no income tax at the time of exercise unless the alternative minimum tax rules apply, as discussed in section 3.5 below. Further, no payroll tax withholding of any kind is required upon the exercise of an ISO.

3.4 Dispositions of ISO Stock

So long as ISO shares are held for the statutory holding period, the entire gain or loss ultimately realized upon the sale of such shares (a "qualifying disposition") will be treated as long-term capital gain or loss rather than as ordinary income. Such gain or loss is equal to the difference between the amount received in the qualifying disposition and the amount paid upon exercise of the ISO. If the optionee realizes a loss on the disposition, the optionee's basis in the ISO shares is adjusted and a capital loss is taken, as necessary. Exhibit 3-1 below illustrates the tax consequences to the optionee of exercising an ISO and holding the ISO shares for the required statutory holding period.

ISO shares sold before the end of the statutory holding period are said to be sold in a "disqualifying disposition" under Section 421 of the Code. A disqualifying disposition literally disqualifies the option from beneficial ISO treatment and instead causes the option to be treated as if it were an NSO. As described in chapter 2, this means that the optionee will be required to include the spread in ordinary income in the year of exercise, and any subsequent appreciation in value of the stock after exercise and before disposition of the shares will be characterized as capital gain.[28] Section 422(c)(2) limits the recognition of gain on disposition of ISO shares to the shareholder's *actual gain*. Accordingly, a disqualifying disposition of ISO shares at a loss (i.e., for a price less than that originally paid for the ISO shares) will not give rise to tax on the spread (if any) realized at exercise.[29] Note that this limitation rule does not apply if the disposition is a sale or exchange with respect to which a loss (if sustained) would not be recognized by the individual.[30]

The employer is entitled to a compensation deduction in the amount of the spread included in the optionee's income upon a disqualifying disposition,[31] although the amount deductible by a public company may be limited by the $1 million cap on compensation of certain senior executives.[32] The company is not required to withhold on a disqualifying disposition of an ISO in order to qualify for the deduction. Exhibit 3-1 below illustrates the tax consequences of a disqualifying disposition.

Exhibit 3-1. Comparison: ISOs Versus NSOs: Consequences to Optionee

Assumptions:
Option price: $1
Fair market value at exercise: $5
Sale price: $10

	NSO	ISO
Include in Income:		
At exercise	$4 (ordinary income)	$0 (unless alternative minimum tax applies)
	New "adjusted basis" in stock equals option price plus spread = $5	
	Subject to withholding	
At sale	$5 (capital gains)	$9
	Capital gains on difference between sale price and adjusted basis: $10 – $5 = $5	*If holding periods are met:* $9 long-term capital gains
		If holding periods are not met: $4 ordinary income $5 capital gains

3.5 Alternative Minimum Tax (AMT) Issues

As described in detail below, the spread on exercise of an ISO is subject
to AMT in the year of exercise. When the stock market bubble popped
in 2000, optionees who failed to focus on the effects of the AMT were
unpleasantly surprised to see a substantial tax bill despite the fact that
the value of their stock may have subsequently declined below the
exercise date price.[33] The experience of the dot-commers emphasizes
the need to respect the special rules for ISOs in regards to AMT and
disqualifying dispositions. These rules require careful consideration of
potential effects that the AMT rules will have on filing Section 83(b)
elections for ISO purposes. It is advisable for many employees who
exercise ISOs for restricted stock to file Section 83(b) elections exactly
as though they were exercising NSOs. Moreover, the rules will apply to
trigger certain planning possibilities as well as pitfalls for optionees
who expect to make disqualifying dispositions of their ISO stock in a
year other than the year of exercise.

3.5.1 Background on the AMT

Although the specific application of the AMT is too complex to sum-
marize here, generally AMT is exactly what its name suggests: an alternative to the regular tax system. AMT is imposed on alternative minimum taxable income (AMTI) as computed under Sections 56 through
58 of the Code.[34] To arrive at AMTI, the taxpayer computes regular
taxable income (as defined in Section 55(c) of the Code) and then
adjusts that amount by any adjustments or "tax preference items"
(i.e., items that reflect certain deductions and tax deferral benefits
allowed under the regular tax system) taken in the taxable year. The
spread on exercise of an ISO has always been treated as a tax preference
item.

Under Section 55 of the Code, AMT is computed on the amount
of AMTI in excess of the applicable exemption amount ($58,000 for
married taxpayers filing jointly, $40,250 for single taxpayers in
2005).[35] If the AMT exceeds the taxpayer's regular tax in a given year,
the taxpayer must pay the AMT amount rather than the regular tax

amount. The difference between AMT and regular tax in any year is allowable as a credit against regular tax in future years pursuant to Section 53 of the Code. Thus, AMT payment essentially serves as a prepayment of regular tax and accordingly offsets any deferral benefit that the taxpayer would otherwise enjoy in a year when AMT exceeds regular tax.

3.5.2 Effect of AMT on ISOs

Section 56(b)(3) of the Code (relating to adjustments applicable to individuals in computing AMTI) states the following:

> (3) Treatment of incentive stock options—Section 421 shall not apply to the transfer of stock acquired pursuant to the exercise of an incentive stock option (as defined in section 422). Section 422(c)(2) shall apply in any case where the disposition and the inclusion for purposes of this part are within the same taxable year and such section shall not apply in any other case. The adjusted basis of any stock so acquired shall be determined on the basis of the treatment prescribed by this paragraph.

Under this special provision, an ISO is not considered to be a statutory option (accorded special treatment under Section 421 of the Code) for AMT purposes. The effect of this language is to treat ISOs for AMT purposes as though they were NSOs subject to the rules of Section 83 of the Code. Accordingly, as further discussed below, employees who exercise ISOs that are not fully vested at the time of exercise should be advised regarding whether to file a Section 83(b) election for AMT.[36]

3.5.3 Effect of Disqualifying Dispositions on AMT

A disqualifying disposition of an ISO has no effect on the optionee's AMT liability unless the AMT liability arises in the same calendar year as the disqualifying disposition. AMT amounts paid with respect to the spread will be subject to recapture as a credit over subsequent tax years. If the taxpayer makes a disqualifying disposition in the same calendar year as exercise, the AMT liability will be canceled.[37]

3.5.4 When to File a Section 83(b) Election for ISO AMT

The same risk factors described above that apply on filing a Section 83(b) election for NSOs apply for filing a Section 83(b) election for AMT.[38] The decision as to each optionee is highly individual and must take into account all of the factors influencing the optionee's tax position. In particular, the disqualifying disposition issue puts an additional gloss on planning considerations when exercise of an ISO produces AMT in the year of exercise. If, in such a case, the optionee believes that the ISO shares will appreciate considerably before vesting and the optionee intends to hold the stock for the statutory holding period, a Section 83(b) election should be filed for AMT. If, however, the optionee intends to make a disqualifying disposition of the ISO shares in the year of vesting, it may be disadvantageous to make a Section 83(b) election at the time of exercise. Making such an election will accelerate the AMT into the year of exercise, and there will be no opportunity to effectively cancel AMT by making a disqualifying disposition in the year of vesting.[39] Of course, if the optionee has no intention of making a disqualifying disposition of the ISO shares, a Section 83(b) election will always be advisable in an up market.[40]

3.6 Modifying Statutory Options

With few exceptions, Section 424(h) of the Code and its regulations provide that a "modification" of an ISO or Section 423 employee stock purchase plan option (discussed in detail in chapter 4) will require that the exercise price of the option be adjusted to match the fair market value of the option stock on the date of amendment, if that price is higher.[41] For purposes of the statutory option provisions of the Code, modification is defined to mean a change in the original terms of the option that gives the option holder *additional benefits* under the option.[42] Examples of modifications cited in regulations include: extending the period for exercise, providing an alternative to the exercise of the option (such as a stock appreciation right), providing an additional benefit upon exercise (such as a cash bonus), and making an offer to change the terms of the grant if that offer remains outstanding for more than 30 days or if it is accepted.[43] If an ISO is modified only with respect to a portion of the optioned shares, or if the modification is solely for the purpose of increasing the number of shares under option, only the portion of the ISO relating to such shares will be deemed modified for these purposes. The affected options will be considered to be a newly granted option.[44] Under the 2004 regulations, if a company inadvertently modifies its ISOs, it can undo the modification without disqualifying the option as long as the modification is reversed by the earlier of the last day of the calendar year when the change was made or the date of exercise of the option.[45]

Accordingly, if an ISO exercisable at $1 per share is amended at a time when the underlying stock has a value of $5 per share, the option exercise price will have to be increased to $5 per share to maintain the ISO status of the option. Options that are not repriced in the event of a modification are treated as NSOs. If an ISO is modified, the grant date is deemed to be the date of the modification rather than the date of the original grant. This will mean that the optionee's statutory holding period must be extended for an additional two years. Note that even if the modification occurs in a down market without repricing (because the exercise price is greater than current fair market value), the statutory holding period will re-start on the date of the modification.

Section 424(h)(3) of the Code provides that a change in the terms of the option attributable to the issuing or assuming of an option pursuant to a corporate reorganization (or other Section 424(h) transaction) or a change attributable to accelerating the time within which to exercise the option will *not* be a modification for Section 424(h) purposes.[46] To avoid modification problems in a corporate transaction where new options will be issued, the old options must be canceled and the new (substituted) options must not offer any new benefits. Furthermore, in terms of the whole grant, the aggregate difference between the option exercise price and the fair market value of the underlying shares cannot be greater after the transaction than before. The number of shares subject to the new option can be adjusted to compensate for any change in the aggregate spread between the exercise price and the fair market value of the shares subject to the option immediately after the change.[47]

No amendment to or modification of a statutory option should be made without careful tax consideration, because such changes can result in significant tax problems that must be understood fully by both the employee and the company. Further, note that modifications can carry accounting consequences. See chapter 10 for a detailed discussion of accounting issues.

Notes

1. See Alisa J. Baker, "Incentive Stock Options Continue to Be a Viable Choice Despite TRA '86," 68 *Journal of Taxation* 164 (1988).

2. Treas. Reg. §§ 1.421-1 through 1.424-1. The new regulations include various renumbering and clean-up changes as well as substantive changes.

3. For a complete discussion of fair market value in the ISO context, see section 3.2.5 of this chapter.

4. Treas. Reg. § 1.421-1(h). See also IRS Notice 87-41, 1987-1 CB 296 (the "20-factor test").

5. For a summary of the substantive changes between the 2004 regulations and the 1984 proposed regulations, see chapter 12 .

6. Treas. Reg. § 1.422-2(b).

7. Treas. Reg. § 1.422-2(b)(4). If the plan otherwise meets the requirements of Section 422, it may be structured in any way that is not inconsistent with the Code. See, e.g., PLR 200513012 (ISO plan with ESPP-type structure still qualifies).

8. Treas. Reg. § 1.422-3.

9. Treas. Reg. § 1.422-2(b)(2).

10. Treas. Reg. § 1.422-2(b)(1)(iii).

11. Governance requirements vary from state to state. For example, Delaware corporate law allows the board to delegate to an officer the authority to grant stock options pursuant to an option plan. See Delaware General Corporation Law, Section 157 (as amended, July 1, 2001). California corporate law, on the other hand, does not permit such delegation.

12. Treas. Reg. § 1.421-1(c)(2). It is important to remember that this regulation governs for tax purposes (i.e., ISO purposes) only, and prior shareholder approval may nonetheless be necessary to establish a grant date for accounting and securities law purposes.

13. Section 424(f) of the Code; Treas. Reg. § 1.424-1(f)(2).

14. Section 421(b) of the Code (employment requirement); Treas. Reg. § 1.421-1(h)(2) (leave of absence).

15. However, as always the company should make sure that state corporate or securities laws do not impose their own post-termination minimums. For example, the California rules state that when termination occurs other than for cause, an optionee must have a minimum of 30 days (and, in the case of death or disability, a minimum of six months) within which to exercise an option post-termination. See Rule 260.140.42(g) under the California Corporate Securities Law of 1968.

16. See chapter 2.

17. Treas. Reg. § 1.421-1(e)(2); Treas. Reg. § 1.422-2(e)(1).

18. Section 422 (c)(7). In other words, vesting requirements in and of themselves do not factor into fair market value.

19. Section 422(c)(1) also applies to safeguard fair market value calculations for purposes of the $100,000 first exercisable rule under Section 422(d).

20. Treas. Reg. § 1.422-2(e)(3).

21. Valuation problems frequently arise when private companies grant stock options at one price to employees at a time when the company is simultaneously raising capital through the sale of similar stock to outside investors at a considerably higher price. The board should be advised that granting an option at a low price in such a situation might result in the option not qualifying as an ISO, thereby depriving the employee option holder of ISO tax benefits. This is one of many reasons that a company is advised to sell a different class of stock when raising capital from nonemployee third parties.

22. The Technical and Miscellaneous Revenue Act of 1988 (TAMRA) amended prior law to provide that an option that otherwise satisfies the ISO requirements of the Code will not be considered to be an ISO if it is designated as an NSO (the so-called "inadvertent ISO" problem). The terms of options granted after the 1986 Act but before TAMRA could have been amended to designate the option as an NSO, provided that the amendment was made before February 8, 1989.

23. Before the Tax Reform Act of 1986 (the "1986 Act"), ISOs were subject to the "sequential exercise rule." Under that rule, an ISO could not be exercised before any prior ISO granted to the same optionee by the same employer until the earlier ISO had been exercised in full or had expired (by lapse of time) under the terms of the grant. Moreover, ISOs were further encumbered by the operation of a $100,000 grant limitation. Under the grant limitation,

no employee could be granted ISOs for more than $100,000 worth of stock in any calendar year. Both the sequential exercise rule and the $100,000 grant limitation rule were repealed by the 1986 Act and apply only to ISOs granted before January 1, 1987. Note that by virtue of the 10-year maximum term imposed by Section 422, these pre-1987 rules never apply to outstanding options after January 1, 1997.

24. TAMRA repealed the prior law provision of the Code requiring that ISOs, *by their terms*, be granted for stock with an aggregate value of no more than $100,000 in any year.

25. Section 422(c) of the Code.

26. Treas. Reg. § 1.422-4(b)(5).

27. In nearly all cases, the note should be a full recourse note bearing interest at a rate governed by IRS regulations under Sections 483, 1274, and 7872 of the Code. Please note that if a nonrecourse note is used, there is a risk that the purchase of the stock will be treated for tax purposes as if it were only the grant of an NSO. The result of such treatment is that the employee will recognize ordinary income when he or she pays off the note in an amount equal to the difference between the value of the stock on the date the note is paid and the actual purchase price of the stock. Moreover, if the rate of interest on the note is not high enough to satisfy the regulations, the IRS will impute additional interest for tax purposes. This can result in additional taxable interest income to the company without a corresponding receipt of cash, as well as causing the employee's ISO to be treated as an NSO. See chapter 5 for a discussion of the many issues relating to employer loans.

28. Note that in one important respect—the ability to file an 83(b) election—ISOs exercised for unvested stock are *not* treated as NSOs upon a disqualifying disposition. In past years, practitioners argued that ISO holders could file a "protective 83(b) election" at the time of exercise for unvested shares in order to limit taxation of the spread in the event of a disqualifying disposition. The 2004 regulations specifically clarify that such a "protective election" is not available for ordinary income tax purposes, although it is available for purposes of the AMT. Treas. Reg. § 1.422-1(b)(3), example 2.

29. This special rule does not apply to limit recognition of gain on a disqualifying disposition of ESPP stock. Furthermore, recognition of AMT with respect to the spread at exercise is not canceled by the operation of Section 422(c)(2). See section 3.5 below.

30. For example, a "wash sale" under Section 1091 of the Code, a gift or other non-arm's-length transaction, or a sale between related persons. See Treas. Reg. § 1.422-1(b)(2)(ii).

31. Treas. Reg. § 1.83-6(a)(2).

32. Section 162(m) of the Code. This limitation is discussed further in chapter 8.

33. After the stock market crash of 2000, the newspapers were full of stories about Silicon Valley executives who held onto stock acquired at the height of the boom without considering the AMT consequences. In the down market, these executives found themselves with huge AMT bills and insufficient assets to satisfy the liability. Attempts in 2001 to introduce legislation to "rescue" adversely affected optionees were unsuccessful. See discussion of timing considerations for dispositions below. See also A. Ebeling and J. Novack, "Killer Tax," *Forbes Magazine*, April 2002.

34. The relevant statutory provisions are found in Sections 53 through 59 of the Code.

35. AMT rates are constantly changing. At this writing, the rate is generally 26% of the first $175,000 of AMTI in excess of the exemption and 28% above that amount. Special rules also apply to limit the maximum capital gains rate to 20%. However, the exemption amount is reduced by 25% of the amount by which AMTI exceeds $150,000 for joint returns (phasing out completely at $382,000), $112,500 for single returns (phasing out completely at $273,500), and $75,000 for separate returns (phasing out completely at $191,000). Optionees with AMT concerns should consult their tax advisors for information on how AMT applies to them.

36. For options exercised before December 31, 1987, the ISO/AMT liability arose under Section 57(a) of the Code, the section dealing with items of tax preference. Section 57(a)(3) of the Code basically stated that the spread on exercise of an ISO would be treated as a preference item. However, in calculating the spread, Section 57(a)(3)(A) specifically provided that "the fair market value of a share of stock will be determined without regard to any restriction other than a restriction which, by its terms, will never lapse." This meant that an ISO could be fully exercisable for restricted stock (i.e., stock that vested over a period of years) and still be treated as an item of tax preference on the *date of exercise* rather than on the date of vesting. Under TAMRA, Congress deleted Section 57(a)(3) entirely, and replaced it with Section 56(b)(3), significantly altering the ISO/AMT treatment for subsequent tax years.

37. Until 1987, most tax practitioners believed that an optionee could make a disqualifying disposition of an ISO within 12 months of exercise of the ISO (whether or not in one calendar year) and avoid the AMT. This was logical because, at the time of disqualification, the optionee would be taxed at ordinary income rates on the entire appreciation between the purchase price and the sale price under the regular income tax system. Accordingly,

any benefit from the optionee's AMT preference would be wiped out by the regular tax liability. Depending upon when the optionee exercised the option, the optionee would either have no obligation to include the preference in an AMTI calculation or would be entitled to file for a refund of any AMT paid because of the now-inapplicable preference. The legislative history to the original ISO provisions contained language that supported this reading of the law. In 1987, the IRS issued a private letter ruling (PLR) in which it confirmed this view, holding that an optionee who disqualified ISO stock in a year after the year of exercise but within 12 months of exercise was entitled to wipe out the tax preference. One year later, however, the IRS issued another ruling in which it revoked the prior ruling for the same taxpayer and held that a disqualifying disposition that occurred within 12 months but not within the same calendar year of exercise would not wipe out the AMT preference. A subsequent PLR issued in May 1988 reaffirmed the IRS version of the new AMT calendar-year window. The IRS was not clear, however, as to the effective date for operating under these new rules. See PLRs 8821076, 8809061, and 8713054. The Committee Reports to TAMRA state that options exercised on or before the effective date of the Act and disposed of in a disqualifying disposition should receive the same minimum tax treatment as regular tax treatment in both year of exercise and year of disposition. Thus, Congress appears to have recognized that before TAMRA, a disqualifying disposition effectively cancelled any AMT consequences.

38. The 2004 regulations specifically clarify that such an election is permissible for AMT purposes. Treas. Reg. § 1.422-1(b)(3), Example 2.

39. Before the 1991 SEC rules, exercises by Section 16(b) insiders presented the most frequent use of this planning opportunity. Under the pre-1991 SEC rules, insiders were unable to make "same-day-sales" of ISO stock. Under Section 83(c)(3) of the Code, stock transferred to an insider was considered to be unvested for tax purposes (regardless of whether it was otherwise fully vested) until the securities restrictions lapsed. Thus, if an insider exercised an ISO in the second half of the calendar year, vesting would not occur for AMT purposes until six months later, i.e., in the subsequent year. The Section 83(b) election provided the insider with the opportunity to take advantage of the six-month window to extend the time available for canceling AMT liability.

    Under the 1996 rules, insiders are no longer automatically subject to the six-month waiting period on exercise (unless the option itself has been held for less than six months and no other securities law exemptions apply). Accordingly, the Section 83(b) election for AMT must be evaluated on the same basis for insiders as for all other ISO optionees.

40. Accordingly, where appropriate, optionees should file Section 83(b) elections for AMT within 30 days of the time ISOs are exercised for restricted shares. Again, various factors may influence the decision on filing the election, including whether the optionee intends to hold the ISO stock for the statutory holding period.

41. For modifications of ESPP options, the regulations provide that fair market value will be the higher of the fair market value on (1) the original grant date, (2) the date of the modification, or (3) the date of any intervening modification. Treas. Reg. § 1.424-1(e)(3).

42. Not all significant changes represent "additional benefits" for these purposes. For example, a change to the length of an ESPP offering period may or may not be an additional benefit. See, e.g., PLR 200418020 (Apr. 30, 2004) (suspension of offering period followed by an extension to permit exercise was not a modification).

43. Treas. Reg. § 1.424-1(e)(4)(i), (ii).

44. Treas. Reg. § 1.424-1(e)(4)(v).

45. Treas. Reg. § 1.424-1(e)(4)(viii)

46. Section 424(h)(3)(C) of the Code and Treas. Reg. § 1.424-1(e)(4)(ii) specifically state that a modification does not include a change in the terms of the option to accelerate the time within which the option may be exercised. However, this begs the question of whether acceleration of vesting—which also results in a acceleration of exercisability—constitutes a modification. IRS rulings on this issue suggest that vesting and exercisability are considered the same for these purposes, but the issue has never been directly addressed by the IRS. See Rev. Rul. 74-504, 1974-1 C.B. 105; PLR 89094011. Note, however, that the addition of a provision to accelerate on a change of control will result in a modification, but this is clearly distinguishable from a provision that simply provides for acceleration. See PLR 8330103. For more on change of control issues, see below.

47. Treas. Reg. § 1.424-1(a)(5). For these purposes, a former employee who has been gone for less than three months is treated as a current employee and can receive the tax-free benefits of the 424(h) issuance.

CHAPTER 4

Employee Stock Purchase Plans

Contents

An employee stock purchase plan (referred to variously as an ESPP, "423 plan," or "Section 423 plan") is a special form of employee stock plan that operates like a subscription purchase plan but is treated for tax purposes like a stock option plan. It may be used in conjunction with or as an alternative to a discretionary stock option plan and/or restricted stock purchase plan. ESPPs are typically designed to give employees the opportunity to make regular, ongoing purchases of employer stock through accumulated payroll deductions, usually at a substantial discount from fair market value on the date of purchase. Generally, all purchases under an ESPP take place on a pre-determined date, at a formula price that is based upon market factors. At this writing, the majority of publicly disclosed domestic ESPPs are tax-qualified Section 423 plans, and as such are subject to various limitations and requirements (described in detail below). However, in some cases employers adopt ESPPs that do not meet the requirements of the Code. These "non-Section 423 ESPPs" are also discussed briefly below.

Because there is a high degree of tax and administrative complexity inherent in a typical ESPP, such plans generally are not adopted by private companies.[1] Public company planners, however, will discover that they have a great deal of flexibility to tailor an ESPP to meet both corporate and employee needs, even when the ESPP is subject to the special tax limitations set out in Section 423. As with any stock-based compensation plan, a company that implements an ESPP must be careful to comply with state and federal securities laws, which are discussed in chapter 7. As always, securities counsel should be consulted to determine the applicable rules.

This chapter discusses planning and design considerations and techniques that have developed over the years for ESPPs. The reader should note that while such techniques are still available under the Internal Revenue Code, changes to the accounting treatment of Section 423 plans may make many historically popular design features such as "look-backs" difficult for companies to use after 2005. For further details, see chapter 10.

4.1 Statutory Requirements for Section 423 Plans

Section 423 plans are governed by the specific requirements prescribed in Section 423 of the Code and its regulations, as well as the general requirements for statutory options set out in Sections 421 and 424 of the Code. As with an ISO plan, the employer must have a written Section 423 plan that sets forth the maximum number of shares that may be issued under the plan and the employees (or class of employees) who are eligible to receive options under the plan.[2] The plan must receive shareholder approval within 12 months of its adoption by the company's board of directors.[3]

However, unlike an ISO plan, administration of a Section 423 plan is subject to specific limitations on employee eligibility, participation, and availability. In order for options granted under an ESPP to be eligible for statutory option treatment, the plan must adhere to strict nondiscrimination rules, including a requirement that it be offered on a nondiscriminatory basis to all non-highly compensated employees of the company and that greater-than-5% shareholders be excluded from participation in the plan. These rules are intended to insure that Section 423 plans are not used as a vehicle for executive compensation. In fact, employers may wish to simply exclude top executives from participation entirely in order to ensure that the plan benefits only employees who do not ordinarily receive discretionary option grants under the company's stock option plans. This is an acceptable strategy under Section 423, which prohibits discrimination *in favor* of highly compensated employees, but does not prohibit discrimination *against* such employees.[4]

Specifically, the statutory prerequisites set out in Section 423(b) of the Code include:

1. Options may be granted only to employees of the employer corporation or its designated parent or subsidiary corporations to purchase stock in any such corporation.[5]

2. The plan must be approved by the shareholders of the granting corporation within 12 months before or after the plan is adopted.

3. Under the terms of the plan, no employee may be granted an option if such employee, immediately after the option is granted, owns stock having 5% or more of the voting power or value of all classes of stock of the employer or its parent or subsidiary corporations.[6]

4. Under the terms of the plan, if any options are granted to any employees, they must be granted to all employees of the corporation[7] with the exception of any or all of the following:

    a. Employees employed less than two years;

    b. Employees whose customary employment is 20 hours or less per week;

    c. Employees whose customary employment is for not more than five months in any calendar year; and

d. "Highly compensated" employees (as defined in Section 414(q) of the Code).

5. Under the terms of the plan, all employees granted such options must have the same rights and privileges, except that the amount of stock that may be purchased by any employee under such option may bear a uniform relationship to the total compensation, or the basic or regular rate of compensation, of employees, and a limit may be placed on the maximum number of shares that an employee may purchase under the plan. The key to satisfying the "equal rights and privileges" rule is to apply any administrative rules uniformly to all participants. For example, the plan may define compensation to include only base salary, or may also include bonus compensation, so long as the same definition applies to all. Another example: if the plan imposes administrative limitations on the number of shares that may be purchased during any offering period—such as an overall cap on number of shares, a cap determined by formula, or a maximum percentage of payroll—these limitations must apply across the board.[8]

6. Under the terms of the plan, the option price may not be less than the lesser of 85% of the fair market value of the stock determined either (1) at the time of grant of the option or (2) at the time of exercise of the option.

7. Under the terms of the plan, options may not be exercised after the expiration of (a) five years, if the option price may not be less than 85% of fair market value on the date of exercise, or (b) 27 months, if the option price may be the lesser of 85% of fair market value on the date of grant or exercise.

8. Under the terms of the plan, no employee may be granted an option which permits his rights to purchase stock under all Section 423 plans of the employer company (and its parent and subsidiary corporations), to accrue at a rate which exceeds $25,000 worth of stock (determined cumulatively on the basis of fair market value at the time of grant) for each calendar year in which such option is outstanding at any time.[9]

9. Under the terms of the plan, such options may not be transferable except by will or the laws of descent and distribution, and must be exercisable during the employee's life only by such employee.

4.2 ESPP Design

4.2.1 ESPP Design Vocabulary

The unique ESPP form has spawned the evolution of its own special vocabulary to describe plan design and operation. An understanding of the following terms is essential before working through all of the design elements of an ESPP:

1. *Offering Period:* The period during which rights to purchase stock under an ESPP are outstanding. The period begins for all participants on the offering date and ends on a pre-determined exercise date.

2. *Offering Date* or *Enrollment Date:* The first day of the offering period. Same as "date of grant" for tax purposes.

3. *Option:* The participant's right to participate in an offering period. For tax purposes, a Section 423 plan option begins on the offering date and has a term equal to the duration of the offering period.

4. *Exercise Date* or *Purchase Date:* Predetermined date upon which stock is purchased for all participants during an offering period. There is always an exercise date at the end of the offering period. There may also be interim exercise dates at the end of multiple exercise periods during a single offering period.

5. *Exercise Period:* Period during the offering period that is shorter in duration than the offering period. There is always an exercise date at the end of an exercise period. Although the first day of an exercise period may not be the offering date, the use of the term "exercise period" generally indicates that the exercise price will be determined with reference to the offering date rather than with reference to the first day of the exercise period.

6. *Exercise Price* or *Purchase Price:* The exercise price for a share of stock purchased at the end of an exercise period, generally determined as of the exercise date (frequently by applying a discount to fair market value on either the offering date or the exercise date).

7. *Overlapping Offering Periods:* Offering periods that run concurrently, but have different offering dates (and accordingly, may have different exercise prices).

8. *Automatic Low Offering Period:* An offering period that automatically terminates as of any exercise date on which the fair market value of a share of stock is lower than the fair market value of a share of stock was on the offering date.

9. *Participant* or *Optionee:* Employee who enrolls in an offering period.

These terms are used in connection with ESPPs throughout this book. Exhibit 4-1 illustrates the application of these terms to overlapping offering periods that include multiple exercise periods and an automatic low offering period.

4.2.2 Statutory Design Limits for Section 423 Plans

As the above requirements show, while Section 423 plans are a type of statutory option plan, they differ significantly from ISO plans. First, eligibility is strictly controlled under Section 423(b): while *all* employees must be eligible (subject to the four specific exclusions set out above) if any are to be eligible, an employee who owns 5% or more of the employer's stock immediately becomes ineligible as of the date he or she crosses the 5% threshold.[10] Second, the term "option" for purposes of a Section 423 plan generally refers to the right to participate in an offering period under the plan, rather than to an individual option grant.[11] All option grants are uniformly subject to a limitation on how much stock can be optioned by a single participant on a calendar-year basis, and the maximum number of shares under option for any offering period must be determinable on the offering date.[12] Third, the plan may not be drafted or operated in any manner

Exhibit 4-1. ESPP Offering Periods

Overlapping two-year offering periods (OP) with four six-month exercise periods (EP). Each purchase price (PP) is lower of 85% FMV on Offering Date (OD) or Exercise Date (ED).

	1/1/01	7/1/01	1/1/02	7/1/02	1/1/03	7/1/03	1/1/04	7/1/04	1/1/05
FMV	$20	$10	$5	$10	$20	$30	$35	$30	$40
OP1	OD1	*ED ------	ED -------- |					
PP($)		$8.50	$4.25						
			|						
OP2		OD2 ------	*ED ------- |					
PP($)			$4.25						
				|					
OP3			OD3 ------	ED --------	ED -------	ED -------- ED			
PP($)				$4.25	$4.25	$4.25	$4.25		
OP4				OD4 -------	ED -------	ED --------	ED -------- ED		
PP($)					$8.50	$8.50	$8.50	$8.50	
OP5					OD5 ----	ED --------	ED --------	ED -------- ED	
PP($)						$17.00	$17.00	$17.00	$17.00

*Automatic Low Offering Periods (OP1 and OP2): Terminate on any ED when ED price is lower than OD price, automatically purchasing shares and then enrolling all participants in next OP.

that would result in different classes of employees having unequal "rights and privileges."[13]

It can be very challenging to ensure that both the plan design and its operation comply with all of these rules. For example, the application of uniform rules with different results will not violate the "equal rights and privileges" requirement. This means that if a plan provides that all participants may set aside up to 10% of compensation for purchases under an offering period, the fact that employees with different levels of income will accordingly be able to purchase different amounts of stock does not violate the rule even though the number of shares under option may vary widely. Another difficult application of the rules arises from the $25,000 limitation, because of the complexities of computing the annual limit on an accrual basis. Under Section 423(b)(8) and its regulations, the option value is measured when the option first becomes exercisable, i.e., the offering date. The key to the calculation, however, is *accrual in accordance with the annual $25,000 limit*, not purchase in accordance with the limit. This means that, if the plan so permits, a participant could purchase zero shares in the first year of a 24-month offering period, and $50,000 worth of stock (computed as of the offering date) in the second year of such offering period, although this cannot be reversed—i.e., the unaccrued right to purchase $50,000 worth of stock may not be anticipated in the first year of the offering period. If the employee is participating in more than one offering period at any time, the total accrual under all offering periods will be added together to determine when the limit has been achieved, but amounts accrued under one offering period may not be used in a subsequent (or concurrent) offering period, even if the limit has not been exhausted with respect to any particular calendar year.

By way of illustration, assume that the offering period is 24 months and the offering date is January 1. If the stock was worth $10 per share on the offering date, each January 1 participant may buy up to 2,500 shares of stock for each calendar year of the offering period (subject to whatever percentage or other limitations have otherwise been imposed by the company). However, now assume that a new offering period begins every six months, and the price on July 1 is $15 per share. For the offering period beginning on January 1, a participant has an option to purchase up to 2500 shares. However, assume that he is only actually able to purchase 1000 shares (shares with a value of $10,000) by the end of the first offering period, leaving a 1,500-share deficit. The unused portion of the January 1 option—1,500 shares—terminates on the last exercise date of the offering period (June 30), and may not be carried over to any subsequent offering period. For the offering period beginning July 1, the participant's available maximum would be the difference between $25,000 (the total calendar year maximum) and $10,000 (the amount of value purchased), over $15 (the value of a share on the offering date), or 1,000 shares. This calculation can become even more complicated when short offering periods straddle two calendar years.

In practice, companies need to ensure that the pool of shares allocated to the ESPP doesn't get used up too quickly and that the plan can be administered without excessive attention to arcane calculations. This is particularly important during a downturn in the market when the discounted price of shares drops, and the number of shares purchasable with participant funds rises accordingly. The best way to handle this may be threefold: (1) percentage of compensation, (2) cap on total number of shares that may be purchased during the offering period, notwithstanding percentage, and (3) the $25,000 limit.

It is easy to see that the interplay of these limits means that employers must take special care to monitor day-to-day operation of a Section 423 plan. Failure to stay within the limits can result, at best, in disqualification of a single option from Section 423 plan status and, at worst, in disqualification of the entire offering or plan. Pursuant to the regulations, disqualification of the entire offering period may result if an individual is permitted to participate who is ineligible under Section 423(b)(4), if an option is priced below the minimum pricing requirements of Section 423(b)(6), if an offering period exceeds the durational limits of Section 423(b)(7) and if the purchase (or right to purchase stock) during an offering period accrues at a rate in excess of that permitted in 423(b)(8). Such inadvertent disqualification can result in serious adverse tax consequences to employees who were expecting to be eligible for the tax benefits of Section 423.[14]

4.2.3 Typical Structure of an ESPP: Payroll Deduction Plans

As detailed above, Section 423 sets out a long laundry list of requirements for tax qualification under the Code. However, although one would assume that non-Section 423 ESPPs offer greater possibilities for plan design, employers have been able to develop remarkably flexible plans for employees within the confines of the rules. By incorporating Section 423 compliance into ESPP planning, employers have been able to provide plan participants with a substantial discount from market price (as well as tax deferral). In practice, non-Section 423 ESPPs often look identical to Section 423 plans—but they can operate without concern for statutory limitations. For example, like most Section 423 ESPPs, most non-Section 423 ESPPs are designed to be payroll deduction plans. However, the company may decide to limit or expand its eligible class of participants, vary the types of benefits extended to different participants, and extend or reduce the length of offering periods. In their simplest form, ESPPs may be "open market plans" that offer little or no discount to the participant but provide an ongoing investment vehicle for regular stock purchases.[15]

Although ESPPs that do not conform with Section 423 can offer share-price discounts, any discount will be considered to be deferred compensation subject to Code Section 409A and thus be subject to immediate taxation and penalties at vesting. Under proposed regulations to 409A, a discounted equity award can be canceled and replaced with an option whose exercise price matches the fair market value from the original grant date any time before December 31, 2006, without triggering 409A, but exercise of a discounted option in 2006 will cause the shares to be treated as deferred compensation under the section's rules. Section 423 ESPPs can offer discounts without being considered deferred compensation.

The most widely used form of ESPP has been the payroll deduction plan (PDP), pioneered largely by Silicon Valley companies in the early 1980s. When designing a PDP, the employer must consider two levels of issues: (1) the overall structure of the offering period and (2) the enrollment procedure/participation level permitted for participants. The limitations of the Code act as an overarching framework to the design, but administrative convenience will generally govern the operation of the plan.[16]

Offering Period Structure

In a typical PDP, the employer first decides whether it will establish long or short offering periods, and whether such offering periods will be consecutive or concurrent. Offering and exercise periods may be six months or less. However, an offering period should not be less than three months or it runs the risk of violating the rule in Section 421 of the Code that requires an optionee to be continuously employed for at least three months prior to exercise of a statutory stock option.[17] Options offered under such an offering period would be disqualified from Section 423 status.

A short, consecutive offering period structure has the advantage of being straightforward and easy to administer. It has a single exercise date, after which the offering period ends and a new offering period (with a new offering date price) begins. The exercise price for each option is computed as the lower of 85% of fair market value on the offering date or the exercise date. At the exercise date, the number of optioned shares which may be purchased with the funds credited to the participant's account for that period are purchased. If the participant has withdrawn from the offering period prior to the exercise date, his option terminates on the date of the withdrawal and all payroll deductions that have been withheld so far in the offering period are returned to him. The plan as a whole may be easily terminated without adversely affecting any individual participant's rights to purchase stock, since there are no concurrent offering periods. Because the offering period is short, the stock price is unlikely to undergo large fluctuations between offering date and exercise date, making it possible to realistically predict the number of shares needed to fund the plan on an ongoing basis.

A long offering period may be more administratively complex, but it has the advantage of providing exceptional price benefits to employees and as such will be perceived very favorably as an employee benefit. Such an offering period might last as long as two years, including multiple exercise periods: for example, a 24-month offering period might have four 6-month exercise periods. During the offering period, participants who were enrolled on the offering date have an option to make four purchases (one on each exercise date). The exercise price for each purchase is computed as the lower of 85% of fair market value on the offering date or the exercise date. Although the exercise date price may change, the offering date price remains constant.[18] Because each offering period has only one offering date, employers who establish long offering periods will generally set them up as overlapping, concurrent offering periods so that new employees may participate without waiting until the first offering period terminates. If new offering periods begin every six or 12 months, the plan administrator must be aware that in an up market, there will be multiple exercise prices on any given exercise date (i.e., if the stock price is steadily rising, the first offering period will always have the lowest exercise price because the discount will be taken from the earliest offering date price). In a down market, the number of shares purchasable in any offering period will increase as the price drops. In a worst case scenario, this can result in the plan running out of stock mid-offering period.[19]

Plan designers should be aware that while the regulations permit complicated accruals for plans that have long offering periods, the plan itself may be designed to avoid such complications. For example, a plan could limit the amount of stock value that may be accrued under all plans of the company during any six-month period to $12,500 worth of stock, notwithstanding the $25,000 annual cap. A plan could also provide that eligible participants may participate in only one concurrent offering period at a time (so long as this rule is applied uniformly to all participants).

Obviously, in an up market, the discount from fair market value at the date of grant can increase dramatically with the fair market value of the shares under this type of ESPP. Assume, for example, that the fair market value of the stock is $20 at the date of grant and that, with a 15% discount, the purchase price would be $17 (85% of $20). Assume further that at month 24 the fair market value of the stock is $40. By allowing an employee to purchase the shares at 85% of the lesser of date of grant or date of exercise, the 15% discount would increase, in this example, to a discount of 42.5% of the value on the date of purchase. However, what happens in a down-market scenario? The cash amount reserved to the participant's account remains the same, but as the stock price decreases the number of shares purchasable with the static cash reserve will increase. Ironically, in a falling market participants are unlikely to want to purchase more stock. They are more likely to choose to withdraw from the offering period (after the end of the exercise period) and immediately re-enter at a different percentage on the next offering date, so as to lock in the lower prices being set for subsequent offering periods.[20] See Exhibit 4-1 above for an illustration.

Enrollment Procedures/Participation Level

A major administrative asset of a PDP is its automatic purchase feature.[21] This is made possible by establishing participant accounts that are pre-funded through (after-tax) payroll contributions. To become a participant, each employee completes a subscription or enrollment agreement prior to the offering date of the first offering period that they are eligible to join. The enrollment agreement states the percentage of after-tax earnings that the participant wishes to set aside for use in purchasing stock optioned under the plan.[22] During the offering period, the company accumulates the deducted amounts in accounts for the plan participants. Unless a participant withdraws from the plan before the exercise date, his or her option is exercised automatically by the company on that date. The number of shares purchased is the maximum number of shares that may be purchased with the accumulated payroll deductions in the participant's account at the applicable option price, up to the overall number of shares subject to the option (as determined on the offering date).[23] If there are not enough shares available under the plan to be purchased at the end of an exercise period or if the amounts accumulated in the participant's account would purchase an amount of shares exceeding the maximum available to a participant under the plan, the balance of the funds can be returned to the participant (with or without interest at the discretion of the company) or can be carried over to the next exercise or offering period. At the discretion of the company, the initial enrollment agreement may stay in place indefinitely until withdrawn by the participant or the participant may be required to file a new enrollment agreement for each offering period.[24]

There are a variety of ways of dealing with withdrawals or percentage changes under the plan, particularly in a down market when employees may want to reduce their investment in company stock so as to diversify their portfolios. Plans should always permit the participant to withdraw completely from an offering period, or options granted under that offering period may be deemed to be exercised for tax purposes on each date that payroll deductions are accumulated in the participant's account.[25] Otherwise, there are no statutory restrictions on how employee contributions must be handled: it is purely a matter of administrative design for the company. Some employers permit participants to make withdrawals and changes in their election percentage at any time during the offering period, while some limit the number of times that changes can occur, or permit withdrawals and percentage decreases but not increases during an exercise period.

A well-designed plan will also include provisions for automatic withdrawal in certain circumstances. The best example of this is automatic withdrawal from the plan (and return of all contributions) when a participant terminates employment during an offering period. This ensures that the plan does not actually authorize disqualification based on employment-related requirements.[26] Another administratively useful example is automatic withdrawal as part of an automatic low offering period mechanism. This feature provides that when multiple overlapping offering periods exist, the plan automatically (1) withdraws participants as of any exercise date where the exercise date price is lower than the offering date price and (2) enrolls such participants in a new offering period beginning on the day after the exercise date. This provision needs to be included in the plan prior to the beginning of the affected offering period, otherwise its addition may be deemed to adversely modify rights granted under the plan and accordingly require the consent of all participants to be effective. Note that the automatic low offering period mechanism may be viewed as dilutive by nonemployee stockholders. However, since participants are always free to withdraw from an offering period and re-enroll in a later period, the technique is really just for administrative convenience. Moreover, in plans that limit the number of times that changes can occur, the automatic low offering period may be the only way to avoid penalizing employees who have a higher offering date price because of seniority.[27]

4.3 Tax Consequences

The tax consequences of ESPP options, like the tax consequences of stock options generally, depend on whether or not the options are statutory stock options. ESPPs intended to qualify under Section 423 of the Code are statutory stock option plans, and in addition to the specific rules set out in Section 423 are governed (along with ISO plans) by Sections 421 and 424 of the Code.[28]

ESPP options that are not granted under a Section 423 plan are NSOs for tax purposes, and as such are governed by Section 83 of the

Code (discussed more fully in chapter 2 above). Accordingly, in the year of exercise, the participant will be required to include in ordinary income the difference between the exercise price and the fair market value of the stock on the exercise date. As a general rule, the employer will be entitled to take a tax deduction in an amount equal to that included in income by the participant.[29] If a non-qualified ESPP offers a discount from the stock's price on the first day of the offering period, then that amount is treated as deferred compensation under Code Section 409A. Gain recognized on the disposition of ESPP shares will be treated as long-term capital gain if the shares were held for more than one year from the exercise date. The mechanics of reporting and withholding on the exercise of an NSO are described in chapter 9, "Tax Law Compliance Issues."

4.3.1 Employee Income Taxes

If a plan satisfies all of the Section 423 requirements, the ultimate tax consequences depend on the actions of the employee and the option price of the stock purchased in relation to its fair market value. A plan participant will not recognize income for federal income tax purposes either upon the grant of an option (the offering date) or upon the exercise of an option (exercise date) under the plan. Instead, all income tax consequences will be deferred until the participant sells the stock or otherwise disposes of the shares.

If stock granted at less than fair market value is held for the statutory holding periods (more than one year from exercise date and more than two years after the offering date), or if the participant dies while owning the shares, the participant will realize ordinary income on a sale (or a disposition by way of gift) to the extent of the lesser of: (1) the difference between the fair market value of the stock and the option price at the *date of grant* or (2) the actual gain (the amount by which the market value of the shares on the *date of sale or disposition* exceeds the purchase price).[30] All additional gain upon the sale of stock is treated as long-term capital gain. If the shares are sold and the sale price is less than the purchase price, there is no ordinary income, and the employee has a long-term capital loss for the difference between the sale price and the purchase price.[31] To get the benefits of a qualifying disposition, the employee must, at all times during the period beginning with the date of grant and ending on the day three months before the option is exercised, be an employee of the corporation granting the option (or of a parent or subsidiary corporation of the employer corporation).[32]

If the participant makes a disqualifying disposition of Section 423 plan stock, the participant recognizes ordinary income at the time of sale or other disposition taxable to the extent of the spread on exercise—i.e., the difference between fair market value and purchase price on the *exercise date*. This excess will constitute ordinary income in the year of sale or other disposition even if no gain is realized on the sale or if a gratuitous transfer is made. The difference, if any, between the proceeds of sale and the fair market value of the stock at the exercise date is a capital gain or loss (which is long-term if the stock has been held more than one year). Ordinary income recognized by an employee upon a disqualifying disposition constitutes taxable compensation which must be reported on a W-2 form.[33]

4.3.2 Employer Income Taxes

Neither income tax nor payroll tax withholding is required on a disqualifying disposition of ESPP stock. The American Jobs Creation Act of 2004 settled a 33-year dispute between employers and the IRS over whether withholding was required by stating specifically that it is not.[34] Subject to any limitations otherwise imposed by the Code,[35] the employer company is entitled to take a deduction for federal income tax purposes to the extent that a participant recognized ordinary income on a disqualifying disposition. The company is not entitled to a deduction if the participant meets the statutory holding period requirements. In order to enable the company to learn of disqualifying dispositions and ascertain the amount of the deduction to which it is entitled, participants should be required to notify the employer company in writing of the date and terms of any disposition of stock purchased under the plan. As with ISOs, the employer will be unable to take the deduction unless the disqualifying disposition has been properly "tracked." The mechanics of reporting and withholding on disqualifying dispositions are further described in chapter 9, "Tax Law Compliance Issues."

Exhibits 4-2 and 4-3 illustrate the tax consequences of exercising Section 423 options.

4.3.3 Quirky Tax Outcomes for Section 423 Plans in Down Markets

Notwithstanding the general tax treatment described above, the operation of the Section 423 rules can produce some surprising results in plans that follow the "typical" formula (purchase price computed as a discount from the fair market value at either offering date or exercise date, whichever is lower). In a rising market, we assume that the market value of the stock at the purchase date will be higher than it was at the offering date, and thus the purchase-price discount will be taken from the fair market value on the *offering date*. In a down market, however, it works the other way: the purchase-price discount is taken from the fair market value on the *exercise date*.

If the optionee satisfies the statutory holding period requirements, Section 423(c) treats as ordinary income the portion of the gain equal to up to 15% of the offering date price, *regardless of the actual purchase price for the stock*. This contrasts with tax treatment on a disqualifying disposition, which characterizes *only the spread at exercise* as ordinary income.

Thus, in a down market, it is possible to get a better tax benefit from a disqualifying disposition than from a qualifying disposition. Although counterintuitive, the optionee's tax outcome may be improved by selling earlier, particularly if the shares were held just long enough for the capital gains to be taxed at the lower long-term rates (i.e., one year from purchase but not two years from grant).

In the down-market scenario, optionees need to be aware that they may control tax consequences by timing the disposition. Exhibit 4-4 illustrates this strange tax result.

4.4 International Planning Considerations

Although a detailed discussion of international ESPP issues is beyond the scope of this chapter, it is important to note the key question of

Exhibit 4-2. 423 Plan Options—Illustration: Gain on Disposition

	Qualifying	Disqualifying
Fair market value:		
First day	$10.00	$10.00
85%	8.50	8.50
Last day	20.00	20.00
85%	17.00	17.00
Exercise price:		
Lesser of 85% first or last day	8.50	8.50
Sale price	30.00	30.00
Exercise price	8.50	8.50
Gain	$21.50	$21.50
Ordinary income:	$1.50 (15% at grant)	$11.50[a]
Capital gain:	$20.00 long-term capital gain	$10.00[b]

[a]Ordinary income on discount at exercise

[b]Long-term capital gain or short-term capital gain, depending on holding period

Exhibit 4-3. 423 Plan Options—Illustration: Loss on Disposition

	Qualifying	Disqualifying
Fair market value		
First day	$10.00	$10.00
85%	8.50	8.50
Last day	$20.00	$20.00
85%	17.00	17.00
Exercise price:		
Lesser of 85% first or last day	8.50	8.50
Sale price	5.00	5.00
Exercise price	8.50	8.50
(Loss)	($3.50)	($3.50)
Ordinary income:	-0-[a]	11.50[b]
Capital loss	($3.50) long-term capital loss	($15.00)[c]

[a] Lesser of discount at offering date or actual gain

[b] Discount at exercise

[c] Short-term or long-term capital loss (sale price minus fair market value at exercise)

Exhibit 4-4. Disqualifying Disposition in a Down Market

Facts: 6-month offering period, 85% FMV pricing

Offering date FMV: $20; 15% discount = $3 (85% = $17)

Exercise date FMV: $10; 85% (actual exercise price) = $8.50; 15% discount = $1.50

Sale prices: (a) $50 (b) $15 (c) $5

Scenario 1: Qualifying dispositions (QDs): Sections 423(c) and 1.423-2(k) provide that the lesser of the difference between option price and FMV on date of grant and actual amount of gain on sale is included in ordinary income (OI). The remainder is capital gain (CG) or capital loss (CL), which is either long-term (LT) or short-term (ST). For these purposes, the first day of the offering period is the date of grant even if the price is not yet determinable, and the option is treated as having been exercised on that date.

Scenario 2: Disqualifying dispositions (DDs): Section 421(a) does not apply. Apply Section 83 on exercise date to difference between FMV and option price.

(a) *$50 sale price*

    QD: Discount at offering date: $3

           Gain on sale: $50 − $8.50 = $41.50

           Lesser of $3 or $41.50 = $3.

           OI =$3, LTCG = $38.50.

    DD: OI on discount at exercise date: $1.50

           CG on sale: $50 − $10 = $40

(b) *$15 sale price*

    QD: Discount at offering date: $3

           Gain on sale: $15 − $8.50 = $6.50

           Lesser of $3 or $6.50 = $3

           OI = $3, LTCG = $3.50

    DD: OI on discount at exercise date: $1.50

           CG on sale: $15 − $10 = $5

(c) *$5 sale price*

    QD: Discount at offering date: $3

           Gain (loss) on sale: $5 − $8.50 = ($3.50)

           Lesser of $3 or ($3.50) = ($3.50)

           OI = $0, LTCL = $3.50

    DD: OI on discount at exercise date: $1.50

           CL on sale: $5 − $10 = ($5)

when—and whether—to include international employees as participants in the plan. Companies that employ non-U.S. employees (both
resident and nonresident) should be aware that even when Section
423 provides no tax benefits to such employees, they must be eligible
to participate in the company's plan if not otherwise excluded under
Section 423(b) of the Code. This rule can cause serious conflicts for the
company if local laws require employees to receive special treatment
that is not otherwise available to U.S. employees under the plan: i.e.,
that results in a violation of the "equal rights and privileges" requirement set out in the regulations. Notwithstanding this conundrum,
failure to extend participation to non-U.S. employees who should
otherwise be included in any offering period—and to take such employees into account for purposes of Section 423 nondiscrimination—
can result in disqualification of the individual option, the plan, and/
or the offering period.

The saving grace with respect to this problem is that although an
ESPP must be offered to all employees of designated companies if it is
offered to any employees of such companies, it is *never necessary to
include all subsidiaries for participation*. In fact, unless a parent or subsidiary is specifically designated as a covered entity in the plan, the employer is not required to extend participation to its employees. This
design element may help global companies that employ non-U.S.
employees through foreign subsidiaries, as it provides one permissible
way to avoid raising eligibility and nondiscrimination issues with respect to such employees.[36]

Notes

1. In particular, most ESPPs are designed around an ongoing, automatic calcu-
    lation of fair market value and an automatic purchase technique that pre-
    sents a practical nightmare for the nonpublicly traded company. ESPP ad-
    ministration (including reporting and tracking) is frequently handled by the
    company's broker or transfer agent, an alternative not available to a privately
    held company. Moreover, employees are unlikely to choose to make ongo-
    ing, automatic after-tax investments when there is no guarantee that there
    will ever be a public market for sale of the stock. Unless the employer is
    willing to provide for a put to the company on ESPP stock (a bad idea for

many reasons!), employees of privately held companies are better off when they can control the timing of stock purchase (i.e., under an ISO or NSO).

2. Treas. Reg. § 1.423-2(c)(3), (4). As with an ISO plan, any changes to the number of shares or class of employees eligible to receive shares under the plan require additional shareholder approval.

3. Treas. Reg. § 1.423-2(c)(1), (2).

4. Section 423(a)(3), (5) of the Code; Treas. Reg. § 1.423-2(d), (e).

5. For these purposes, and for all statutory options, "employee" is defined with reference to the common-law definition of employee as used for purposes of wage withholding under Section 3402 of the Code. Treas. Reg. § 1.421-1(h). See also IRS Notice 87-41, 1987-1 CB 296 (the "20-factor test"). The definitions of "parent" and "subsidiary" for statutory option purposes are set out in Section 424 of the Code.

6. Section 423(b)(3) of the Code. The rules for determining the percentage of stock ownership are set out in Section 424(d) of the Code.

7. Section 423(b)(4) of the Code.

8. See Treas. Reg. § 1.423-2 (f).

9. Section 423(b)(8) of the Code.; See also Treas. Reg. § 1.423-2(i) and the examples in Treas. Reg. § 1.423-2(i)(4).

10. Section 423(b)(4); Treas. Reg. § 1.423-2(d), (e).

11. See Treas. Reg. § 1.421-1(a)(2).

12. Treas. Reg. § 1.423-2(h) (option period); Section 423(b)(8), Treas. Reg. § 1.423(i) ($25,000 annual limit). The IRS has agreed with the position that the incorporation of the $25,000 annual limit under the plan is adequate to establish the maximum number of shares available, since the number may be computed on the offering date by dividing $25,000 by the fair market value of the shares on that date. See Rev. Rul. 73-223, 1973-1 C.B.206. But see PLR 9414042 (formula that resulted in maximum price determinable only on last day of offering period was not sufficient to fix maximum number of shares purchasable on offering date, even though a maximum number of shares was included). The 2004 regulations did not discuss this issue. Although a maximum number is not *per se* required to be stated to meet the requirements of Section 423, the conservative approach is to include such a number.

13. Section 423(b)(5); Treas. Reg. § 1.423-2(f).

14. See Treas. Reg. § 1.423-2(i).

15. See, e.g., Ryan Weeden et al., "Introduction," *Employee Stock Purchase Plans* (Oakland, CA: NCEO, 2001).

16. For some practical thoughts on plan administration, see Barbara A. Baksa, "Administering an Employee Stock Purchase Plan," in *Employee Stock Purchase Plans* (Oakland, CA: NCEO, 2001).

17. Section 421(b) of the Code; Treas. Reg. § 1.421-1(h).

18. See Section 423(b)(7) of the Code.

19. See chapter 13 ("Shareholder Approval Considerations") and chapter 15 ("Reloads, Evergreens, Repricings, and Exchanges") for more on issues related to running out of shares in a statutory stock plan.

20. See discussion of "automatic low offering periods" below.

21. The plan can provide that options are exercisable by cash payment or by promissory note at the date of exercise as well as by payroll withholding. However, few ESPPs have this feature because of the administrative difficulty of obtaining timely payment from optionees on the exercise date.

22. The amount of the percentage is purely discretionary to the company, although typical caps are in the 10–15% range. As noted above, the Code requires only that each participant be limited to $25,000 worth of stock, computed as of the offering date, under all Section 423 plans of the company during any calendar year.

23. The exact number is computed by dividing the actual amount in the participant's account by the exercise price set on the exercise date, and then applying any additional caps (e.g., number of shares equal to $25,000 on offering date, company-imposed per-participant offering cap) to that number.

24. Note that this is where the difference between offering period and exercise period becomes important in a long offering period: "excess" funds will always be carried over (unless otherwise withdrawn by the participant) to the next exercise period, even if re-enrollment and return of funds is required for subsequent offering periods.

25. See Treas. Reg. § 1.421-1(f).

26. For example, options (or the entire offering period) could be disqualified if exercised more than three months after termination of employment (Section 421(a)) or if only some participants are afforded the right to participate after termination (Section 423(b).

27. Of course, it's not necessary for the company to "rescue" employees from unfavorable stock prices (and it is noteworthy that in this type of ESPP, an "underwater" offering date price will be ignored in favor of a discount from the exercise date price anyway).

28. As a general rule, the same rules apply to modifications of Section 423 plan options as apply to ISOs. See discussion on "Modifying Statutory Stock

Options" in section 3.5 above. However, note that—unlike an ISO—an ESPP right that is modified, renewed, or extended must be priced at the higher of fair market value at the date of grant, the date of modification, or the date of any previous modification. Section 424(h)(2) of the Code; Treas. Reg. § 1.424-1(e)(3).

29. Section 83(h) of the Code; Treas. Reg. § 1.83-6(a).

30. Different rules apply on disposition of statutory option stock as a result of death. See chapter 16. In addition, Section 421(d) (added by the American Jobs Creation Act of 2004) provides that after October 22, 2004, a person who is required to sell ESPP stock for purposes of complying with federal conflict of interest laws is treated as satisfying the statutory holding period regardless of how long the stock was held.

31. Section 423(c) of the Code; Treas. Reg. § 1.423-2(k).

32. Section 421(a) of the Code.

33. See Section 421(b) of the Code; Treas. Reg. § 1.83-6(a)(2). Compare this treatment to the treatment of a loss on a disqualifying disposition of ISO stock described in section 3.3 of chapter 3.

34. For the history of the withholding dispute see Rev. Rul. 71-52, 1971-1 CB 278. The application of this Revenue Ruling to ESPP stock was long the subject of much controversy. See, e.g., Alisa J. Baker and Renee R. Deming, "Disqualifying Dispositions of Statutory Option Stock Subject to Withholding?" *Journal of Taxation* 72 (1990): 218; Mary Hevener, "Tax Withholding Changes Under Consideration for ISOs and Employee Stock Purchase Plans," *Tax Management Compensation Planning Journal* 18 (1990): 249. See also Alisa J. Baker, "Withholding FICA on ESPP Options," *NASPP Stock Plan Advisor,* summer 1998. For many years, the IRS inconsistently applied a withholding requirement in private letter rulings. See, e.g., PLRs 9407013, 9243026, 8926010, 8921027, 8920030, 8919004, and 8912039 (requiring withholding on disqualifying dispositions from ESPP plans), and PLRs 9452012, 9309035, and 9245020 (declining to comment or rule on withholding). In public forums during the 1990s, representatives of the IRS stated that withholding should be required for both FICA and federal income tax purposes, and in 1999 the IRS issued a field service advisory (FSA 199926034) that restated this position for the benefit of its auditors. Until publication of the Proposed Withholding Regs in 2001, however, there was no public ruling or statement on this issue.

35. For example, the limitations on deductions in Sections 162(m) and 280G of the Code. See section 9.5 of chapter 9 ("Tax Law Compliance Issues").

36. Counsel should always be consulted before making decisions with regard to international plan matters. For general information on international plans see, e.g., *Equity-Based Compensation for Multinational Corporations* (Oakland, CA: NCEO, 2002). Current updates on international issues are readily available online at *www.naspp.com* and *www.geo.org*. In addition, various international law and accounting firms maintain subscription-based reporting services aimed at keeping companies updated on changing rules in one or more countries.

CHAPTER 5

Financing the Purchase of Stock Options

Contents

For the optionee, receiving a grant is only the first step in realizing the compensation aspect of equity compensation. To get the benefit of an option, the optionee must actually purchase the underlying stock. Of course, the easiest way (for all concerned!) for an optionee to exercise an option is with cash. However, a company that wants to encourage its employees to buy and hold stock may decide to offer alternative financing methods. As this chapter will show, there are numerous alternatives available, ranging from stock swaps to loans. Each alternative raises its own set of issues and procedures, and these issues have increased along with the increased politics around executive compensation. As will be discussed, in many cases the benefits of stock option financing arrangements to the employee are now far outweighed by their negative impact on the employer (at least in the public company setting).

5.1 Alternatives to Cash

Compensatory stock options always may be exercised by tender of cash in the amount of the exercise price stated in the option grant. However, many companies are willing to provide their employees with alternative financing mechanisms to assist in option exercises. This chapter discusses several of the most popular alternatives, including stock swaps, same-day-sale arrangements for public companies, and company-provided loans.

In all cases, alternative financing must be authorized in the company's stock option plan as well as in the option grant itself. If the plan and agreement do not allow for alternative financing, the company will find itself severely limited as to what it can legitimately offer to optionees at the time of grant. Moreover, if a company allows an employee to exercise an ISO using an alternative method when that method has not been authorized in both grant and plan, the exercise will result in a Section 424(h) modification of the ISO at time of exercise. If the ISO is not repriced at that time, it will be treated as an NSO for tax purposes. Finally, financing modifications carry accounting consequences that will be discussed in chapter 10. Plan administrators need to be aware that these issues will arise if the board decides to amend an option to allow for new forms of payment.

5.2 Stock Swaps

If the company has made multiple grants to employees, it may wish to allow them to exercise their options with previously owned stock (a "stock swap"). The rules governing the tax consequences of stock swaps are extremely complex, and the following discussion only touches upon the key issues. For NSO purposes, the general principles regarding "like-kind exchanges" under Sections 1036 and 1031(d) of the Code will apply. For ISO purposes, stock swaps are specifically authorized by Section 422(c)(4)(A) of the Code (and are also subject to Sections 1036 and 1031(d)). The compensation planner should study Treas. Reg. § 1.422-5(b)(1) and the examples in Treas. Reg. § 1.422-5(e) for a detailed explanation of the IRS position on stock swaps of statutory options.[1] Both the FASB and the SEC look favorably on such swaps, but companies should be aware that securities and accounting issues may arise when using this technique.[2]

For those options that do permit stock swaps, the key to analyzing the tax consequences on the swap is to focus on three separate levels of stock purchases: (1) the original purchase of the shares that will be exchanged in the swap, (2) the purchase of shares under the current option, and (3) the character of the sale on the acquired stock. The following discussion considers both levels of a stock swap when (1) an ISO is exercised with stock other than restricted stock, (2) an NSO is exercised with stock other than restricted stock, and (3) an ISO or NSO is exercised with restricted stock. Exhibit 5-1 provides an example illustrating stock swaps. *(Note: For purposes of this chapter, when we discuss "restricted stock," we are referring to tax, not securities, restrictions—i.e., nonvested stock.)*

For convenience, this discussion uses the following terminology in describing stock swaps. Shares that were acquired previously and are swapped or surrendered to exercise a new option are referred to as "swapped shares." Shares that are received in the swap in a one-to-one like-kind exchange for the swapped shares (pursuant to Section 1036 of the Code) are referred to as "replacement shares." Shares that are received in excess of the replacement shares (which constitute the compensation element of the swap) are referred to as "additional shares."

5.2.1 Exercise of an ISO with Stock Other Than Restricted Stock

Under Section 422(c)(4)(A) of the Code, an ISO may be exercised using stock of the granting corporation so long as all other ISO require-

Exhibit 5-1. Stock Swap:

First Level: *Shares Purchased Pursuant to Option*
Assumptions are for an option on 50 shares at $50 per share

	ISO	NSO
Exercise price	$2,500	$2,500
FMV at exercise	$5,000	$5,000
Amount included	-0-	$2,500
Basis$2,500	$5,000	

Second Level: *Option Exercised with Swapped Shares*

100 shares purchased at $100 per share using the 50 shares purchased pursuant to option above	**1** ISO shares for ISO shares, old Section 422 holding period met	**2** ISO shares for ISO shares, old Section 422 holding period *not* met
FMV on 1/1/2002	$20,000	$20,000
Total exercise price	10,000	10,000
Spread on exercise (AMT)	(10,000)	(10,000)
Amount included as compensation on exercise	-0-	2,500 (DD)
Basis:		
50 swapped shares	2,500	2,500
100 new shares:	2,500	5,000
50 replacement shares	2,500	5,000
50 additional shares	-0-	-0-

Third Level: *Sale of New Shares*

Total sale price	30,000	30,000
Total gain on sale	27,500	25,000
Character if sold on:[a]		
7/1/2002 (DD)		
Ordinary income	10,000	10,000
Capital gain[b]	12,500 LT, 5,000 ST	15,000
1/1/2003 (QD)		
Ordinary income	-0-	-0-
Capital gain	27,500 LT	25,000 LT

[a] If shares are sold in more than one transaction, the IRS treats the lowest-basis shares as sold first, absent a designation under Code Section 1012.

[b] The character and amount of capital gain for replacement shares (long-term or short-term) depends on the original purchase date of swapped shares.

Analysis of Tax Consequences

Abbreviations:

FMV	= fair market value	ST	= short-term capital gain
AMT	= alternative minimum tax	LT	= long-term capital gain
DD	= disqualifying disposition	QD	= qualifying disposition

3	4	5
NSO shares for ISO shares	ISO shares for NSO shares	NSO shares for NSO shares
$20,000	$20,000	$20,000
10,000	10,000	10,000
(10,000)	10,000	10,000
-0-	10,000	10,000
5,000	2,500	5,000
5,000	12,500	15,000
5,000	2,500	5,000
-0-	10,000	10,000
30,000	30,000	30,000
25,000	17,500	15,000
10,000	-0-	-0-
15,000	17,500	15,000[b]
-0-	-0-	-0-
25,000 LT	17,500 LT	15,000 LT

ments are met and the option plan and the grant allow exercise with stock. Special rules apply if the stock has been purchased pursuant to an ISO or Section 423 plan (referred to here as "statutory option shares"). Columns 1 and 2 of Exhibit 5-1 give an example of a swap using statutory option shares.

Basis Rules[3]

Treas. Reg. § 1.422-5(b)(3) provides that exercise of an ISO with previously acquired stock is a tax-free exchange under Section 1036 of the Code to the extent that old shares are exchanged for an equal number and kind of new shares (the "replacement shares"). Generally, the employee will take a "carryover basis" in the replacement shares under Section 1031(d) of the Code—i.e., a basis equal to his or her original cost basis in the swapped shares—*increased* by any amount included in income as compensation under Code Sections 421 through 424 or Code Section 83 as a result of the swap. The exception to this occurs when ISO shares that have been held for the full ISO holding period are used to effect the exchange, and the new ISO shares are subsequently disposed of in a disqualifying disposition. In that case, the optionee will take a "stepped-up basis" in the replacement shares equal to the fair market value of the shares on the date of the swap for purposes of computing ordinary income under Section 421(b) of the Code. For all other purposes (i.e., computing capital gain with respect to the replacement shares), the optionee takes a carryover basis.

As a rule, the optionee will not include any amount in income as compensation upon exercise of an ISO with swapped shares. Instead, he or she will defer recognition of the income and tax on such income until the time that he or she disposes of the ISO shares. The exception to the deferral rule occurs when statutory option shares that have not been held for the full ISO holding period are swapped for new ISO shares. In that case, the swap constitutes a disqualifying disposition of the swapped shares under Section 424(c) of the Code. The employee must include in income as compensation the difference between his or her original purchase price for the statutory option shares and the fair market value of those shares at time of exercise (the spread on the original exercise). Accordingly, his or her basis in the replacement shares will be equal to his or her original cost basis in the statutory option shares *plus* the amount included in income as a result of the swap.

Regardless of the kind of stock used in the swap, the employee will take a zero basis in the new, non-replacement shares received in the swap (the "additional shares"). The second level of exhibit 5-1 illustrates the basis rules.

Holding Periods

ISO shares acquired with stock are subject to the statutory holding period,[4] which starts (for ISO purposes) at date of exercise of the new ISO. The employee may not "tack" (add on) his or her holding period in the old swapped shares onto the statutory holding period of the new ISO replacement shares, no matter how long he or she held the swapped shares. However, for purposes other than the statutory holding period, the employee's holding period in the swapped shares may be tacked onto the replacement shares (i.e., for computation of short-term or long-term capital gain on a disqualifying disposition).

As described above, the exercise of an ISO with previously acquired stock results in the taxpayer taking a zero basis in the additional shares acquired in the swap. The regulations provide that in the event of a disqualifying disposition of the shares received in the swap, the employee is deemed to have disposed of the shares with the lowest basis first (i.e., the zero basis additional shares). As noted above, if the swapped shares have been held for the statutory holding period, they will take a stepped-up basis for purposes of computing ordinary income on a disqualifying disposition only. The third level of exhibit 5-1 illustrates the effect of the holding periods on the tax consequences of a stock swap.

5.2.2 Exercise of an NSO with Stock Other Than Restricted Stock

The rules with respect to stock swaps for NSOs are fairly straightforward. As with any exercise of an NSO, the employee is required to include and pay tax on the spread (between the exercise price and fair market value of the stock) in ordinary income as compensation. The employee then takes a carryover basis in the replacement shares and a basis equal to the spread in the additional shares.[5] The employee is permitted to tack his or her holding period for the swapped shares to the holding period for the replacement shares under Section 1223(1) of the Code.

An NSO may be exercised with statutory option shares even if the employee has not held the shares for the statutory holding period. The stock swap is not considered to be a disqualifying disposition (and the employee continues to hold the same number of ISO shares as were swapped) and accordingly does not result in a change in basis or an extra inclusion in income.

Columns 3, 4, and 5 of exhibit 5-1 set out an example of a stock swap using NSO stock.

5.2.3 Exercise of an ISO or NSO with Restricted Stock

As a general rule, an employee is taxed at the time of vesting on the difference between the amount paid for unvested stock (also called "restricted stock" for these purposes) and its fair market value. The regulations provide that a sale or other disposition of "substantially nonvested property" is treated as a taxable event under Section 83(a) of the Code, and the IRS has taken the position in private letter rulings that the exercise of an option with restricted stock may qualify as a disposition for these purposes.[6]

Restricted Stock for Restricted Stock

Under Section 83(g) of the Code, Section 83(a) and its regulations will not apply if restricted ("substantially nonvested") stock is exchanged for other restricted stock. However, the IRS has indicated that ISO shares, even when restricted, will not be considered to be subject to the same kind of restricted stock as restricted non-ISO stock.[7] Accordingly, if an employee uses non-ISO restricted shares to exercise an ISO for restricted replacement shares, Section 83(a) will apply to treat the stock swap as a taxable disposition of the restricted shares.[8] The employee will include the amount realized (i.e., the difference between the amount paid for the non-ISO restricted shares and the fair market value of the stock at the time of the disposition) in income in the year of the swap and take a basis in the replacement shares equal to the original cost basis of the non-ISO restricted shares *plus* the amount included in income. The additional shares received in the swap will have a zero basis. [9]

If an employee uses restricted shares to exercise an NSO for restricted replacement shares, however, there should be no adverse consequences on the surrender of the swapped shares at the time of exercise. The normal Section 83(a) rules for exercise of an NSO will apply to require the employee to include the spread on exercise in income as compensation. The additional shares received in the transfer take a basis equal to the included amount and need not be restricted shares.

Section 83(b) Election

Neither the Code nor the regulations addresses the exercise of stock options with nonvested stock for which a valid Section 83(b) election has been made, and the IRS has not considered this possibility in private or published rulings. However, Section 83(b) and its regulations provide that the substantial vesting rules of Section 83(a) will not apply to property for which the Section 83(b) election has been made. If such stock is subject to no other restrictions, it should be treated as ordinary vested stock for purposes of exercising both ISOs and NSOs. [10]

Section 83(c)(3)

If employees who exercise options with restricted stock are public company insiders, their stock may be subject to restrictions in addition to vesting restrictions. Under Section 83(c)(3) of the Code, stock is considered restricted if the beneficial owner of the stock would be subject to suit upon sale of the stock under Section 16(b) of the Exchange Act. The Exchange Act provides a six-month "short-swing sale" period, during which time if an officer, director, or more-than-10% shareholder of a public company sells his shares at a profit, he or she must disgorge the profits to the company. He or she is subject to suit for the profits during the six-month period.[11]

The Section 83(b) election resolves the vesting problem, but does not remove the Section 16(b) restriction. If the employee is still subject to suit under Section 16(b), his or her new shares will also be restricted for purposes of Section 83(c)(3). Thus, assuming that there are no other restrictions on the swapped shares, the swap will be treated as an exchange of shares with "substantially similar" restrictions under Section 83(g) of the Code (as described above).

If the employee is no longer an insider at the time of the swap, the employee's new shares will not be subject to the Section 16(b) restriction. Accordingly, Section 83(g) will not apply, and the swap will be treated as a disposition of the swapped shares for tax purposes. The employee will include the amount realized in income in the year of exercise and take an increased basis in the replacement shares.[12]

5.2.4 Procedure for Stock Swaps

The optionee can actually deliver the shares at the time of exercise. The easier way, though, and one expressly sanctioned by the IRS and the SEC, is to use a certification/attestation process for constructive delivery of the swapped shares. If the shares are held in street name, the IRS suggests that the optionee give a notarized statement attesting to the number of shares owned that are intended to be used in the swap. Otherwise, the optionee can simply provide certificate numbers to the issuer at the time of exercise. If this procedure is followed, there is no need for an actual physical transfer of the certificates.[13] In addition, the IRS now permits optionees to exercise a stock swap by e-mail, either by attesting to the number of shares (if held in street name) or to the certificate numbers (if the optionee holds the certificates). No notarization is required to support constructive delivery in this type of paperless exercise.[14] This is a convenient and cost-effective method of accomplishing a stock swap.

A company that allows stock swaps should provide a form or e-mail procedure to employees who wish to exercise their options with stock. The company will have to develop its own criteria and instructions for determining the fair market value of the swapped shares on the exercise date. The criteria adopted will differ for private and public companies.[15]

5.3 Same-Day Sale Transactions

A same-day sale allows an optionee to exercise an option for stock in a public company with the proceeds from the sale of stock acquired under the option. For practical purposes, it gives the same result as a tandem option/stock appreciation right (SAR) or stock swap with less complication: the appreciation on stock is used to finance the exercise of the option and no additional cash is needed for the exercise.[16]

5.3.1 Mechanics

To accomplish a same-day sale, the company must make arrangements with a broker to provide the following services:[17]

1. The optionee completes and delivers to the company an option exercise notice and agreement and a stock power that authorizes the broker to trade shares as necessary.

2. The optionee indicates that the cash purchase price for shares is to be derived from the sale of the purchased shares and provided by the broker.

3. The company notifies the broker of the authenticity of the options and instructs the broker to open an account for the optionee.

4. The broker borrows the same number of company shares from another shareholder who has an account with the broker and sells those on behalf of the optionee.

5. Upon receipt of sale proceeds from the broker, the option exercise is complete, and the company instructs the transfer agent to issue a stock certificate in the optionee's name.

6. The certificate is sent directly to the broker.

7. Using the stock power executed by the optionee, the broker directs the transfer agent to issue two new stock certificates: (1) for

number of shares sold on optionee's behalf out of another shareholder's account, and (2) for the balance of the shares purchased.

The company should not be a party to the agreement between the optionee and the broker, and as such will not be liable to issue shares to the broker if the optionee attempts to rescind the agreement with the broker.

5.3.2 Tax Issues

In the case of an ISO, the use of a same-day sale technique raises the Section 424(h)(3) modification issue discussed throughout here unless the technique is permitted in the ISO grant. Furthermore, the addition of a same-day sale program to a stock option constitutes a modification of the option.[18] However, if the company is not a party to the same-day sale agreement, it should not be deemed to be giving additional benefits to the optionee, and the result should be the same as if the optionee secured a third party loan to finance the transaction.

Note, however, that the use of ISO shares for a same-day sale will necessarily constitute a disqualifying disposition of those shares (because the ISO holding period will not be satisfied). Also, payment of the exercise price must occur on the same day as the sale, or there is a risk that the broker's margin loan will be deemed an interest-free loan under Section 7872 of the Code.[19]

5.3.4 Insider Issues

Before the 1991 SEC rules, an optionee who was a public company insider could not sell stock within six months of exercise of the option under Section 16(b) of the Exchange Act. Thus, insiders were unable to take advantage of same-day sale programs. Under the 1996 SEC rules, this restriction no longer applies to insiders. However, restrictions on employer loans to directors and executive officers (i.e., "extensions of credit") under Section 402 of the Sarbanes-Oxley Act of 2002 generally operate to prevent cashless exercise by insiders.[20]

5.4 Employer Loans

Another alternative available to employers to help employees finance their stock options is an employer-provided loan. However, the type of loan used may have serious securities, accounting, and tax consequences. If a note is insufficient, the employee may be unpleasantly surprised to find that neither the tax nor securities holding periods on the stock have begun to run until the loan is paid off. Further, after August 29, 2002 (the effective date of the Sarbanes-Oxley Act of 2002), issuers are prohibited from making personal loans to their most common recipients: top executives who are public company insiders.[21] Before providing for any loan arrangements, the following issues must be explored in depth by the compensation planner.

5.4.1 Recourse Notes

Companies typically wish to provide the most favorable terms possible when making a stock purchase loan to employees. Although a note may legally be drafted to limit the lender's recourse in the case of default (for example, recourse against the underlying property only), there are many reasons why limited or nonrecourse notes are unwise. First, as a corporate and securities law matter, when offered to officers or insiders such notes appear self-dealing and may raise fiduciary and governance issues for the stockholders. As noted above, under the Sarbanes-Oxley Act of 2002, public companies are largely prohibited from making any personal loans to insiders. Further, SEC Release No. 33-8040 requires public companies to disclose any material contracts with insiders, including loans.[22] Second, for tax purposes, company-provided loans for stock purchases must put the optionee at risk for the underlying property. A statutory option that is exercised with a promissory note will not be considered to have been exercised at all "unless the optionee is subject to personal liability" on the loan under Treas. Reg. § 1.421-1(f). Similarly, for NSOs, Treas. Reg. § 1.83-3(a)(2) provides that the purchaser must show that he or she has taken on the rights and obligations of an investor, including risk of loss, with respect to the property. The purported purchase of property using a nonrecourse note will be considered to be an option. In either case, stock paid for with a nonrecourse note will not be considered to be transferred until the note is fully paid or collateralized.[23]

5.4.2 Collateral

For tax purposes, collateralizing a recourse loan to purchase stock with the underlying stock will suffice to trigger the capital gains holding period. However, for securities law purposes, the holding period under Rule 144, which offers a safe harbor for the sale of stock that holds securities-law restrictions and is explained in detail in chapter 9, will not start unless and until shares are fully paid or collateralized with security other than the underlying stock.[24]

5.4.3 Authorization in ISO Plans

The IRS specifically permits employer-provided loans for statutory option exercises.[25] However, the modification issue discussed in section 3.6 of chapter 3 will arise if the loan provision is added to the grant at the time of exercise. Note that a third-party loan (e.g., a broker loan) arranged without the involvement of the employer will not constitute a modification to the ISO.

5.4.4 Providing Adequate Interest

Employer-provided loans for employer stock are subject to the rules respecting "below-market" loans for seller-financed transactions under Sections 483 and 1274 of the Code.[26] If a seller-financed loan is deemed to be below market because it carries insufficient stated interest terms, the principal of the loan will be recharacterized by the IRS and adequate interest will be calculated based on that principal. The chief impact of such recharacterization for both ISO and NSO purposes will be that the employee will be deemed to have paid less than fair market value for the stock at exercise. Accordingly, the option will in any case be treated as a discount NSO under Section 409A, subject to the tax and penalties at vesting.[27] If the option was an ISO, it will also be disqualified from statutory option treatment under Section 421 of the Code.[28] In the case of an NSO, the option will be treated as a discount option under Section 409A. In either case, the employee's basis in the optioned stock will be reduced because the imputed interest will be subtracted from the total amount paid under the note.[29]

The rules regarding imputed interest are exceedingly complex and are far beyond the scope of this chapter. For tax purposes the issue will never arise if all promissory notes are rated at the applicable federal rate (AFR) prescribed under Section 1274(d) of the Code (published monthly by the IRS).[30]

5.4.5 Loan Forgiveness

Companies that wish to encourage executives to exercise their options and hold option stock will sometimes provide for loan forgiveness, either in the loan contract itself or as a side agreement. Typically such arrangements set out a forgiveness schedule tied to continued employment, underlying vesting (e.g., same vesting schedule as stock) or other performance milestones. Companies may also agree to forgive stock-related loans when the underlying stock is valued well below the original purchase price.[31]

Loan forgiveness provisions, regardless of where stated, raise a number of issues that must be carefully considered by the company and the borrower. For tax purposes, the amount of the forgiveness is ordinary income, which must be recognized as received, withheld upon, and reported by the company on the optionee's Form W-2.[32] If forgiveness is in installments, so is the tax liability. A final comment: after Sarbanes-Oxley, as noted above, public companies are essentially prohibited from making loans to insiders. In certain circumstances, there may be "grandfathered" loans still outstanding to such executives, and those may be subject to forgiveness. However, the final rule in SEC Release No. 33-8048 provides that public companies will be required to disclose and file any material contract with an insider. This would presumably include any but the most de minimis loan forgiveness agreement.

5.4.6 Recommendations

Employer-provided stock option loans, while seductive, raise an inordinate number of issues for the company (particularly the public company). Given the increasing number of constraints on such loans, a better alternative might be for the company to assist the employee in obtaining a third-party loan. Such loans frequently include favorable terms (e.g., nonrecourse, secured by underlying stock), and they avoid the issues described above.[33] However, given the lack of guidance from the SEC, companies should tread carefully when considering providing insiders with access to third parties, as even the "arrangement" of such access may violate Section 402 of the Sarbanes-Oxley Act.

Notes

1. Rev. Rul. 80-244, 1980-2 C.B. 234 (original application of stock swap principles to qualified stock options). See also PLR 99901006 (stock swap does not result in constructive receipt under trust formed to fund plan).

2. EITF 84-18.

3. For purposes of this discussion, basis is the amount a taxpayer is deemed to have paid for the shares and is used to calculate the amount of tax payable upon sale of the shares.

4. Treas. Reg. § 1.422-5(b)(2).

5. See Sections 1036 and 1031(d) of the Code.

6. See Treas. Reg. § 1.83-1(b)(1); see also PLRs 8645073, 8642025, and 8321020. Note that with regard to exercise using restricted (nonvested) stock, if the employee filed a Section 83(b) election at the time of purchase of such stock, it is treated as unrestricted stock for tax purposes (even though it is still subject to vesting restrictions for non-tax purposes). See "Section 83(b) Election" in 5.2.3.

7. Treas. Reg. § 1.422-5(e), example 5. See also PLR 8645073.

8. Although the 2004 regulations do not specifically address this point, an employee should suffer no adverse consequences on exercise of an ISO for restricted shares with restricted shares that were previously acquired by the exercise of an ISO.

9. Treas. Reg. § 1.422-5(e), example 5.

10. Note that the facts to example 5 of Treas. Reg. § 1.422-5(e) specifically state that the optionee did *not* make a Section 83(b) election at the time the original restricted shares were purchased.

11. See the discussion in chapter 7 regarding the effect of the 1996 SEC rules on Section 83(c)(3).

12. The tax consequences described above are completely separate from consequences under the securities laws. The fact that stock subject to a Section 16(b) restriction may be disposed of for tax purposes or swapped for stock subject to the same restriction will not affect the employee's liability to suit under Section 16(b).

13. In PLR 9736040, the IRS stated that "this procedure is sufficient to constitute the constructive exchange of stock for federal income tax purposes." See also PLRs 9628028, 8650045, and 8210098.

14. See PLR 200207005 (approving paperless exercise of ISOs using e-mail).

15. Note that for Rule 144 transactions in public company stock, specific procedures must be in place to satisfy the SEC's "T+3" settlement date requirement. See, e.g., Smith Barney, SEC No-Action Letter (June 20, 1995).

16. See section 6.2 of chapter 6 on "Stock Appreciation Rights (SARs)."

17. Note that same-day sale transactions are facilitated by the Federal Reserve Board Amendment to FRB Regulation T (January 25, 1988). Under Rev. Proc. 2002-50, brokers may no longer be required to file 1099-Bs for same day sale transactions. The 1099B requirement will be eliminated so long as the company certifies in writing that it intends to report compensation from the sale (measured using the actual sale price) on the service provider's W-2 or Form 1099, as appropriate.

18. Treas. Reg. § 1.424-1(e)(4)(i).

19. For more on employer loans generally, see section 5.4.

20. See section 5.4. The SEC has not issued specific guidance on cashless exercise as of December 2005. However, under the act, third-party loans are not prohibited so long as the company does not participate in arranging for the extension of credit. As a result, it has become commonplace for brokers to work with executives to execute a cashless exercise using a margin loan (i.e., the broker sells the shares, remits the exercise price and withholding taxes immediately to the company, and treats that amount as a margin loan until the settlement date a few days later).

21. Section 402 of the Sarbanes-Oxley Act. As a general rule, an issuer may not extend credit in any form to a director or executive officer after July 30, 2002. Although the SEC has not issued specific guidance regarding the interpretation of Section 402 as yet, most practitioners believe that the language of the act is intended to encompass virtually any kind of loan to an insider, including stock-related loans. See fn 20 supra regarding cashless exercise.

22. See section 7.4.3 of chapter 7.

23. However, what constitutes sufficient recourse to avoid characterization as "nonrecourse" for these purposes? Treas. Reg. § 1.83-3(a)(2) sets out some

factors for weighing risk, but as a rule the IRS will not give guidance on whether a transfer has occurred when property is acquired with partial recourse debt. See, e.g., Rev. Proc. 2002-3, 2002-1 IRB 117 § 3.01(3) (January 17, 2002). Tax lawyers generally suggest that the underlying property be valued at no less than 25% of the face value of the note, but this is based on anecdotal evidence rather than IRS guidance.

24. Rule 144(d)(2).

25. Treas. Reg. § 1.421-1(b)(2).

26. Section 483 applies to seller-financed sales greater than $3,000 and up to $250,000, where some or all payments are due more than one year after sale or exchange. Section 1274 applies to seller-financed sales over $250,000 where some or all payments are due more than six months after the date of sale or exchange. In the case of publicly traded stock, the "original issue discount" rules of Section 1273 of the Code govern to produce similar results. Employer-provided loans that are not for seller-financed property are governed by Section 7872. With respect to third-party loans for employees, Section 7872 of the Code establishes rules for taxing any loan made in connection with the performance of services that is (1) not for a seller-financed sale (under Sections 483 and 1274) and (2) deemed to be a "below-market loan" (BML). If an employee loan is a BML, the difference between the amount of interest paid and the amount that should have been paid (pursuant to the rules described below) is treated as "forgone interest" that has been transferred from the lender/employer to the employee/borrower, and then retransferred from the employee/borrower back to the lender/employer. The forgone interest amount is taxable as compensation and may result in an adjustment to the loan principal. Section 7872 and its extensive set of regulations are extremely complicated, but the basic gist of the rules is that employee loans will not be BMLs if they (1) carry market interest rates and (2) such rates are not entered into with a principal purpose being tax avoidance.

27. See chapter 2.

28. See chapter 3. Treas. Reg. § 1.422-2(e)(v) specifically provides that amounts treated as interest are not includible in the ISO exercise price. Furthermore, the regulation states that a fair market value set by adjusting the option price to reflect amounts treated as interest will not be a "good-faith attempt" and thus will result in a discount option.

29. Treas. Reg. § 1.83-3(g). See also Treas. Reg. § 1.422-2(e)(v) (below-market loan results in disqualified ISO).

30. For seller-financed sales, Sections 483 and 1274 of the Code generally provide that AFR is the lowest rate for the relevant term as between the month

of sale and the two preceding months. Loans for an amount below $2.8 million are subject to a maximum AFR of 9%. However, it is unclear under Section 7872 of the Code and its proposed regulations whether these special minimum AFR rules will apply to a note issued by an employee for the purchase of employer stock. The safest course in most cases will thus be to use the prescribed monthly rule and so avoid any risk of selecting a below-market rate. See note 26 above for more on the operation of Section 7872.

31. This issue arose more frequently in the wake of the technology crash of 2001. Executives with loans and AMT liabilities for underwater stock were anxious for quick solutions, without full awareness of the tax consequences described below. See also discussion of AMT in chapter 3.

32. Treas. Reg. § 1.83-4(c). The employer company is entitled to a corresponding tax deduction in the amount included in the employee's income.

33. From the tax perspective, the company's involvement with third-party loans should not trigger tax: this is essentially the same mechanism as obtaining a third-party broker loan for a same-day sale. See section 5.3 of this chapter.

CHAPTER 6

Other Forms of Equity Compensation

Contents

In recent years, discussions of equity compensation have expanded beyond stock options to include grants of tax-restricted stock, stock appreciation rights (SARs), phantom stock, and restricted stock units (RSUs).[1] The forces contributing to the increasing popularity of these instruments are varied. For one thing, accounting rules that favored stock options over other forms of equity compensation have been replaced.[2] For another, corporate governance trends and shareholder approval rules have led companies to look for forms of equity-based compensation that are more palatable to shareholders—who must approve most public company equity compensation plans and who tend to prefer plans that give out fewer actual shares. Companies that grant equity compensation are by no means abandoning traditional stock options wholesale, but these other vehicles for sharing equity with employees are increasingly relevant to discussions of equity compensation.

So what are they?

- *Restricted stock plans* provide employees with the right to purchase shares at fair market value or a discount, or they simply grant shares to employees outright. In this case, "restricted" refers to restrictions the company puts on the stock that defer taxation, *not* to securities restrictions.

- *SARs* give their holder the right to the appreciation in a set number of shares of the underlying stock. They can be paid out in cash or shares. Like options, SARs can be underwater, and thus worthless to the holder, if the stock price drops.

- *Phantom stock* offers holders the right to the value of a set number of shares on a set date.

- *RSUs* are essentially phantom stock that pays out in shares instead of cash.

6.1 Restricted Stock

Under restricted stock plans, companies grant shares to employees or nonemployees but restrict them for a time after grant. The recipients, who may or may not have to pay anything for the shares, cannot take possession of them until the specified restrictions lapse, and thus are not taxed until they receive the shares. The most common restriction requires the employee to continue to work for the company for a certain number of years, often three to five. This time-based vesting may occur all at once or gradually. The company is free to choose which restrictions it will set. It could, for example, restrict the shares until certain corporate, departmental, or individual performance goals are achieved. The company must also decide whether to pay restricted stock holders dividends, provide voting rights, or give the employee other benefits of being a shareholder before the restrictions lapse.

In most cases, a company will grant fewer shares of restricted stock than it would options because the restricted stock has value to the recipient even if the share price drops after the grant date.

In this scenario, "restricted stock" means stock that is restricted for tax purposes. However, in other cases the "restricted" aspect of restricted stock may be a securities law restriction. For example, the stock may be unregistered and thus subject to securities laws governing whether it can be transferred to someone else. Or the term can refer to restrictions imposed by the company. For example, companies often limit executives' trading or impose special blackout periods when they aren't allowed to sell their shares. Nonprofessionals are frequently unclear about what they mean by "restricted stock"; equity planners would be wise to clarify the nature of the restrictions desired by the company before designing a restricted stock plan.

For the purposes of tax-restricted stock, Section 83 of the Code applies to require the recipient to include the difference between the price paid for the shares and their fair market value on the vesting date as compensation income at that time, and the employer is entitled to a tax deduction in the year the recipient must include that amount in his or her income taxes. Subsequent changes in value are capital gains or losses.

Award recipients who want to avoid being taxed at the time of vesting have the right to make Section 83(b) elections, much as they can for stock options. If they make the election, they are taxed at ordinary income tax rates on the "bargain element" of the award at the time of grant. If the shares are simply granted at no cost to the employee, then the bargain element is their full value. If the employee does have to pay for them, then the tax is based on the difference between what is paid and the fair market value. If the recipient must pay the full price of the shares, there is no tax. Any future increase in the value of the shares until they are sold is then taxed as capital gains, not ordinary income.

A Section 83(b) election carries some risk. If the employee makes the election and pays tax, but the restrictions never lapse, for example because the employee leaves the company before they vest, then he or she paid unnecessary taxes that are not refundable.

As for the employer, it can take a tax deduction only for amounts on which award recipients owe income taxes, regardless of whether a Section 83(b) election is filed.

Restricted stock is exempt from taxation as deferred compensation under Code Section 409A as long as the payment of the stock is not deferred past vesting.

6.2 Stock Appreciation Rights (SARs)

A SAR is a contractual right that allows the holder to elect to receive the appreciation in the value of a set number of shares of stock between the grant date and the exercise date. SARs may be paid in cash, stock, or a combination of the two as prescribed in the grant. SARs may not have a specific settlement date; like options, the employees may have flexibility in when to choose to exercise the SAR.

In some cases, SARs are issued in tandem with an option. In a tandem option/SAR, the exercise of one right typically cancels out the complementary right. For example, an employee may be granted a tandem SAR/NSO for 2,000 units. The employee might choose to partially exercise for stock with cash obtained by exercising the appropriate number of units as SARs. With careful planning, the employee may be able to use the SAR to avoid investing any out-of-pocket cash in the stock *and* have cash in hand for paying tax on the spread as well. The IRS has specifically provided that a tandem ISO/SAR is a "permissible provision" for purposes of the ISO rules.[3]

6.2.1 Tax Issues: Employees

SARs trigger income tax for the employee when they are exercised.[4] SARs that are exercised for stock are taxed under Code Section 83, which also governs NSOs. Those that are exercisable for cash, however, are not taxed under Code Section 83 because they are considered to be unfunded and unsecured promises to pay money rather than property.[5] Instead, the recipient is taxed under the constructive receipt rules of Code Section 451.

Under Treasury regulations proposed in September 2005, SAR are specifically excluded from deferred compensation treatment under Code Section 409A as long as their exercise price is no lower than the stock's fair market value on the grant date. This applies to SARs issued by public and private companies, and to SARs settled in both cash and stock.[6]

6.2.2 Tax Issues: Employers

The employer is entitled to a compensation deduction in the year the SAR is exercised by the employee.[7] If the SAR is exercised for cash, the

IRS takes the position that the timing of the deduction is governed by Section 404(a)(5) of the Code. That section provides for a deduction in the employer's taxable year in which or with which the employee's taxable year of inclusion ends.[8] The employer is required to withhold taxes on exercise of the SAR.[9]

6.3 Phantom Stock

Phantom stock plans provide cash or stock bonuses based on the value of a stated number of shares, to be paid out at the end of a specified period.

Unlike most SARs, phantom stock is considered to be deferred compensation. When the payout is made, it is taxed as ordinary income to the employee as long as the details of the plan follow the requirements of Code Section 409A and the attendant proposed regulations. As with other forms of equity compensation, the employer is entitled to deduct from its taxes the amount the employee must include as income in his or her own taxes.

If the recipient has not followed the deferred compensation rules, he or she suffers adverse tax consequences in which all amounts considered deferred are immediately taxed as income unless they remain subject to a substantial risk of forfeiture and haven't been taxed previously. The recipient must also pay a 20% penalty tax on the additional amount taxed, and pay cumulative interest at the IRS underpayment rate plus one percentage point.

Some phantom plans condition the receipt of the award on meeting certain objectives, such as sales, profits, or other targets. These plans often refer to their phantom stock as "performance units." Phantom stock and SARs can be given to anyone, but if they are given out broadly to employees, there is a possibility that they will be considered retirement plans and will be subject to federal retirement plan rules. Careful plan structuring can avoid this problem.

6.4 Restricted Stock Units (RSUs)

RSUs are essentially phantom awards that pay out in stock rather than in cash. RSUs' moment in the sun came in 2003 when Microsoft announced it would discontinue granting stock options in favor of RSUs that would be transferred to recipients only when they vest, thus limiting dilution.

RSUs are simply a form of equity-based deferred compensation, most frequently seen at the private company level in the form of "phantom stock units" or "performance units." Such awards have always had the benefit of flexibility: they can be drafted to provide for payment in cash or stock, they can be indexed to real or phantom investments, and they can be awarded under a broad-based stock plan or pursuant to individual contracts. The Achilles' heel of the RSU has been its accounting consequences; but new accounting rules that went into effect in 2005 ended stock options' accounting advantages over other forms of equity compensation.

In Microsoft's version of the RSU plan, shares of stock are transferred only when they vest. From the company's perspective, the new design stabilizes the total number of shares outstanding to employees (i.e., it eliminates the need to predict forfeiture or repurchase of unvested shares for accounting purposes).[10]

From the employees' perspective, capital gains treatment is reduced because the stock is not transferred until it is already fully vested and so no Section 83(b) election is available before the transfer. However, most employees will be able to finance the tax due by cashing out part of the award at the time of transfer. Microsoft, of course, will be entitled to the full market value tax deduction for each vested RSU.

Exhibit 6-1 on pages 98 and 99 shows a comprehensive comparison between stock options, restricted stock, and restricted stock units.

Notes

1. Portions of this chapter were adapted with permission from *"Ownership Solutions"* by Corey Rosen (Oakland, CA: NCEO, 2004). For fuller explanations of these vehicles, see Corey Rosen et al., *Beyond Stock Options*, 4th ed. (Oakland, CA: NCEO, 2006).

2. For more on this, see chapter 10.

3. Treas. Reg. § 1.422-5(d)(3).

4. Rev. Rul. 80-300, 1980-2 C.B. 165, *as amplified by* Rev. Rul. 82-121, 1982-1 C.B. 79. However, note that a "naked SAR" (i.e., a stand-alone SAR) that is

subject to a cap on appreciation payable will be considered to be constructively received at the time the cap is reached under Treas. Reg. § 1.451-2. See generally PLR 9904039; PLR 9903037 (tandem option/SARs).

5. Treas. Reg. § 1.83-3.

6. Earlier proposed rules would have limited this exemption to SARs issued by publicly traded companies and that could be settled only in stock. However, Prop. Treas. Reg. 158080-04 opted to treat stock- and cash-settled SARs the same way.

7. Code Section 162(a).

8. See, e.g., PLR 8230147. Note that the effect of Section 404(a)(5) is to give a fiscal year employer a deduction in a different year than the calendar year employee. Treas. Reg. § 1.404(a)-12(b)(1).

9. Code Section 3402.

10. In fact, Microsoft decreased the allocation of shares to its 2001 plan by 100,000 shares to reflect the impact of the new RSU program. See the Microsoft 2003 Proxy Statement.

Exhibit 6-1.

	Restricted Stock
Is employee taxed at grant?	No, unless 83(b) election is made; otherwise, ordinary income tax paid when restrictions lapse.
Is employee taxed at vesting?	Yes, unless employee makes 83(b) election.
Is employee taxed at exercise?	N/A
Can employees receive capital gains tax treatment?	Yes, any gain between grant date and sale is taxed as capital gain if an 83(b) election is made.
Can tax be deferred until sale?	Yes, if 83(b) election made.
Can alternative minimum tax apply?	No.
Does the employer get a deduction?	Yes, for amount recognized as ordinary income by employee.
Does the employee get dividends?	Can be separate arrangement, but payment of accrued dividends upon exercise leads to deferred compensation treatment.
Voting rights for employees	Can be attached to restricted shares before restrictions lapse.
Is there value if the share price drops below grant price?	Yes.
Do the awards affect dilution and EPS calculations?	Yes, but fewer restricted shares than options are normally issued because of their downside protection.
Can employees delay exercise after vesting?	No, shares belong to employee when restrictions lapse.
How is value affected by volatility?	Better in less volatile companies.

Restricted Stock vs. Stock Options vs. RSUs

ISOs	NSOs	RSUs
No.	No.	No.
No.	No.	Yes (at time of transfer).
No.	Yes.	Yes (at time of transfer).
Yes, any gain on shares received on exercise is taxed as capital gain, provided holding period rules are met.	Only for gains on shares held after exercise.	No. Full value of stock award at vesting/transfer is taxed at ordinary income rates. Capital gain only on subsequent appreciation (if any).
Yes, if requirements met.	No, unless purchase of unvested shares is permitted.	No.
Yes, to spread on exercise if shares not sold in year of exercise.	No.	No.
Only for disqualifying dispositions for amounts taxed as ordinary income.	Yes, for amount recognized as ordinary income by employee.	Yes, for amount recognized as ordinary income by employee.
Not until shares are actually purchased.	Not until shares are actually purchased.	Not until shares are actually transferred.
Not until shares are actually purchased.	Not until shares are actually purchased.	Not until shares are actually transferred.
No.	No.	Yes for RSUs, no for SARs.
Yes, even if the awards are underwater.	Yes, even if the awards are underwater.	Yes, but fewer shares than options are normally issued because of their downside protection.
Yes, under terms of option.	Yes, under terms of option.	No, shares belong to employee at time of transfer.
Better in more volatile companies.	Better in more volatile companies.	Better in less volatile companies.

CHAPTER 7

Overview of Securities Law Issues

Contents

This chapter briefly looks at some of the substantive provisions related to stock plans under the securities laws, as well as related securities law reporting requirements, including recent SEC rules expanding equity compensation disclosure requirements for public companies. Attention to this area of the law has been intense for the past several years. On July 30, 2002, President Bush signed the Sarbanes-Oxley Act of 2002 (H.R. 3763), which in the words of the White House "imposes tough penalties to deter and punish corporate and accounting fraud and corruption, ensures justice for wrongdoers, and protects the interests of workers and shareholders." Regulations and interpretations of this law have followed in the ensuing years. Updated sources should always be consulted before relying on the rules described below.[1]

7.1 State Blue Sky Laws

As a general rule, public companies are eligible for stock exchange-related exemptions from state securities laws and regulations (these laws and regulations are commonly referred to as "blue sky laws") for granting employee options. Non-public companies, however, must check carefully with counsel to determine whether permit and/or notice requirements are imposed by any states in which the company intends to issue options. In addition, public companies that are traded on foreign stock exchanges should be equally cautious, as not all states provide a blanket exemption for non-U.S. traded companies.[2]

7.2 Federal Securities Rules: Section 16

Under Section 16 of the Securities Exchange Act of 1934 (the "Exchange Act"), officers, directors, and more-than-10% shareholders of a public company are considered to be "insiders." Public company insiders are subject to special restrictions on their ability to buy and sell company stock, including the obligation to publicly disclose all stock holdings and transactions on reports filed with the SEC. Most importantly, under Section 16 of the Exchange Act such insiders are subject to the "short-swing" profit rule. This rule gives the company the right to sue to recover any "profits" (as defined in the statute) realized by an insider from any purchases or sales of the issuer's securities within a six-month period. Purchases and sales are "matched" during the six-month period, and "profit" is measured with respect to all transactions, not merely transactions involving the same shares.[3]

Until 1996, most public companies that sponsored employee stock option plans had to qualify their plans as "Section 16b-3 plans" under the Section 16 regulations (the "pre-1996 rules"). Assuming the pre-1996 rules were met, purchases made under the exempt plan were not subject to matching with sales for purposes of the short swing profit rules. The pre-1996 rules were the product of a complicated and extensive revision and comment process that began in the late 1980s and produced several new versions of the rules, including 1991 regulations that appeared for some time to be final.[4]

The rules that were adopted in 1996 completely shifted the focus of the Section 16 exemption process for compensatory stock options from the *plan itself* to *transactions* under the plan.[5] Generally, new Rule 16b-3 provides that a grant will be exempt from the operation of Section 16(b) if either (1) it has been approved in advance by the issuer's board of directors; (2) it has been approved in advance by a committee comprised solely of two or more "non-employee directors" (a term that has a specific definition under Rule 16b-3); (3) it has been approved in advance or subsequently ratified by the issuer's shareholders; or (4) neither the option nor the underlying shares are disposed of within six months of the date of grant.[6] Further, so long as the grant itself is exempt, the exercise of the grant is a non-event for purposes of Rule 16b-3.[7]

Under the pre-1996 rules, certain practices were common that are no longer required for securities law purposes. For example, it is no longer necessary for Section 16(b) purposes to establish separate plans for employees and outside directors, to impose a formula grant for directors, to require a written plan, or to require options to be held six months before exercise (unless that is the transactional exemption used by the optionee).[8] Transactional exemptions are now more appropriately geared to the underlying nature of the option exercise rather than to an arcane system of unrelated technical requirements. Because the 1996 rules provide a choice of transactional exemptions, most public company insiders will be able to participate in broad-based plans without running afoul of the Section 16 limitations.[9]

Section 16(a) also sets out comprehensive reporting requirements for Section 16 transactions. These requirements are discussed briefly below in section 7.4.

7.3 Federal Securities Rules: Rules 144 and 701

Before securities can be offered or sold to employees, they must either be registered under the Securities Act of 1933, as amended (the 1933

Act) or sold pursuant to an exemption from registration. Obviously, an exemption is necessary for options and sales of private company stock. However, public company optionees frequently hold securities that were issued before the company's initial public offering ("restricted securities"). If such restricted securities are not subsequently registered (for example, on a Form S-8 registration statement), they must also be sold pursuant to an exemption. The most commonly used exemptions for employee-related restricted securities are Rule 144 and Rule 701, described below. Note that in all cases, resales of restricted securities in reliance on an exemption must be cleared with company counsel prior to transfer, and appropriate notice and disclosure filings must be made with the SEC upon sale.[10]

7.3.1 Rule 144 Generally

Rule 144 is a safe harbor exemption created by the SEC to permit public resales of restricted securities under Section 4(1) of the 1933 Act by persons who are neither issuers, dealers, nor underwriters of the stock.[11] Such persons are categorized as either "affiliates" or "nonaffiliates."[12] Rule 144 sets out a list of requirements which must be met by sellers of restricted securities in order to satisfy the safe harbor, including minimum holding period of one year from purchase (Rule 144(d)), volume sale limitation measured over a three-month rolling period (Rule 144(e)), requirement to sell through a broker (Rule 144(g)), and notice obligation (Rule 144(h)).[13] Rule 144(c) also requires that the issuer provide current public information (pursuant to the reporting requirements of the 1934 Act) in order for the seller to take advantage of the rule. As long as a sale of restricted securities is made in full compliance with Rule 144, the seller (whether affiliate or nonaffiliate) may rely on the exemption to sell such securities after satisfying the one-year holding period. After holding restricted securities for two years, a nonaffiliate may be released from most of the safe harbor requirements and permitted to sell the shares without restriction under Rule 144(k). However, affiliates will always be subject to the full compliance requirement, regardless of how long they hold their stock. As a rule, executive officers, and directors are deemed to be affiliates.

If Rule 144 is unavailable or undesirable, other exemptions may be useful. For example, private sales that do not comply with Rule 144 may be eligible for an exemption under Section 4(1) or "Section 4(1½)" (a term used for a hybrid exemption using some of the criteria from both Section 4(1) and 4(2) of the 1933 Act). Public sales may also be exempt under SEC Regulation A, Rule 145, or Section 3(a)(10) of the 1933 Act. However, there are many requirements for such exemptions, and no sales should be made in reliance on any exemption without consulting counsel.

7.3.2 Rule 144 Decision Tree

The following three-point decision tree may be used as an initial step in determining how (or whether) Rule 144 applies:

1. *Is the Seller an Affiliate?*
   * If yes, then Rule 144 may offer protection for sales relying on Section 4(1); go to step 3.
   * If no, then go to step 2.
2. *Are the Securities "Restricted Securities"?*
   * If yes, then Rule 144 may apply; go to step 3.
   * If no, then no limits on resale apply.
3. *How Will Sales Be Made?* (Note: must be a trade, not a "distribution.")
   * If sale is private (i.e., not made on a public market), the hybrid "Section 4(1½)" exemption mentioned above may apply (i.e., as if the seller were an issuer making a private placement) or Rule 144(a) may apply (to institutional investors only).
   * If sale is made on the public market, affiliates must always rely upon Rule 144. Nonaffiliates may sell without restrictions after two years (Rule 144(k)).

By using this decision tree, one can see that sales of *unrestricted securities* by a *nonaffiliate* will never be required to comply with Rule

144. On the other extreme, sales of *any securities* (regardless of whether they are restricted securities) by an *affiliate* will always be required to comply with either Rule 144 or another exemption.

7.3.3 Rule 701

As described above, Rule 144 provides a safe harbor exemption from registration under the 1933 Act for *persons* who wish to resell restricted securities. In contrast, Rule 701 provides a safe harbor exemption from registration under the 1933 Act for *pre-IPO issuers* with respect to offers and sales of restricted securities to nonaffiliates under an employee stock plan. For these purposes, a written compensation agreement between the issuer and a single employee will still be a plan. For transactions after April 7, 1999, Rule 701 covers securities held by employees, family member transferees, and former employees that were acquired under an eligible plan. However, the offer to acquire such securities (e.g., option) must be made at the time the recipient is providing services to the company in order for Rule 701 to apply, even if the exercise occurs after termination of the services.[14] If its conditions are satisfied, Rule 701(c) permits securities acquired under the plan by covered offerees to be sold as quickly as 90 days after the IPO (subject, of course, to any lock-up or market stand-off requirements contractually imposed by the underwriter).

The issuer's ability to rely upon Rule 701 turns on whether *before the IPO*, the issuer satisfied certain mathematical tests with respect to securities sold or optioned under its employee plans. Under Rule 701, in any given 12 month period the sum of (1) the exercise price of outstanding options plus (2) the aggregate dollar amount of sales made in reliance on Rule 701 during the preceding 12 months, cannot exceed the greater of (a) $1 million, (b) 15% of the company's total assets at the end of its most recent fiscal year, or (c) 15% of the outstanding securities of the same class of stock. In order to ensure post-IPO availability of Rule 701, privately held companies need to track stock and option issuances on a rolling basis during the life of the employee plan. After the first time the thresholds are exceeded, Rule 701 will be unavailable for subsequent grants (although shares that previously came in under the thresholds will still be eligible to use the exemption).

The issuer must deliver to investors a copy of the employee plan. In addition, if the aggregate sales price or amount of securities sold during any consecutive 12-month period exceeds $5 million, the issuer is subject to additional disclosure requirements before the date of sale. Under Rule 701(e), such disclosure obligations include:

1. If the plan is subject to ERISA, a copy of the summary plan description;
2. If the plan is not subject to ERISA, a summary of the material terms of the plan;
3. Information about the risks associated with investment in the securities sold pursuant to the compensatory benefit plan or compensation contract; and
4. Financial statements required to be furnished by Part F/S of Form 1-A under Regulation A (§§ 230.251–230.263) as of a date no more than 180 days before the sale of securities in reliance on this exemption (including financial statements of parent if parent assets are used to compute asset test).
5. If the sale involves a stock option or other derivative security, the issuer must deliver disclosure a reasonable period of time before the date of exercise or conversion.[15]

A sample Rule 701 tracking worksheet is set out on Exhibit 7-1.[16]

7.4 Securities Law Information and Reporting Requirements

As noted throughout this book, the grant of a stock option may be unlawful if the option plan has not been properly qualified under or exempted from applicable securities laws. If an option grant is unlawful, the optionee may have the right to rescind any stock purchase made under his or her option and to demand repayment of the purchase price with interest, as well as other rights under applicable state

Exhibit 7-1. Rule 701 Test Sheet

I.   Information needed for the calculations:

    A. *Dollar amount* of aggregate sales price for securities offered or sold under Rule 701 in the last 12 months (sum of all cash, property, notes, cancellation of debt, or other consideration received or to be received by the issuer for the sale of the securities. Value options at exercise price of the option on date of grant): $____

    B. *Number of securities* sold under Rule 701 in the last 12 months (treat the securities underlying all currently exercisable or convertible options, warrants, rights, or other securities, other than those issued under this exemption, as outstanding): ____

    C. *Total company assets* at end of last fiscal year: $____

    D. *Outstanding securities of the class* at the end of the last fiscal year (the "class" being the securities being sold under Rule 701, e.g., common), including securities of that class issuable pursuant to exercise of outstanding options, warrants, rights, or convertible securities that were not issued under Rule 701:

    ____

II. Rule 701 qualification tests (to qualify under Rule 701, the company must satisfy test 1, 2, or 3):

    1. *Dollar Cap Test*
        Does A exceed $1 million? Yes ____ No ____
        If "no", then company is qualified under this test.

    2. *Assets Test*
        Does A exceed 15% of C? Yes ____ No ____
        If "no", then company is qualified under this test.

    3. *Stock Test*
        Does B exceed 15% of D? Yes ____ No ____
        If "no", then company is qualified under this test.

laws. In addition, the securities laws impose various reporting obliga-tions with respect to the option plans and transactions under such plans. These obligations (along with many others unrelated to op-tions) were significantly expanded by the Sarbanes-Oxley Act of 2002, enacted July 30, 2002 (P.L. 107-204). The SEC is engaged in ongoing rulemaking under the Act, and to date not all of the outstanding issues have been settled (or even commented upon).[17] Accordingly, the fol-lowing reporting information is intended as a basic summary only. Before any securities reporting is attempted, careful consultation must be undertaken with legal counsel to determine the status of the law.[18]

7.4.1 1933 Act: S-8 Prospectus

Assuming that the issuer is not relying on Rule 701 to provide an exemption from registration for shares issued under its employee stock plan, the issuer will generally register such shares on a Form S-8.[19] By using the Form S-8, the issuer may take advantage of a simplified prospectus delivery requirement with respect to the registration of shares of stock to be issued under such plans. Participants need not receive a "prospectus" per se; instead, they may have access to a num-ber of documents that provide material information regarding the plan, its operations, and the securities to be issued. Specifically, Form S-8 requires that participants be furnished with (among other things): the name of the plan and the registrant, the administrator's telephone number, information about the plan's administration, a description of the securities being offered under the plan, the rules for eligibility, the manner of determining the price, tax consequences and any re-strictions (including restrictions on resale), and forfeiture events.[20] Generally, employers satisfy the prospectus requirements by incorpo-rating the company's public documents by reference and providing a detailed, "user-friendly" plan summary (including a copy of the plan) to all employees. The SEC has ruled that such documents may be made available electronically to employees (including by e-mail), as long as employees who are not able to have electronic access are pro-vided with an alternative way of receiving the information.[21] In com-panies where e-mail and intranets (intra-company Web sites) are used, this method of disseminating the prospectus is both efficient and cost-effective.

7.4.2 Exchange Act: Section 16(a) Filings

Under Section 16(a) of the Exchange Act, public company insiders must file information reports with the SEC disclosing their holdings of, and transactions in, the equity securities of their companies. Although most of the transactions discussed here will be exempt for Section 16(b) purposes, they may still be subject to reporting under Section 16(a), as follows:

- *Form 3:* To report equity holdings the first time a person becomes subject to Section 16;[22] filed within 10 days of event that triggers the insider status.

- *Form 4:* To report non-exempt transactions (including any occurring during the six months after terminating insider status), exercises and conversions of derivative securities (whether or not exempt), and certain acquisitions.[23] For transactions occurring on or after August 29, 2002, Form 4 is required to be filed before the end of the second day on which the transaction was executed.[24] Prior to the enactment of the Sarbanes-Oxley Act of 2002, Form 4 was required to be filed within 10 days after the end of the month in which the transaction occurred.

- *Form 5:* To report exempt transactions (other than those covered by Form 4).[25] Form 5 must be filed within 45 days after the end of the company's fiscal year. For transactions occurring on or after August 29, 2002, most filings that previously were made on Form 5 are now required to be made on Form 4 (and thus are subject to the expedited filing rules). The kinds of transactions that may still qualify as reportable on Form 5 include gifts of stock, transfers to family members for estate planning purposes, and small acquisitions of less than $10,000 that aren't directly from the company.

For each form, the insider is required to electronically file three copies: one with the SEC, one with each applicable stock exchange, and one with the company. The filer must keep a manually signed copy for five years after filing. The Sarbanes-Oxley Act required electronic filing of all Section 16 disclosures no later than July 30, 2003. Further, since June 30, 2003, both the SEC and the issuer have been required to post Section 16 statements on publicly accessible Web sites no later than the end of the business day following the filing and to keep them accessible for at least a year.[26]

For its part, the company must report any delinquent filings in its annual proxy statement. In 2004, the SEC proposed rules that would mean companies could no longer assume that forms 3, 4, or 5 were filed in a timely manner with the SEC just because the insider notified the company of the change in beneficial ownership in a timely manner.

7.4.3 Exchange Act: Equity Compensation Disclosure Rules

In addition to the Section 16(a) rules described above, the Exchange Act imposes extensive disclosure and reporting obligations on public companies, including obligations with respect to equity compensation awarded to employees and consultants. In 2001 and 2002, the SEC responded quickly to public outcry over perceived corporate failures to adequately disclose executive compensation.[27] Among its numerous initiatives and statements, two are of particular importance for equity compensation planners to be aware of: SEC Release No. 33-8048 (final rules on disclosure of equity compensation information) and SEC Releases Nos. 33-8400 and 34-49424 (final rules for Form 8-K disclosure of certain management transactions). As noted above, there is likely to be additional regulatory activity in this area, particularly with respect to executive compensation. Furthermore, certain provisions of the Sarbanes-Oxley Act overrode the SEC's previously proposed rules. These provisions have required the SEC to do substantial rulemaking during the years following the act's enactment.

SEC Release No. 33-8048[28]

This release sets out the final rules for disclosure of equity compensation plan information, adopting amendments to the Exchange Act that enhance disclosure requirements applicable to annual reports on Form 10-K and Form 10-KSB (annual reports) and to proxy and information statements filed in connection with annual meetings (annual meeting materials). Generally, the final rule prescribes a new form of stock plan disclosure table that must be filed each year with annual reports and with annual meeting materials in any year when any compensation plan is submitted for shareholder action.[29] The table breaks down equity plans into two categories: those that have been approved by shareholders, and those that have not been approved (including individual arrangements and plans assumed in an M&A transaction). For each category, the company must supply the following data in tabulated form:

1. Column A: Number of securities to be issued upon exercise of outstanding options, warrants, and rights;

2. Column B: Weighted-average exercise price of outstanding options, warrants, and rights; and

3. Column C: Number of securities remaining available for future issuance under equity compensation plans (excluding securities reflected in column A).

The data may be aggregated within each category. For each non-approved plan or individual arrangement, the company must file copies of the documents (unless immaterial) and provide a brief narrative describing the material features of the plan or arrangement.[30] This requirement for a narrative description may be satisfied by cross-referencing information already set out in the company's financial statements in accordance with FAS 123(R).[31] The final rule became effective on March 15, 2002, for annual reports filed with respect to fiscal years ending on and after that date, and on June 15, 2002, for annual meeting materials filed on or after that date.

SEC Releases Nos. 33-8400 and 34-49424

In implementing Sarbanes-Oxley, the SEC initially sought to expand the number of transactions that would need to be reported on Form 8-K, which acts as the reporting mechanism for significant transactions between public companies and management under the 1934 Act. These changes would have required accelerated disclosure of most garden-variety equity compensation transactions by public company insiders, and would have significantly raised the stakes for entering into special agreements with such insiders.[32] However, commenters were highly critical of the proposals and ultimately very few disclosure items specifically related to equity compensation were included in the final requirements under Form 8-K. Note, however, that if a material amendment is made to a stock incentive plan or an award document, or if the board of directors adopts a new benefit plan (with or without shareholder approval) that includes insiders, it must be reported on Form 8-K within four business days under Item 1.01 because it represents a "material definitive agreement" with the company.[33]

7.5 ESPP Securities Law Considerations

Generally, ESPPs are subject to the same accounting and securities laws as those described above with respect to stock options. However, there are a few distinctions that should be noted with respect to Section 423 plans. Note also that these distinctions may apply to non-Section 423 plans as well if they are designed as broad-based, noncompensatory plans but simply do not satisfy all of the requirements of the Code.

7.5.1 Securities Act of 1933

Section 423 plans are subject to the federal securities laws described above. However, because most companies offer Section 423 plans only after going public, sponsors typically register such plans with the SEC on Form S-8.[34] Accordingly, Rule 144 will apply (to sales by affiliates) only on a limited basis.

7.5.2 Securities Exchange Act of 1934

With respect to Section 16(b), the 1996 SEC rules provide a specific exemption for transactions under a "tax-conditioned plan." For these purposes, Rule 16b-3 provides that a tax-conditioned plan is an em-

ployee benefit plan that meets the coverage and participation requirements of Sections 423(b)(3) and 423(b)(5) of the Code. This means
that, as a general rule, the grant and acquisition of securities under a
Section 423 plan will be exempt from Section 16(b). However, as noted
above, transactions under Section 423 plans are required to be reported
on the Form 4 (and are subject to expedited filing rules).[35]

   Nonstatutory ESPPs are not eligible for "tax-conditioned plan"
status. Such plans will need to comply with a different Section 16(b)
exemption, as discussed in section 7.2 above.

7.6   International Securities Law Issues

Non-U.S. employees who receive securities in U.S. companies are generally subject to U.S. securities laws with respect to transactions in such
securities. However, additional issues may arise if local country law
limits or restricts ownership of U.S. securities by residents, or if the U.S.
issuer is required to comply with local country permit rules. Foreign
countries frequently impose disclosure and reporting requirements on
transfers of employee-owned securities (regardless of where the issuer
is located). Exchange/currency controls are also common, including
restrictions on sending currency outside of the country for the purposes of purchasing securities. As always, both U.S. and local country
counsel must be consulted to ensure compliance before grant.

Notes

1.   News of congressional action (including links to current activity in both
      houses) may be obtained from *www.firstgov.gov*, among other resources.
      Information on and copies of the latest SEC releases may be obtained from
      the SEC Web site at *www.sec.gov*.

2.   See, e.g., the California Commissioner's Rules, which impose a variety of
      restrictions on plans sponsored by privately held corporations pursuant to
      Section 25102(o) of the law and Reg. § 260.140.41-45. See also Matthew
      Topham, "State Securities Law Considerations for Incentive Stock Plans,"
      Selected Issues in Equity Compensation, 3rd ed. (Oakland, CA: NCEO, 2006).

3.   Section 16(b)(3) of the Exchange Act. For stock option purposes, the six-
      month period begins on the date of grant unless the grant is exempt (as

further discussed below). Once a non-exempt transaction occurs, it is matched against any other non-exempt purchase or sale that occurs within six months (i.e., within the year beginning six months before the transaction and ending six months after the transaction).

4. The SEC adopted sweeping changes to its Section 16 rules in Release No. 34-28869, as amended no less than five times through 1994 (the "1991 rules"). Generally, the 1991 rules were effective May 1, 1991. However, public companies were permitted to defer compliance with the rules, and ultimately they were superseded by the 1996 rules.

5. The 1996 rules became mandatory on November 1, 1996. See SEC Release No. 34-37250, § VII.B (1996).

6. Release No. 34-37250 (1996); Rule 16b-3(c),(d). A different exemption may apply for Section 423 plan options, as discussed in section 7.5 below.

7. This is because the acquisition of a derivative security (the option grant) is considered to be the acquisition of the underlying equity for purposes of Section 16. See Rule 16b-6.

8. See 1991 rules. Note, however, that for other purposes, such as shareholder relations and (as to written plans) tax and stock exchange requirements, some of these devices may survive regardless of the flexibility of the 1996 rules.

9. This is a brief overview of a very complicated area of the law and is not intended to provide definitive guidance. For in-depth discussion of the 1996 rules and changes to the 1991 rules, see Peter Romeo's *Comprehensive Section 16 Outline* (2001, updated annually each August). See also chapter 6 of Herbert Kraus, *Executive Stock Options and Stock Appreciation Rights* (New York: Law Journal Press, 2004).

10. Typically, in the case of legended restricted securities, company counsel will issue an opinion letter to the issuer's transfer agent authorizing the transfer of the Rule 144 or Rule 701 securities, with a copy to the selling brokerage firm.

11. Rule 144 is based on the exemption provided by Section 4(1) of the 1933 Act, which allows securities to be sold by any person *other* than an issuer, underwriter, or dealer without registration of the shares with the SEC and without delivery of a prospectus in a form approved by the SEC. Application of the rule is extremely complex, and this chapter is not intended to provide detailed guidance on its application. For a comprehensive current treatise on all aspects of the rule, refer to J. William Hicks, *Resales of Restricted Securities, 2005 ed.* (Eagan, MN: Thomson West). For some targeted examples, see Robert A. Barron, "Some Comments on the Usual Rule 144 Scenario and Related Matters," 25 Securities Regulation Law Journal 431 (winter 1997).

12. Rule 144(a)(1) defines "affiliate" to mean a person who directly or indirectly controls, is controlled by, or is under common control with the issuer. All persons who are not affiliates are nonaffiliates for these purposes.

13. 1933 Act Reg. § 203.144. Upon sale, Rule 144(h) requires that three copies of Form 144 must be filed with the SEC for any shareholder who relies upon Rule 144 to sell more than 500 shares during any three-month period *or* who sells shares having an aggregate sales price of more than $10,000. If the shares are listed on a stock exchange, a Form 144 must also be filed with the listing exchange. For specific instructions see Form 144, SEC Release No. 52231 (1975), as amended.

14. 1933 Act Reg. § 203.701; SEC Release No. 33-7645 (Apr. 7, 1999).

15. 1933 Act Reg. § 203.701(e).

16. For more information on Rule 701, see Kirk Maldonado, "Rule 701: Parameters and Nuances," *Journal of Employee Ownership Law and Finance* 14, no. 3 (summer 2002).

17. For example, a new set of rules regarding (among other things) accelerated filing was proposed by the SEC on September 21, 2005.

18. Please note that this section does not discuss the executive compensation and stock option disclosure requirements under the 1934 Act, nor does it analyze the Section 16(a) reporting obligations. For an in-depth analysis of the latter rules, see Romeo, note 9 above.

19. Form S-8 is available to public company employers that have complied with all required reporting obligations in the 12 months prior to its use. See general instructions to Form S-8, Section A. The Rule 701 exemption may apply to permit sales of restricted stock optioned under an employee stock plan before the issuer's IPO. See section 7.3.3 above.

20. See Form S-8, Items 1, 2.

21. SEC Release No. 33-7288, IV, Example (1). The example specifically provides that if e-mail is used in the "ordinary course" of employee business, an alternative is provided for those that do not otherwise access e-mail, and paper versions are available, then electronic delivery is a satisfactory way of meeting the prospectus delivery requirement. This analysis may be logically extended to Internet or intranet delivery (e.g., via a corporate Web site) if access is readily available to all employees.

22. Rule 16a-3(a).

23. Rule 16a-3(f), 16a-6.

24. Sarbanes-Oxley Act of 2002, Section 403(a). As mandated by the act, the SEC adopted final rules for implementation of the Section 16(a) amendments as of August 29, 2002, in SEC Release No. 34-46421 (Aug. 27, 2002).

25. Rule 16a-3(a), 16a-3(f).

26. Section 403(a) of the Act (new Section 16(a)(4)); SEC Release No. 33-8230 (May 7, 2003).

27. In press releases and media interviews discussing the various initiatives, then-SEC Chairman Harvey Pitt repeatedly stressed that the SEC would aggressively pursue a "regulatory agenda" to address issues raised by investors and Congress, including financial disclosure and reporting, accounting standards, regulating the accounting profession, and corporate governance. See, e.g., SEC Rel. 2002-22 (Feb. 13, 2002). Similar statements have been made by SEC representatives since that time, including by new (as of June 2005) SEC Commissioner Christopher Cox. See, e.g., Cox comments to SEC proposals of 9/21/05.

28. 67 F.R. 232 (Dec. 21, 2001). Readers are strongly encouraged to review the text of SEC Release No. 33-8048, which contains a comprehensive discussion of the amendments and rationale for their adoption in layman's language, and illustrates the form of table required to be included in each filing.

29. See new Item 201(d)(1) of Regulations S-B and S-K.

30. See new Item 601(b)(10) of Regulations S-B and S-K (filing); new Item 201(d)(3) of Regulations S-K and S-B (narrative).

31. See Final Rule Discussion Section IIB (setting out cross-reference disclosure chart).

32. See SEC Release 8090 (April 11, 2002). The SEC proposed rules regarding insider transactions that, if adopted, would have required public companies to file current reports on Form 8-K that describe directors' and executive officers' transactions in company equity securities, directors' and executive officers' Rule 10b5-1 arrangements for the purchase and sale of company equity securities, and loans of money to a director or an executive officer made or guaranteed by the company or an affiliate of the company.

33. SEC Release No. 33-8400A (August 23, 2004).

34. For information on Form S-8, see section 7.4.1 above.

35. See Rule 16b-3(b)(5). The only exception to this broad exemption arises if a transaction is considered to be a "discretionary transaction" under Rule 16b-3(b)(1). Generally, discretionary transactions will occur only in the context of a retirement plan. For detailed information, consult Romeo, note 9, and see above.

CHAPTER 8

Preliminary Planning Concerns

Contents

As we have seen, the technical requirements governing stock option plan design are detailed and numerous. As such, companies should give themselves the broadest possible flexibility when they design equity compensation plans. This chapter looks at the broader issues companies should consider in designing their equity compensation plans as well as the more specific issues to be considered when choosing whether to offer ISOs or NSOs.

8.1 General Considerations for the Company

The adoption of a broad, flexible stock option plan will permit a company to grant ISOs or NSOs to employees and NSOs to outside directors and consultants who are not employees of the company. As we have seen, the rules regulating stock option plans are complex and subject to frequent change for legal and political reasons. This means that companies are best served by adopting "umbrella"-type option plans that set out the broadest parameters available under applicable laws. Broad discretionary language will allow the plan administrator to devise specific solutions to a wide variety of granting situations, without requiring an amendment to the plan each time a new approach or policy is adopted.

For example, unless required by state securities laws, a company is ill-advised to include specific vesting and exercise terms in the plan document itself.[1] Instead, the document should set out the plan administrator's authority to provide for limitations on vesting and exercise. Specific schedules (including early exercise provisions) may then be included in the individual notices of grant, thus providing the opportunity for the administrator to impose vesting schedules of differing lengths (including performance vesting) for each optionee.[2]

Examples of other provisions that should be included in individual grant and exercise documents rather than in the umbrella plan document include contract rights of the company (e.g., rights of first refusal), nonstatutory definitions related to termination or severance (e.g., constructive termination), limitations on forms of consideration for exercise, and valuation formulas.

Similarly, plan provisions that are governed by substantive company policy should refer to such policies *as in effect from time to time* without incorporating them into the plan. The plan should not set out specifics because it may be legally permissible for such policies to change at the company's discretion. Examples of policies best adopted outside the plan include fair market value methodology, hiring and performance grant matrices, repricing guidelines, global plan administration, and option vesting on a leave of absence or change of employment status.[3]

Finally, companies should be careful to ensure that tax restrictions set out in the plan apply only where necessary. An oft-overlooked mistake can occur when the plan language inadvertently applies ISO limitations to all grants, NSOs as well as ISOs. A common example of this mistake is language that sets a post-termination exercise period of three months for all options. While this is an ISO requirement, it is inapplicable to NSOs and unnecessarily ties the plan administrator's hands. Other examples of this mistake include generic restrictions on transferability, pricing requirements and overbroad application of U.S. law to international grants.[4] Exhibits 8-1 and 8-2 set out basic guidance regarding the types of plan provisions that should be included in (or excluded from) the plan document.

8.2 ISOs or NSOs?

Many companies have found that ISOs are a useful tool for providing tax-advantaged achievement incentives to key personnel. With ISOs, if the statutory holding periods and other rules are met, the optionee incurs no tax liability upon exercise (unless the optionee is subject to the alternative minimum tax), but instead incurs tax liability only upon the sale or other disposition of the shares, and even then is taxed at the long-term capital gains tax rates rather than the (higher) ordinary income rates. However, because ISOs are statutory creatures, they must be granted and exercised in accordance with the technical conditions of Section 422 of the Code and the IRS regulations thereunder in order to preserve the tax benefits that ISOs are designed to achieve. The grant and exercise of ISOs are also regulated by state and federal securities laws as well as by state corporation laws. A further drawback is that, assuming the optionee complies with all the ISO rules, the employer will not be entitled to receive a compensation deduction as a result of either the grant or exercise of an ISO. Chapter 3 sets out the details of using ISOs.

In contrast, the grant of an NSO is not limited by federal income tax laws as to the number of shares, price per share, length of term, or identity of the recipient of such option (although the company's plan usually will stipulate the eligibility requirements for an NSO). As detailed in chapter 2, upon the optionee's exercise of the NSO, the company is entitled to receive a compensation deduction in the amount of the spread between the option price and the value of the stock at time of purchase. The tax consequences of an NSO, however, are generally less advantageous to the employee than are the tax consequences of an ISO, and the employer has a withholding obligation on the spread at time of exercise.[5] The details of using NSOs are set out in chapter 2.

Exhibits 8-3 below and 3-1 in chapter 3 set out the relative advantages and disadvantages of using NSOs and ISOs.

8.3 International Planning Considerations

When stock options first became popular in the United States, U.S. companies that operated globally were faced with practical, as well as

Exhibit 8-1. Basic Plan Features

FEATURE	PURPOSE	NOTES
Discretionary Plan Scope	Permit administrator to exercise broad discretion in awarding options in a variety of compensation situations, also in interpreting plan to allow for repricings, regrants, acceleration etc.	*Trend to limit equity plans to specific purposes only (e.g., option plan, restricted stock plan, advisors plan) and to require shareholder approvals for special transactions etc.*
Statutory Provisions	Tax rules for ISOs (and 423 plans)— set out in Code Sections 421–424; administrative requirements for exclusion under Section 162(m); deferred compensation concerns under Section 409A	*Tax code requires specific language, approvals and %/$ limitations for valid incentive stock option plans and for avoidance of $1 million cap on compensation deductions attributable to options for top employees in public companies; adverse tax consequences for discount options or options that permit deferral of compensation*
Change of Control Provisions	Provide guidance for plan termination and/or acceleration on acquisition	*Note effect of revised proposed Code Section 280G regulations for factoring options into "golden parachute" definition of reasonable compensation; deferred compensation concerns under Section 409A for severance arrangements*
Limitations on Value of Stock Grants	Plan must state maximum number of shares that may be awarded under plan	*Code Sections 422 and 423 require shareholder approval of total number of shares in plan and impose certain $ value limitations; Code Section 162(m) safe harbor requires a stated maximum number of shares available to any individual at a public company*
Basic Corporate Governance	Statutory option plans require shareholder approval for number of shares and certain material provisions; delegation of authority to committee of board is generally otherwise permitted	*Recent shareholder vigilance may result in increased oversight, particularly with respect to executive grants. Public company SEC disclosure requirements are widening*
State Securities Law Requirements	"Blue sky" rules differ from state to state—some states require very specific language to take advantage of permits or exemptions, others require notice only	*California, e.g., has numerous specific rules that must be satisfied for the 25102(o) exemption*
Federal Securities Law Requirements	Sale of stock under any plan, private or public, requires federal securities law compliance. Language generally incorporated in disclosure documents rather than plan itself, but some exceptions	*Rules 701 and 144 generally explained in investor reps to pre-public company investors; Section 16 for public company insiders is transactional and so generally included in disclosure docs rather than plan document. Ever-increasing SEC reporting requirements for equity compensation*

Exhibit 8-2. Policies Outside of the Plan

FEATURE	DESCRIPTION	NOTES
Grant Policies	Provide employment grade matrix for hire grants, reload options, retention grants	*Particularly useful for routine grants delegated to committee; have board adopt and approve from time to time*
Vesting Policies	Default vesting schedule adopted for all grants	*Performance vesting used as incentive on a case-by-case basis*
Repricing/Regrant Policies	Guidelines to avoid accounting issues	*Shareholder approval not de rigueur for these kinds of transactions*
Tax Planning	No withholding on ISOs; provide for FICA/FUTA withholding for NSOs	*Monitor legislation for new developments*
Adding Shares to Plan	Long term planning for additional shares—requires shareholder approval	*With recent reluctance of investors, the fewer times company needs to ask for more shares the better*
Leaves of Absence	Coordinate general LOA policies with effect under plan—does vesting stop? Partial vesting?	*Also applies to change in status; e.g., does vesting change if employee goes from full time to part time?*
Global Plan Administration	Decisions about when to adopt specific country plans; approvals	*Need to assess importance of tax advantages in each country*

Exhibit 8-3. Comparison: ISOs Versus NSOs: Consequences to Company

	ISOs	NSOs
Option Price	Must be fair market value at date of grant; "good faith" valuation necessary	No tax requirement; state corporate law may govern. Section 409A consequences may apply to discount grant
Qualification Requirements	Must meet all requirements of Section 422 at time of grant; must be granted under qualified ISO plan	None; may require state corporate securities permit or exemption if issued under a plan
Who Is Eligible	Employees only	Employees, consultants, directors, other independent service providers
Limitations	(a) $100,000 first exercisable per year; (b) grant and plan both have 10-year term only; (c) more-than-10% shareholders subject to special limitations	No tax limitations (but watch for Section 162(m) cap); discount options will cause tax consequences under Section 409A
Deduction	None if optionee holds for ISO holding period; deduction for spread if optionee makes disqualifying disposition and report timely filed by company	Deduction for spread in year of exercise provided income included (or "deemed included") by optionee
Withholding Obligation	None	Withhold at supplementary rates (income tax and FICA) at exercise by employee
Reporting	Information (Section 6039) and disqualifying disposition tracking (W-2, W-2(c))	W-2, 1099

technical, concerns about whether to offer the same equity incentives to their international employees (i.e., non-U.S. employees resident in foreign countries) as they offered to their U.S. employees. For the most part, throughout the 1980s and well into the 1990s stock options were perceived as a dubious benefit at best in all but a few European countries.[6] Many international employees were accustomed to receiving compensation packages that included fringe benefits (such as car and housing allowances) as well as state-mandated retirement and leave payments. Culturally, equity was not considered to be a particularly valuable or prestigious component of the compensation package, particularly if offered in lieu of more traditional benefits. Further, the regulatory environments found in most foreign countries were not conducive to use of securities in lieu of (or in addition to) cash compensation. Many countries imposed punitive tax or regulatory schemes on stock options, or appeared to have ambiguous rules that were difficult for either U.S. or local counsel to interpret with confidence.[7]

Because worldwide stock option plans can be a potent tool for creating a companywide ownership spirit that bridges cultural gaps, U.S. multinationals have continued to find ways to extend equity compensation to international employees wherever possible. In some cases this has involved simply adapting the U.S. plan to meet global needs; in others, an assessment of local tax and corporate issues result in adoption of mirror plans or subplans for individual country use.

On August 26, 2003 (and effective as of the same date) the IRS published final regulations (T.D. 9088) with respect to the tax treatment of compensatory stock options for purposes of qualified cost-sharing (transfer pricing) arrangements between U.S. companies and their foreign affiliates. Under the final regulations to Section 482 of the Code, all costs attributable to stock-based compensation must be taken into account in determining the controlled participant's operating expenses. The spread on a statutory stock option, even if not otherwise includable in employee compensation, will nonetheless be shared for these purposes. U.S. multinationals need to work carefully with their tax advisors to ensure compliance with these complex rules when extending equity compensation to the non-U.S. work force.

Communicating the benefits of options has become easier with the increased mobility of the international workforce and accordingly, higher levels of interest in (and awareness of) equity compensation worldwide. In addition, as foreign-based companies with U.S. employees have sought to add employee stock plans, they have worked with their governments to amend local country rules to enable their use.[8] In any case, decisions regarding whether and how to grant to international employees must be subject to a careful review of the issues, including (without limitation): local country securities, corporate, and employment law/social tax requirements; exchange control regulations; tax impact on employees; tax impact on company in the U.S. and locally; requirements for tax-approved or other government review status; effect on (or necessary amendments to) design of overall plan; perceived benefit/value to local country employees vs. cost of compliance.

A complete discussion of international plan issues is beyond the scope of this book, although where appropriate, the text flags areas of concern for global equity planners. There are a growing number of resources and professional organizations that are devoted entirely to exploration of these issues, and the reader is encouraged to seek them out for general information and guidance.[9] Before designing or implementing any global features in an equity plan, however, companies are best advised to consult both U.S. and local country counsel.

Notes

1. For example, California has extensive plan requirements, described in its securities regulations, which must be met before filing a required notice. See California Corporate Securities Act of 1968, Sections 25100 et al.; Rules § 260.140.41-46 (the "California Commissioner's Rules"). California employers should note that in recent years, changes have been made to the California Commissioner's Rules that have loosened the restrictions considerably and, at the urging of the bar, the Commissioner continues to examine the viability of these rules. Companies should always check with counsel for the latest rules before adopting plans that cover employees resident in California.

2. Such terms may be subject to regulation but still not be required to be included in the plan document. See, e.g., California Commissioner's Rules 260.140.41(k) (setting minimum pricing and repurchase requirements).

3. While Treas. Reg. § 1.421-1(h)(2) provides a definition of "leave of absence" for purposes of determining when a statutory option terminates, and thus when the three-month post-termination exercise period begins, the plan document should provide that the company's policy governs as to the treatment of the option itself during a leave.

4. The specific ISO rules required to be set out in the plan are discussed in detail in chapter 3.

5. Until 1995, an employer was not entitled to a tax deduction for the amount included under Section 83(a) by the service provider on exercise unless it withheld on that amount. However, Treas. Reg. § 1.83-6(a)(2) now provides that the employer may take the deduction so long as it reports the included amount on the employee's (or former employee's) W-2 form before reflecting the deduction on its tax return. This provision, however, does not relieve the employer of its withholding obligation under Section 3402 or of any of the penalties associated with failure to withhold. The employer deduction is discussed at greater length in chapter 2.

6. Notable exceptions to the rule were the United Kingdom (England, Ireland, and Scotland) and France, where versions of tax-qualified option plans have long been available. However, holding periods and other requirements for buying stock under these plans are far more restrictive than those imposed under the Code.

7. For example, until the late 1990s, the Scandinavian countries and the Netherlands imposed substantial tax on both the grant and exercise of stock options. However, the most common concern throughout the world (especially in Japan and Asia) were corporate, securities, and exchange control laws that prevented local country corporations from granting employees equity at all. For multinationals operating through local subsidiaries, or attempting to transfer parent stock through such subsidiaries, these regulatory controls could be a major stumbling block.

8. Most countries now tax employee options on exercise, rather than on grant. See Virginia Gibson, "Implementing and Maintaining Compliance of Equity Compensation Programs Globally" in *Equity-Based Compensation for Multinational Corporations*, 7th ed. (Oakland, CA: NCEO, 2005).

9. See, e.g., *Equity-Based Compensation for Multinational Corporations*, note 8 above; and the Global Equity Organization (GEO) at *www.globalequity.org*.

CHAPTER 9

Tax Law Compliance Issues

Contents

Income recognized by an optionee on the exercise of a stock option is subject to a variety of reporting and disclosure requirements under the Code. In addition, the employer may be entitled to take a compensation deduction with respect to such income in the year of inclusion by the optionee. This chapter reviews the relevant requirements for withholding, reporting, disclosing, and deducting income realized in connection with stock options.

9.1 Tax Withholding for Stock Options

The compensation element (the spread) on exercise of an NSO by an employee constitutes wages subject to federal income tax withholding under Section 3402 of the Code (and where applicable, state withholding). The spread is treated as "supplemental wages" for withholding purposes.[1] The current supplemental withholding rate is 25% for supplemental payments of $1 million or less, and 35% for supplemental payment amounts that exceed $1 million. (Note that these rates change from time to time.) Exhibit 9-1 summarizes the current withholding rules for NSOs.

No payroll tax withholding is imposed upon the exercise of a statutory stock option. The American Jobs Creation Act of 2004 ended repeated attempts by the IRS to impose FICA and FUTA withholding at the time of exercise.

9.2 Tax Reporting for Stock Options

9.2.1 Nonstatutory Options: Form W-2 or Form 1099

Generally, the spread on exercise of an NSO should be reported on the employee's (or former employee's) Form W-2 for the year in which the exercise occurred. Reporting for nonemployees is on a Form 1099.[2] As noted above, if the optionee is an employee at the time of the grant, the spread will generally be subject to withholding at exercise.

9.2.2 Statutory Options, Code Sections 422 and 423: Form W-2

As described above, no tax withholding is required on the spread on exercise of a statutory option by an employee (or former employee). However, if an employer intends to take a tax deduction with respect to a disqualifying disposition of statutory option stock, deductibility is subject to compliance with Section 83(h) of the Code, which provides that a service recipient may deduct an amount equal to the amount included by the service provider in income. As more fully described in section 2.7 of chapter 2, if the employer timely reports the includible amount on the service provider's Form W-2, the employer may rely upon the "deemed inclusion" rule and deduct the amount reported regardless of whether it has actual proof of the employee's inclusion. Although the Code does not require federal income tax withholding at the time of sale or disposition, it imposes Form W-2 information reporting requirements on any remuneration payments ultimately made to employees which, in the aggregate, exceed $600 annually.[3] For purposes of deductions with respect to a disqualifying disposition, the deemed inclusion rule will be satisfied if the Form W-2 or W-2c (as applicable) is filed by employer on or before the date on which the employer files its the tax return claiming the deduction.[4]

9.3   Section 6039 Information Reporting for Statutory Options

Section 6039 requires information reporting in writing to optionees who exercise an ISO or dispose of ESPP stock. There is no requirement to file an information return with the IRS.[5] As discussed below, failure to satisfy the reporting obligation will result in penalties to the employer company under Section 6722 of the Code (see section 9.3.3).

9.3.1   Information Required to Be Reported to Optionee

The employer must satisfy the Section 6039 information reporting obligation by January 31 of the year following the ISO exercise or ESPP stock disposition. In the case of ESPP stock, the obligation applies only on the first transfer of ESPP stock by its original owner: that is, the company will not be required to provide information statements on interim or subsequent transfers. In a 2001 IRS Chief Counsel Advisory memorandum, the IRS Office of Chief Counsel clarified that the "first transfer" occurs only at the time that the optionee transfers *legal title* in the stock. This means that if ESPP stock is held by a transfer agent in street name, the transfer may not actually occur until the optionee directs a third party sale. The information statement would be triggered by such third party sale, not by the interim transfer to the transfer agent.[6]

Exhibit 9-1. Withholding Information for NSO Exercise

	FIT/SIT Withholding	FICA/FUTA Withholding	Form
1. Employee	Spread on exercise	Spread on exercise	W-2[a]
2. Former Employee			
(a) Year of term	Spread on exercise	Spread on exercise	W-2
(b) Subsequent years	Spread on exercise	Spread on exercise	W-2[b]
3. Retiree: same as former employee[c]			
4. Estate			
(a) Calendar year of death	None	Spread on exercise[d]	1099 MISC[e]
(b) Subsequent years	None	None[f]	1099 MISC
4. Nonemployee Former Spouse (NEFS)[g]			
(a) Employee employed	Spread on exercise: NEFS	Spread on exercise: employee	1099 MISC: NEFS (FIT) W-2: Employee (FICA)[h]
(b) Former employee: calendar year of term.	Spread on exercise: NEFS	Spread on exercise: employee	1099 MISC: NEFS (FIT) W-2: Employee (FICA)
(c) Former employee: subsequent years	Spread on exercise: NEFS	Spread on exercise: employee	1099 MISC: NEFS W-2: Employee (FICA)
5. Transferee[i]			
(a) Employee employed	Spread on exercise: employee	Spread on exercise: employee	W-2: employee[j]
(b) Former employee: calendar year of term.	Spread on exercise: employee	Spread on exercise: employee	W-2: employee
(c) Former employee: subsequent years	Spread on exercise: employee	Spread on exercise: employee	W-2: employee
6. Change to consultant status	Allocate spread on exercise across years of service; withhold on amount attributable to years as employee[k]	Allocate spread on exercise across years of service; withhold on amount attributable to years as employee	W-2 for employee years; 1099 MISC for consultant years

Exhibit 9-1. Withholding Information for NSO Exercise (cont'd)

7. Change of residence			
(a) To foreign country: U.S. expatriate	Allocate spread on exercise across years of service; exclude if IRC §911 applies, otherwise withhold on spread[l]	Allocate spread on exercise across years of service; exclude if totalization agreement requires social security payments to foreign country only[m]	W-2
(b) To different state	Allocate spread on exercise across years of service for state income tax purposes; FIT not affected[n]	Spread on exercise	W-2

a. Code §§ 3401(a) and 3121(a). The spread on exercise is wages for both FIT and FICA purposes.

b. Note that 1.83-6(a)(2) provides that a deduction is available as long as reporting is made, including using a 1099 MISC for a former employee. However, Code § 3401 and its regulations specifically provide that the employment relationship giving rise to a withholding obligation is not dependent on whether the payment is made at the time of the relationship.

c. For these purposes, there is no difference between a retired employee and an employee who has terminated for other reasons. Payments to retirees are excluded only in certain limited situations: some payments from and to qualified plans and certain deferred compensation payments (for which FICA withholding has already occurred). Code §§ 3401(a) and 3121(v)(i).

d. Rev. Rul. 86-109.

e. Report both FIT and FICA but no FIT withholding required.

f. Code § 3121(a).

g. Note that generally, this will apply only in community property states (unless the plan permits transferability).

h. Rev. Rul. 2002-22; Rev. Rul. 2002-31.

i. Note that this will only apply if the option is transferable.

j. Code § 83.

k. Code §§ 83, 3402, and 3121. No withholding is required for independent contractors, so the analysis here is the same as for any former employee, subject to allocation.

l. Code §§ 83 and 1441. The spread is allocated between U.S. source income (i.e., attributable to years resident in the U.S.) and foreign source income, based on where the services were performed. Withholding would ordinarily be required on U.S. source income. PLR 8711107. However, § 911 may provide an overall exclusion that will trump the withholding requirement.

m. Section 3121. The same rules apply, except that certain tax treaties (totalization agreements) may allocate the Social Security payment differently.

n. Each state has different rules. Most states require source income to be allocated on the same basis as USSI/FSI, but enforcement has been spotty.

The specific reporting requirements set out in the Section 6039 regulations provide that the statement furnished to the optionee (the "transferor") contain the following information:

1. The name and address of the company whose stock is being transferred;

2. The name, address, and identifying number of the transferor;

3. The date such stock was transferred to the transferor;

4. The number of shares to which title is being transferred; and

5. The type of option under which the transferred shares were acquired.

A statement is considered to be furnished to the transferor if it is mailed to the person at his or her last known address or, with the transferor's consent, delivered electronically.[7]

9.3.2 Tracking ESPP Qualifying Dispositions

Despite the Section 6039 reporting requirement, limited attention has traditionally been paid to tracking qualifying dispositions of ESPP stock. A "qualifying disposition" is a disposition of ESPP stock that occurs either after the applicable holding periods have expired or upon the death of the employee. As noted above, companies are not entitled to a tax deduction on a qualifying disposition, although the amount included in ordinary income under an ESPP option must be reported by the company on the optionee's W-2.[8] Because there is no perceived tax benefit to the employer in tracking qualifying dispositions, many companies have automatically assumed that there is also no requirement to do so. Section 6039(a), however, imposes an affirmative duty to report even on a qualifying disposition.

The challenge of Section 6039 for ESPP purposes lies not only in the paperwork required for adequate reporting but also in the timing of its requirements. Although it includes historical information, the actual reporting obligation arises only at the time of the qualifying disposition. Because by its terms a qualifying disposition must occur at least two years after grant of the option (or upon death of the optionee), the employee may have left the company long before the disposition takes place. Thus, the stock administrator or transfer agent must be able to recognize that the transferred stock is ESPP stock regardless of whether the transferor is still an employee of the company. In addition, the stock administrator will need to monitor the company's compliance schedule to ensure that statements are sent no later than January 31 for transactions that occur in any prior calendar year. Finally, it will be important to keep qualifying dispositions separate from disqualifying dispositions, so that the correct reporting obligations can be satisfied for each type of transfer and tax deductions taken where appropriate. In many cases, the broker that handles transactions under the plan will already be providing reports to employees that substantially satisfy Section 6039. If the administrator ensures that all of the Section 6039 requirements are satisfied by the broker report, the employer may be able to comply without additional expense. As noted above, the 2004 regulations specifically bless broker reporting in these situations.[9]

9.3.3 Penalties for Noncompliance

Section 6722 of the Code applies generally to impose penalties for failure to furnish payee information statements (including failure to furnish statements required under Section 6039). Those penalties include: (1) $50 for each failure to furnish a correct payee statement, up to a maximum of $100,000 per calendar year; and (2) in the case of intentional disregard of the reporting requirements, $100 per failure with no maximum.[10]

9.4 Procedure for Withholding with Stock

To assist optionees in providing for withholding on exercise of an NSO, many companies allow optionees to elect to provide for withholding by instructing the company to retain shares of stock on exercise of the option. Both the IRS and the SEC have approved stock withholding for tax withholding purposes.[11]

To withhold federal, state, or local taxes with stock, the company simply computes the tax due on the spread and retains shares with a fair market value equal to such amount on the employee's exercise of the option. The company's grant documents should state that the company will withhold on exercise as applicable either by collecting cash from the employee, by withholding from the employee's compensation, by withholding stock, or by a combination of methods.

9.5 Limit on Deductions: $1 Million Cap (Code Section 162(m))

Section 162(m) of the Code provides that a public company may not take a tax deduction with respect to compensation in excess of $1 million paid to the CEO and top four highly compensated employees ("covered employees"). The value of employee stock options will be factored into the $1 million cap calculation unless they are considered to be "performance-based compensation." Section 162(m) and its complex regulations provide a special safe harbor for options in this regard, although the rules for use in computing the limitation set out a veritable maze of definitions and exclusions. As an alternative to using the safe harbor, stock options may be designated as "performance based" under the general rules of Section 162(m)(4)(C) of the Code (requiring disclosure of material terms of performance goals). However, notwithstanding its complexity, the safe harbor generally provides an easier route for most companies.[12]

Generally, options granted to covered employees will be excluded from the $1 million cap if the plan under which options are issued satisfies the following requirements:

1. The plan is administered by a committee of outside directors. For these purposes, an "outside director" may not be a current or former employee of the company (or its affiliates) during the taxable year, must never have been an officer, and must not receive any remuneration from the company other than as a director. This definition differs from that used for Section 16 and other securities law purposes, and accordingly the company may choose to

have a special committee in place purely for the purpose of making Section 162(m) grants.[13]

2. The plan specifies who is eligible to participate, and this is disclosed to the shareholders.

3. The plan states a maximum number of shares that may be granted to any single participant, and this is disclosed to the shareholders.

4. Options are granted at fair market value.

5. The plan, as disclosed, is approved by the shareholders.

Any broad-based option plan that is designed to include ISOs will necessarily satisfy requirements (2) and (5). Requirement (3) can be met by drafting the plan to state a per-person maximum annual grant.[14] Requirements (1) and (4) require an affirmative intention on the part of the company to observe the criteria for the exclusion and are operational rather than a function of the plan itself. Plan administrators should be alert to the type of grant, and the manner in which it is granted, to any officer whose compensation might fall under Section 162(m).

9.6 Limit on Deductions: Golden Parachute Rules

Under Sections 280G and 4999 of the Code, certain employees and consultants ("disqualified individuals") who receive payments, including additional or accelerated stock options, contingent on a "change in control" of the payor company (or its related company) may suffer adverse tax consequences, along with the payor. If such payments are deemed to be "parachute payments," the disqualified individual is permitted to receive an aggregate payment of up to three times his "base amount" without penalty. However, if the present value of the amounts paid is equal to or greater than three times the base amount, the difference between the payment and the base amount will constitute an "excess parachute payment." Section 280G disallows a tax deduction to the payor in the amount of the excess parachute payment paid and Section 4999 imposes a 20% excise tax on the payee (in addition to normal income tax) with respect to the excess parachute payment received.[15]

Any but the most rudimentary overview of these complicated rules is beyond the scope of this discussion. For our narrow purposes, however, equity compensation planners should be aware of the following points.

9.6.1 Final vs. Proposed Regulations

The rules relating to golden parachute payments under Section 280G were in flux for 10 years. The first comprehensive set of proposed regulations to Section 280G were issued in Q/A form in 1989. These regulations were generally effective for payments under agreements entered into on or after June 14, 1984. The 1989 proposed regulations were significantly amended and republished on February 19, 2002, effective for payments related to changes in control occurring on or after January 1, 2004. Between 2002 and 2004, taxpayers could rely on either set of proposed regulations.

On August 4, 2003, the IRS published the final Section 280G regulations, which are effective for any payment contingent on a change in ownership or control if the change in ownership or control occurs on or after January 1, 2004.[16] The final regulations are substantially similar to the 2002 proposed regulations, with certain changes and clarifications, primarily concerning the small-corporation exemption, prepayment of the excise tax, and the definition of change in ownership or control. At the same time, the IRS published Rev. Proc. 2003-68 (discussed further in section 9.6.3 below), which modified and superceded earlier rules regarding acceptable methods for valuing options under Section 280G.[17]

9.6.2 When Are Options Treated As Parachute Payments?

To be a parachute payment under Section 280G(b)(2), a payment must first be "in the nature of compensation." The final regulations make it clear that options are considered to be compensation.[18] Second, the payment must be made "contingent on a change in control"—i.e., the payment would not, in fact, have been made had no change in ownership or control occurred. The easiest case would be when unvested options accelerate and become fully vested on a change in control, or when vested options are granted in connection with a change in control.[19] Things become more difficult when options are only partially amended at the time of the change, or when there is evidence that the option grants (or accelerated vesting) would have occurred anyway in connection with ongoing services; e.g., that the payments constitute "reasonable compensation" rather than parachute payments. Analyzing this issue is one of the trickiest aspects of the rules.[20]

9.6.3 How Are Options Valued for Purposes of Section 280G?

Once it is determined that an option-related payment is a parachute payment, the payment must be valued as part of the overall excess parachute payment calculation. If the full amount of the option is deemed to be a parachute payment, it is valued as of the date it becomes fully vested. If only the accelerated portion of the payment is a parachute payment, that portion must be present-valued and included separately. Treas. Reg. § 1.280G, Q/A 13, specifically requires valuation of transferred options and Rev. Proc. 2003-68 elaborates on the rules, providing that options may be valued using any valuation method that is (i) consistent with generally accepted accounting principles (GAAP) (such as FAS 123), and (ii) that takes into account the factors set out in Treas. Reg. § 1.280G, Q/A 1 (i.e., the spread, the probability of the stock increasing or decreasing in value, and the length of the exercise period). Further, section 4 of Rev. Proc. 2003-68 sets out a safe harbor valuation method for these purposes.[21] Care must be taken in performing these valuations, as option-related payments are often large enough to transform a parachute payment into an excess parachute payment.

For planning purposes, both payees and payors will want to ensure that option-related payments are carefully scrutinized as early as possible to avoid unanticipated golden parachute issues. The goal, of course, is to keep the base amount as large as possible (i.e., to maximize the type and amount of payments that go into that number) while keeping parachute payments to a minimum (i.e. to structure compensation so as to avoid characterization as parachute payments). In many cases, advance planning will result in more "reasonable compensation" and less "excess parachute payments."

Notes

1. See Rev. Rul. 82-200, 1982-2 C.B. 239; Rev. Rul. 67-257, 1967-2 C.B. 359. See also Treas. Reg. § 31.3402(g)-1 (supplemental wage withholding generally). Withholding is not required on exercise by a nonemployee unless he is a former employee of the company. See Treas. Reg. § 31.3401(a)-1(a)(5); see also chapter 15.

2. Typically, this amount has been reported in the "other" or "misc" box on either form. However, from time to time the IRS prescribes the use of various codes, and employers should check for the most up-to-date rules annually under Treas. Reg § 1.83-6(a)(2).

3. Treas. Reg. § 1.6041-(2)(a)(1).

4. Treas. Reg. § 1.83-6(a)(2). As of 2003, employers are required to use a "V" code on the Form W-2 when reporting disqualifying dispositions. See IRS Announcements 2002-108, 2002-49 I.R.B. 952; 2001-92, 2001-39 IRB 301.

5. The proposed regulations originally required that the company furnish the IRS with a copy of each Section 6039(a) information report, a requirement that was suspended by the IRS Office of the Chief Counsel pending final regulations. See CCA 200114001 (April 6, 2001). The requirement was dropped from the 2004 Treasury regulations.

6. Section 6039(b)(2); CCA 200114001 (April 6, 2001).

7. Treas. Reg. § 1.6039-1(d) (mail); § 1.6039-1(f) (electronic).

8. Section 423(c). For ISO purposes, information reporting with respect to the year of exercise would be necessary (although not specifically required) regardless of Section 6039, so as to give optionees the ability to compute AMT. As a practical matter, for public company stock transactions the transfer agent/broker will ordinarily issue an information report to the optionee at the time of exercise.

9. Treas. Reg. § 1.6039-1(b)(3).

10. Under the proposed regulations, the IRS Office of Chief Counsel took the position that Section 6039 penalties would be assessed under Treas. Reg. § 301.6678-1, which imposes less stringent penalties of $10 on each failure to furnish a correct payee statement up to a maximum of $25,000 per calendar year. That position was overruled by the 2004 regulations.

11. See, e.g., PLRs 9736040, 9629028, and 8650045 (withholding for stock swap); Ralston Purina Company, SEC No-Action Letter (Apr. 23, 1991); and Cravath, Swaine & Moore, SEC No-Action Letter (May 6, 1991). Note that this is a different scenario than broker-assisted withholding (e.g., same day sales), which is not considered to be stock withholding for these purposes.

12. Treas. Reg. § 1.162-27(e)(2).

13. Section 162(m)(4)(C); Treas. Reg. § 1.162-27(e)(3). See also PLR 9811029 (compensation committee appropriate for 162(m) purposes).

14. The IRS Chief Counsel has agreed that the stated option pool required in an ISO plan may be deemed to set out an annual per-person limit equal to the total number of shares available under the plan. See CCA 2001133014 (August 17, 2001). However, because this may not always be viewed as adequate disclosure of the cap to shareholders for Section 162(m) purposes, most lawyers suggest that companies state a specific per-person maximum when possible. Note that under the regulations, repriced options will be double-counted (i.e., both the original option and the repriced option will be counted separately) in computing the per-person limit. Treas. Reg. § 1.162-27(e)(2)(vi)(B).

15. The golden parachute rules are highly technical, and each of the terms set off in quotes is specifically defined by the Code and its regulations, along with numerous other definitions. Consideration of options in parachute payments constitutes only one part of the extensive regulatory scheme. See Treas. Reg. § 1.280G-1. For a detailed technical and historical review of Section 280G and its regulations, see Bill C. Wilson and Diane M. McGowan, 396 T.M., *Golden Parachutes* (BNA).

16. The final (corrected) version of the regulations was published at 68 Fed. Reg. 59114 (10/14/03).

17. 2003-34 I.R.B. 398, revoking Rev. Proc. 2002-13, 2002-8 I.R.B. 549, and Rev. Proc. 2002-45, 2002-27, I.R.B. 40.

18. Treas. Reg. § 1.280G-1 Q/A-11. Treas. Reg. § 1.280G-1 Q/A-13 clarifies that the treatment of both nonstatutory and statutory options for these purposes is identical.

19. Treas. Reg. § 1.280G-1 Q/A 22-23.

20. Ibid. See also Treas. Reg. § 1.280G-1 Q/A 25-26 (parachute payment presumption); Q/A 9, 38-44 (when is a payment "reasonable compensation").

21. The safe harbor method is essentially a modified Black-Scholes model, *generally* based on the following factors: (1) the volatility of the underlying stock, (2) the exercise price of the option, (3) the value of the stock at the time

of valuation, and (4) the term of the option on the valuation date. See also Rev. Proc. 98-34, 1998-1 C.B. 983 (valuation methods for compensatory stock options for purposes of gift, estate, and generation-skipping transfer taxes).

Part II
Special Issues: The Changing Landscape

The dynamic field of equity compensation is constantly evolving to meet the challenges posed by the interplay of tax, accounting, corporate, and securities regulations regarding the use of stock as employee incentives. The following chapters provide a survey of some current issues and creative approaches to these issues, and, in some cases, the author's highly opinionated response to them (which the reader is advised to take for what it's worth!). Please note that this discussion is updated as of the end of 2005. Before pursuing any of the suggestions below, companies should always check with their legal and accounting advisors to ascertain the current status of the rules.

Readers are also invited to periodically check the "New Stock Option Topics" section of the author's Web site, *www.alisabaker.com,* for new articles and updates to those that follow.

CHAPTER 10

Basic Accounting Issues

By Alisa Baker and Barbara Baksa*

Contents

There are two basic building blocks of equity compensation accounting: Accounting Principles Board Opinion No. 25, and Statement of Financial Accounting Standards No. 123.

The Accounting Principles Board, or APB, was the precursor to what is now the Financial Accounting Standards Board, or FASB, the

---

Barbara Baksa is the executive director of the National Association of Stock Plan Professionals (NASPP). She is a Certified Equity Professional (CEP) and serves on the Certified Equity Professional Institute's advisory board and the NCEO's board of directors.

private board that sets U.S. accounting standards.[1] Accounting Principles Board Opinion No. 25 (APB 25) was historically the accounting standard under which most companies that grant stock options accounted for them in their financial statements. It set out specific "fixed-award" accounting rules that, when satisfied, effectively permitted the company to show no stock-option-related expense on its financial statements. A company that used APB 25 but failed to satisfy the fixed-award rules was required to fall back on "variable plan accounting," under which the cost of a grant was accounted for quarterly. Predictably, many companies designed their plans to take advantage of fixed plan accounting and avoid variable plan accounting at all costs.

In the mid-1990s, FASB issued its Statement of Financial Accounting Standards 123 (FAS 123), which gave options issuers two choices: (1) continue to rely on APB 25 but add a footnote to their income statements placing a value on the options they granted; or (2) voluntarily switch to FAS 123. This was a compromise. FASB had hoped to set a new mandatory standard, but it backed down after Congress intervened.

In December 2004, FASB issued FAS 123 (Revised 2004), also known as FAS 123(R), a mandatory standard that began to go into effect in mid-2005.[2] FAS 123(R) has leveled the equity compensation playing field by ending the special accounting treatment enjoyed by some forms of stock options under APB 25 that made them more attractive than restricted stock, SARs, phantom stock, and performance shares.

This chapter describes all of the standards, even those that are now of historical value, so as to give the reader an opportunity to understand context when assessing accounting issues for equity plans going forward. Many plans will contain latent design issues and administrative provisions that track back to accounting rules that are no longer applicable; these plans must be reviewed and amended as appropriate. In analyzing these issues, however it is important to remember that none of the rules discussed here affect the tax treatment of equity compensation. Accounting and taxation remain separate concerns for plan designers.

10.1 APB 25

Under APB 25, an employee stock option plan was either compensatory or noncompensatory. To be considered noncompensatory, a plan had to meet the following conditions:

1. substantially all full-time employees are eligible to participate;
2. options are granted equally or based on a uniform percentage of salary;
3. the time allowed for exercise is limited to a reasonable period; and
4. the discount at the grant date is no more than 15% from fair market value (FMV).

APB 25 specifically cited Section 423 ESPPs as noncompensatory. With the exception of Section 423 ESPPs, most equity awards, including stock options, restricted stock, SARs, and similar programs did not meet these noncompensatory tests.

Under APB 25, employers did not have to recognize compensation expense with respect to stock issued under noncompensatory plans. However, most stock option plans were considered to be compensatory. In a compensatory plan, accounting treatment of an option was determined on the "measurement date," or the first date on which the number of shares *and* the purchase price for those shares was fixed. If the measurement date occurred on the grant date, the compensation was measured using "fixed-award accounting," which meant that the intrinsic value of the option was measured as the difference between the option price and the option's fair market value on the measurement date. Any difference was treated as a compensation expense that was recognized in equal installments over the period of service (typically the vesting period) to which the option related.

If the measurement date could not be fixed on the grant date (usually because the price or other unfixed terms of the award might change or because vesting was based on performance), the compensation was measured using variable-award accounting until the measurement date. Using that method, the "intrinsic value" of the option was measured during the service period by taking the difference between the option price and the fair market value quarterly during the vesting period in an approach called "marking to market." This value was treated as a compensation expense, recognized in equal installments, and adjusted as necessary on the company's financial statements until the measurement date, which was generally the date when the option was exercised or expired, but in some circumstances was the date of vesting. For the purposes of APB 25, companies could use stock to withhold taxes without triggering accounting consequences as long as the amount withheld was no higher than the minimum statutory federal and state amount. However, the company could withhold more in cash (for example, from an employee's paycheck) without triggering accounting consequences.

As a general rule, APB 25 meant that employee stock option grants at fair market value whose only vesting requirement was continued employment did not affect a company's financial statements.

10.2 FAS 123

FAS 123, which FASB issued in 1995, sought to require companies to place a "fair value" on employee stock options not otherwise expensed under APB 25 as of the grant date. That amount was either recorded as a charge to earnings during the service period or disclosed in a footnote. The newest standard, FAS 123(R) (discussed in detail below), eliminates the footnote option.

Under both the original FAS 123 and the revised standard, fair value is determined using an option-pricing model, typically the Black-Scholes model. Neither FAS 123 nor the revised standard requires the use of a specific model, but both standards require that the model used consider the risk-free interest rate, the expected life of the option, the exercise price of the option, the current price and expected volatility of the underlying stock, and the expected dividends.

10.3 Interpreting APB 25 Under FIN 44

In 1998, FASB made it clear that it was dissatisfied that companies were continuing to rely on APB 25 instead of switching to FAS 123. After extensive debate, the FASB issued an interpretation titled "Accounting for Certain Transactions Involving Stock Compensation," on March 31, 2000, as FASB Interpretation No. 44 (FIN 44). Although APB 25 survived the issuance of FIN 44, its application was made considerably more complicated by the new rules. FIN 44 applied prospectively as of July 1, 2000.

The FASB considered many issues during its lengthy initial review of APB 25, including:

- Definition of employee
- Definition of grant date
- Reconciliation of approaches to measurement date
- Accounting for plans with puts, calls, and rights of first refusal
- Accounting by a subsidiary of a public company
- Accounting for deferred tax assets
- Accounting for plan modifications
- Accounting for accelerated vesting
- Accounting for cancellation/reissuance of stock awards
- Accounting for linkage between stock and cash bonus plans
- Accounting for pooling
- Accounting for exchange of options in business combination
- Accounting for Section 423 ESPPs with look-back provisions

Not all of these issues were resolved fully by the final interpretation. The March 2000 version of FIN 44 included (among other things) the following important changes and clarifications:

- *Definition of Employee:* Before FIN 44, consultants were often considered employees for purposes of APB 25. FIN 44 defined "employee" with respect to the common-law tax rules only. Under it, options to nonemployees were considered to be outside the scope of APB 25 and accordingly were valued under FAS 123. Once measured, the options were subject to variable award accounting and marked to market quarterly until fully vested. In addition, a change in status (for example, from employee to consultant) created a new measurement date for the unvested portion of outstanding options and resulted in recognition of compensation expense from then on for that portion of the grant. Changes in status as a result of a "spin-off" were excepted from this rule. Note that under FIN 44, nonemployee directors and, in limited cases, leased employees could be treated as employees under APB 25. For these purposes, advisory board members were treated as consultants.

- *Section 423 Plans:* APB 25 specifically mentioned Section 423 plans as noncompensatory plans. FIN 44 retained the status quo, provided that Section 423 plans satisfy a "reasonableness" criterion by offering a discount of no more than 15% as of the day of grant. Moreover, although the FASB had stated that it disapproved of "look-back" mechanisms that base the purchase price on the lower of the stock price on the grant date or exercise date (which is allowed under Section 423 of the Code), FIN 44 allowed those provisions to continue to be permissible as long as they were "reasonable" as of the date of grant.

- *Modifications:* Modifications to otherwise fixed options under FIN 44 generally resulted in a new measurement date and produced expense based on the intrinsic value added by the modification. For these purposes, modifications under FIN 44 included cancellations and reissuances of options, extensions or renewals of an option's term, and the addition of accelerated vesting (including acceleration at the company's discretion) to already outstanding grants (where the accelerated vesting allowed employees to exercise shares that would otherwise have been forfeited). Modifications to otherwise fixed options that changed the exercise price or the number of shares subject to options, or that added a reload feature, resulted in variable award accounting for those options from the date of the modification through the date of exercise. Note that in the case of discretionary acceleration, the new measurement date did not occur unless company actually exercised that discretion.

- *Repricings:* Under FIN 44, repricing resulted in variable award accounting from the time of the repricing until the exercise date. A cancellation followed by a reissuance within six months was considered a repricing for these purposes.

- *Grants to (or Among) Subsidiaries:* If the parent company accounted for stock option grants to employees of subsidiaries on a consolidated basis, the subsidiary could account for parent or sister company stock issued to its employees under APB 25 on its separate financial statements. Under FIN 44, the subsidiary had to be part of the consolidated financial statement to avail itself of compensatory plan accounting in this situation. Grants to employees of joint ventures were not eligible for treatment under APB 25.

- *Tax Withholding:* FIN 44 restated the FASB's position that tax withholding with stock *for no more than the minimum statutory federal and state withholding amount* would not result in variable award accounting at the time of exercise. However, it added the requirement that the plan could not give the optionee discretion to determine the amount of the tax withholding—the terms of the plan had to specify that tax withholding with stock at exercise could not exceed the statutory minimum. Of course, additional withholding from the employee's regular paycheck had no effect on accounting characterization of an option.

- *Cash Bonus Features:* Under FIN 44, variable award accounting was required for stock option grants that included "cash bonus" features that included payment contingent on exercise and bonus amounts that were not "fixed and determinable."

10.4 EITF Issue No. 00-23 Interpretations

The FASB's Emerging Issues Task Force (EITF) continued to study the issues raised by FIN 44 through March 2002, when it finally concluded the project. EITF Issue No. 00-23 ultimately produced guidance on 71 practice issues and subissues related to FIN 44. Some of the most important guidance included the following:

- *Option Repricings at Six Months Plus One Day After Cancellation ("6+1"):* Under FIN 44, any agreement made at the time of option cancellation to replace options in a manner that compensated for stock changes during the 6+1 period resulted in variable award accounting. "6+1" referred to a then-popular approach to replacing options in which employees turned in their underwater options in return for a promise to receive new options (not necessarily on a one-to-one basis) six months and one day later. EITF 00-23 clarified that variable award accounting was not necessary simply because the replacement ratio is greater than 1:1 so long as the replacement formula was not directly or indirectly connected to stock fluctuations during the 6+1 period. However, if it appeared that there was a connection, variable award accounting was required. Note, however, that regardless of whether the offer was accepted, an offer to cancel and replace an option within six months did result in variable award accounting.

- *Transferability:* EITF 00-23 clarified that the addition of a transferability feature to an otherwise fixed option in and of itself was not a modification that resulted in variable award accounting unless circumstances indicated that the transferability feature was for the purpose of reacquisition by the employer or circumvention of accounting rules.

- *Tax Reloads:* Under FIN 44, variable award accounting did not apply to an option that included a tax reload feature in the original grant provided that the swapped shares replaced by the reload were "mature" (i.e., held for six months). EITF 00-23 modified this rule to provide that a tax reload feature for the *minimum statutory amount* did not require variable accounting treatment even if the swapped shares used were not mature.

- *Broker-Assisted Cashless Exercise:* Issue 48 of EITF 00-23 concluded that cashless exercises effected through an *unrelated* (third-party) broker produced no accounting consequences so long as the employee was the legal owner of the stock (i.e., assumed market risk from exercise to sale). If the broker was a *related party*, there was no accounting consequence if the employee was the legal owner of the stock, the broker was a substantive entity with operations separate and distinct from the grantor, the shares were sold on the open market, and the cashless exercise process was the same for all (related and unrelated) brokers. In any case, failure to meet the requirements of Issue 48 resulted in variable award accounting.

- *Early Exercise Provisions:* So long as unvested stock was subject to repurchase at the *lesser* of fair market value or original purchase price and was otherwise in substance a forfeiture provision under the original vesting schedule, no adverse accounting consequences resulted. If the repurchase right was at the original price only, exercise was a prepayment that was recognized as a liability, and options had to be accounted for as the stock vested.

10.5 FAS 123(R)

Ultimately, FASB decided to make expensing mandatory. This reflects a global trend, exemplified by a 2004 International Accounting Standards Board (IASB) standard that requires expensing[3]; FASB worked with IASB and other standards bodies with the goal of bringing about a convergence of accounting standards across the major world capital markets. As a result of this project, in December 2004 FASB released a revision of FAS 123 called FAS 123(R). While FAS 123(R) differs in some respects from the IASB's standard, the two standards are generally very similar. Public companies must adopt FAS 123(R) by the first annual fiscal period beginning after June 15, 2005; private companies and public companies that file as small-business issuers must adopt FAS 123(R) by the first annual fiscal period beginning after December 15, 2005. In many respects, the new standard is very similar to the original. Under it, compensation expense for options and awards granted to employees is determined at grant, and is generally not adjusted for subsequent events (with the exception of forfeitures), provided that the option or award can only be settled in stock. After an employee leaves the company, the former employer can continue to expense options and awards under FAS 123(R) as long as their terms are not modified.[4] The expense for stock options is equal to the fair value of the arrangement, which is determined using an option-pricing model.

Once determined, any expense is recorded over the service period (typically, the vesting period) of the arrangement. In most cases, an expense is recognized only for arrangements that actually vest; expense is not recognized for forfeited shares. If the number of shares forfeited exceeds expectations, previously recognized expense associated with the forfeited shares is reversed. Expense is not reversed, however, for arrangements that vest but subsequently expire unexercised or for underwater options that are cancelled as part of a repricing or option exchange program.

The following discussion highlights some of the significant provisions of the standard, including areas where the final standard differs from the original FAS 123.

10.5.1 Valuation Model

Stock options result in an expense equal to their grant date fair value, as determined using an option-pricing model. FAS 123(R) states that fair value must be measured "based on the observable market price of an option with the same or similar terms and conditions, if one is available." However, in the absence of such an option, fair value must be determined using an option-pricing model. The final standard does not express a preference regarding the type of pricing model that should be used to value employee stock options, other than to require that the model consider the following six factors:

- The exercise price of the option
- The fair market value of the underlying stock
- The expected life of the option
- The expected volatility of the underlying stock
- The expected dividend yield on the underlying stock
- The risk-free interest rate

FAS 123(R) allows employers to use virtually any pricing model that exists today or that is developed in the future, including lattice models, the Black-Scholes model, and Monte Carlo simulations. There are a variety of lattice models and more are likely to be developed. For reasons described below, they are likely to be a popular way for publicly traded companies to value options. However, those switching to lattice models must gather significant amounts of data to develop accurate assumptions. Thus, companies whose options expense is unlikely to be significantly reduced by using a lattice model have opted to continue to use the Black-Scholes model.

Lattice models are mathematically complex tools, but conceptually simple. The idea is to predict a series of outcomes (two in a binomial lattice model, three in a trinomial, etc.) for the exercise of options at different possible future prices. In a binomial model, at each "node" on the lattice (think of a tree with branches, with the branches having more branches in a potentially infinite progression; the nodes are where a branch splits into two more), the price can go up or down. Probabilities are assigned to each outcome based on estimates of the stock's volatility. The value of the option at each node is calculated based on its predicted price at that point. All these calculations are then factored into a formula that weighs their probability and comes up with a single number. Because these models are more dynamic than Black-Scholes (which makes very fixed assumptions about how options are used), they are generally considered to more accurately value options that can be exercised at varying points in time, such as employee stock options.

To apply a lattice model to employee stock options, the model must be modified to consider a minimum of two additional inputs: the "suboptimal exercise factor" and the likelihood that employees will terminate and be forced to exercise the option sooner than they would otherwise. The suboptimal exercise factor is the ratio by which the stock price must increase before employees are expected to exercise. Increases in stock price frequently drive exercise behavior; this factor specifies how much appreciation triggers employees to exercise. It is "suboptimal" behavior because, in theory, it is generally better to wait until near the end of an option's term to exercise, but experience shows that price increases in the interim can induce many employees to exercise sooner. Then, the model emphasizes the outcomes where this ratio has been achieved in calculating the option value. We also know that when employees terminate, they are often forced to exercise earlier than they would otherwise. The probability of this occurring is also factored into the value computed by the model.

Although the standard precludes including the likelihood of forfeiture as a model input, it does allow the use of models that incorporate a variety of other inputs, such as black-out periods, performance criteria, or Rule 10b5-1 trading plans (plans for executives that automatically trigger exercise at set intervals).

10.5.2 Expense Attribution

Once the expense for an option or award is determined, it is recorded over the service period of the award. In most cases, the service period starts on the grant date and ends on the vesting date.

Determination of the grant date has been complicated by the requirement in FAS 123(R) that the grant date occur when the company and award recipient come to a "mutual understanding" of the award's terms and conditions, meaning generally when the award is communicated to the recipient. Because this contravened the common practice of counting the grant date as occurring when corporate governance requirements such as board or compensation committee approval are met, practitioners argued that this provision would unnecessarily complicate plan administration because it would potentially force companies to account for grants that had the same exercise price for tax purposes as having different grant prices for accounting purposes. As a result, FASB in October 2005 amended its definition of "mutual understanding" to state that one exists if (i) the award is unilateral and thus its recipient cannot negotiate its key terms and conditions after it is approved, *and* (ii) "the key terms and conditions of the award are expected to be communicated to an individual recipient within a relatively short time period from the date of approval." A relatively short time period is "that period an entity could reasonably complete all actions necessary to communicate the awards to the recipients in accordance with the entity's customary human resource practices."[5] The practical effect of this in most cases will be that the date of approval will be the grant date.

For options and awards that are subject to cliff vesting (e.g., the entire award vests in full on a single date), expense is accrued on a straight-line basis over the service period (i.e., the vesting period). For options and awards with graded vesting (i.e., monthly, quarterly, or annual), the final standard permits two alternative attribution methods: expense can be recorded on a straight-line basis over the full service period (provided that the amount of expense recorded at any point in time is proportionate to the percentage of the option or award that is currently vested), or expense can be recorded in an accelerated manner where each vesting increment is treated as a separate award.

10.5.3 Service Period

The expense is recorded over the service period of the option or award. Under the new standard, the service period is generally presumed to be the vesting period unless there is clear evidence to the contrary. Where vesting is contingent upon future service, the service period cannot be defined as a prior period. An award that will vest automatically when an employee retires must be fully recognized as soon as the employee becomes eligible to retire, regardless of whether he or she actually retires at that time.

For awards that vest based on performance conditions, the service period can sometimes differ from the vesting period. If vesting will be accelerated upon achievement of a performance goal and it is expected that the goal will be achieved, the service period is the period of time over which the goal is expected to be achieved rather than the stated vesting period. For example, assume a company grants an option that vests upon completion of a specified goal but, if the goal is not achieved, vests in five years after the date of grant. The stated vesting period is five years, but if it is expected that the goal will be achieved sooner, the expense for the option would be recorded over this shorter period.

In some cases, performance-based options and awards may not have a stated vesting period. For these arrangements, the company should estimate when the goal is likely to be achieved and accrue expense for the arrangement over that period. If the performance goal is related to the company's stock price, the company should use an option-pricing model to derive when the goal is likely to be achieved. In some arrangements, vesting may be contingent on multiple goals or service conditions. For example, an option may vest based on the achievement of a specified goal and the optionee's continued service over a specified time period. The company should determine the period of time associated with each vesting contingency. If all of the contingencies must be met for the arrangement to vest, the service period is generally the longest period. If only one of the contingencies must be met, the service period is generally the shortest period. The guidance in this area is complicated, however, and can vary based on the likelihood that the contingencies will be achieved.

10.5.4 Forfeitures

An expense is generally recognized only for options or shares that actually vest. Where vesting is contingent solely upon continued service and options or awards are forfeited before vesting, no expense is recognized for the forfeited shares. If the forfeitures occur after some portion of the vesting period has elapsed, the expense that was previously recorded with respect to the forfeited shares is reversed to the extent that the forfeitures are greater than anticipated.

For arrangements where vesting is contingent upon the achievement of performance goals, the standard distinguishes between performance conditions that are market related and those that are not. Performance goals that are related to the company's stock price, such as a specified price target, shareholder return, or another calculation involving the company's stock price are referred to as "market conditions." Performance goals that are not related to the company's stock price could include specific revenue or earnings targets, or individual or departmental goals. Expense recognized for options forfeited as a result of failure to meet market conditions cannot be reversed.

10.5.5 Modifications

For companies that have experienced a decline in stock price, FAS 123(R) may make repricing a viable alternative once again. Whereas under APB 25, repricing an underwater stock option triggered variable plan accounting, which could ultimately be very costly for the granting corporation, under FAS 123(R) repricings and other option modifications are accounted for using the same general principles that applied under FAS 123.

Under FAS 123(R), a repricing or other modification is viewed as a cancellation of the original option and the grant of a replacement option. None of the expense previously recorded for the cancelled option is reversed and, if the option is not yet fully vested, the company continues to record the remaining unamortized expense along with the additional expense for the replacement option. The expense for the replacement option is equal to its fair value less the fair value of the cancelled option at the time of the cancellation.

One of the longest and most complex discussions in FAS 123(R) concerns modifications of awards that are performance based. There are multiple possibilities described for modifications that have different likelihoods of producing value. Modifying an award to make a performance target higher, or canceling an option and replacing it with one with a performance condition not likely to be met, for instance, would be treated differently from a modification that had a high likelihood of vesting. The details are beyond the scope of this discussion, however.

10.5.6 Employee Stock Purchase Plans

The treatment of ESPPs under the final standard is very similar to the treatment of these plans under the original FAS 123. This treatment differs significantly from that enjoyed by ESPPs under APB 25, where any plans that complied with the requirements of Section 423 of the Code were generally considered noncompensatory. Under FAS 123(R), ESPPs can also be considered noncompensatory, but must meet all of the following requirements to receive this consideration:

1. Where the terms of the plan are more favorable than those available to all shareholders, any discount offered under plan must be equal to or less than the company's costs of raising capital through a public offering. A safe-harbor discount of 5% is allowed without further justification, but companies wishing to offer a higher discount must either offer that same discount to all shareholders or demonstrate that their costs of undergoing a public offering would be greater than that.

2. The plan cannot incorporate any option-like features. A common option-like feature that is prohibited under this requirement is a "look-back" provision, under which the purchase price is based on the lower of the market value of the stock on the enrollment date or the purchase date.

3. Substantially all employees must be permitted to participate in the plan on an equal basis. Plans meeting the rules for Section 423 ESPPs would qualify under this requirement.

Consequently, many employee stock purchase plans that had been considered noncompensatory under APB 25 are considered compensatory under FAS 123(R). If compensatory, the rights acquired by employees are viewed as stock options that are granted on the enrollment date and exercised on the purchase date. Again, this does not affect the tax treatment of Section 423 ESPPs.

10.5.7 Private Companies

For purposes of determining the fair value of option grants, the final standard requires privately held companies to use an option-pricing model that considers stock price volatility; the original FAS 123 permitted privately held companies to use a minimum-value model to measure the expense of option grants. The minimum-value method allowed companies to assume that volatility was zero. Because volatility is often the most important factor in determining option value, and the higher the volatility, the higher the value, this was a substantial concession. Under FAS 123(R) private companies can use volatility indexes for comparable public companies if they cannot establish a volatility measurement otherwise.[6]

10.5.8 Tax Effects

Tax deductions reduce the company's tax expense, to some extent off-setting stock plan expense. In the case of stock compensation, however, the tax deduction received for the arrangement differs in timing and amount from the expense recorded for it. Special procedures are required to account for this difference.

For nonqualified arrangements, the company records an estimated tax benefit at the time it records its expense for the arrangement and reduces its current-period tax expense by the amount of the estimated benefit. The estimated benefit is equal to the expense recorded for the arrangement multiplied by the company's statutory tax rate. If the company's actual tax savings exceed the estimated benefit, the company records additional paid-in-capital on its balance sheet for the excess. Where it is less (or where the company doesn't realize any tax savings because an option expired unexercised), this difference must be recorded as a reduction in paid-in-capital, but only to the extent there is a reserve of paid-in-capital from prior stock transactions that can be reduced. If not, an additional tax expense must be recorded on the income statement.

For tax-qualified arrangements, such as ISOs and employee stock purchase plans (ESPPs) that meet the requirements of Internal Revenue Code Section 423, the company cannot assume any tax benefit up front. Instead, the company records a tax benefit (and reduces tax expense) only when disqualifying dispositions actually occur. (Section 423 ESPPs are explained in chapter 4, and disqualifying dispositions are explained in section 3.4.)

This was true under APB 25, but was rarely an issue since most stock option arrangements resulted in an expense of zero under that accounting standard.

In FAS 123(R), FASB assumed that companies had been tracking the amount of paid-in-capital attributable to excess tax deductions since the implementation of FAS 123. However, many companies had not and were not even certain they had the decade of detailed data on grants and corporate taxes and tax rates needed to determine their reserve of additional paid-in-capital. Thus, FASB in November 2005 approved an alternative method for establishing the beginning balance of paid-in-capital from excess tax deductions that requires less detailed calculations.[7]

Multinational companies facing different tax rates and rules must carefully incorporate these considerations into how these calculations are performed.

10.5.9 Effective Date and Transitional Provisions

Publicly traded companies must adopt the standard by their first annual fiscal period beginning after June 15, 2005, with the exception of publicly traded small-business issuers and private companies, which must use it for annual periods beginning after December 15, 2005. The new standard applies to any options and awards granted after adoption and any options or awards granted before adoption that are not yet vested.

Companies are permitted, but not required, to voluntary restate prior fiscal periods (either just the prior interim periods for the year of adoption or all prior periods included in their financial statements). If choosing restatement, however, it is still not permissible to revalue or change attribution methods for options and awards granted before adoption of the new standard; the restatement must reflect the expense that was originally reported on a pro forma basis for the periods subject to the restatement.

For privately held companies that previously used a minimum-value model to account for stock options under FAS 123, the new standard applies only to options and awards granted after adoption. In addition, these companies are not permitted to voluntarily restate prior fiscal periods.

10.5.10 Accounting for Awards Other Than Options

FAS 123(R) affects a variety of equity compensation awards other than stock options, such as restricted stock and phantom stock, most of which are beyond the scope of this text. However, it is helpful to note that SARs *paid out solely in stock* generally receive the same treatment under FAS 123(R) as do stock options. The expense for the SARs is equal to the fair value of the arrangement at the date of grant, as determined using an option-pricing model, and is recorded over the service period of the arrangement. This preserves the treatment of stock-settled rights under FAS 123 and, many would argue, improves upon the treatment of these rights that applied under APB 25. Generally all SARs, whether paid in stock or in cash, are subject to variable plan accounting under APB 25.

SARs that are (or may be) paid in cash are treated as a liability under the standard. The expense for rights paid in cash is the fair value of the arrangement at the time of exercise or, if never exercised, expiration. Expense is recorded over the service period of the right, based on interim estimates of fair value. The interim estimates are adjusted each financial period until the measurement date occurs.

Notes

1. The Accounting Principles Board (APB) was a committee, organized by the American Institute of Certified Public Accountants (AICPA), that set accounting standards from 1959 to 1972, after which the FASB assumed responsibility for accounting standards.

2. Information on ordering FASB publications, including FAS 123(R), is posted on the FASB Web site at www.fasb.org.

3. For more information on the IASB, see its Web site at *www.iasb.org*.

4. FASB Staff Position 123(R)-1, August 31, 2005.

5. FASB Staff Position 123(R)-2, October 18, 2005.

6. For an analysis of the application of FAS 123(R) on private companies, see McMillan, "The Impact of FASB's New Equity Expensing Rules on Private Companies," 17 *Journal of Employee Ownership Law and Finance* 97 (Spring 2005).

7. FASB Staff Position 123(R)-1, November 10, 2005.

CHAPTER 11

Legislative and Regulatory Initiatives Related to Stock Options: History and Status

Contents

11.1 Legislative History: Stock Option Initiatives

There have been surprising legislative ups and downs with respect to stock options during the 1990s and into the 21st century. This chapter briefly summarizes the history of these legislative initiatives through 2005.

11.1.1 Early Attention: 1991–1997

Before 1991, congressional involvement with stock options had been limited to enacting the implementing tax legislation for ISOs in the Economic Recovery Tax Act of 1981. Aside from those who received options, only lawyers and accountants who worked with equity compensation paid much attention to their status. In fact, in 1991 the status of compensatory stock options seemed clear: the Code and its regulations governed tax treatment, APB 25 established accounting procedures, and Section 16 of the Exchange Act dictated disclosure requirements for insiders. Even the FASB, which started its review of stock option accounting in 1984, had closed down the project in 1988 for lack of interest.

In the early 1990s, however, compensatory options began to get national attention in the press. A number of articles appeared that focused on big option packages for executives without noting the effectiveness of broad-based equity compensation.[1] With an election year around the corner, Senator Carl Levin, D-Michigan, picked up on the negative publicity as a justification for introducing S. 1198, a bill that required companies to include the "cost" of options on financial statements and disclose information about unexercised options to shareholders. Under this June 1991 bill, the SEC was required to figure out and impose a valuation method, with or without the cooperation of FASB or the Treasury Department.

Over the next two years, stock options (now dubbed "stealth compensation") became a hot topic as a wide variety of interest groups and professional organizations loudly participated in hearings, drafted proposed legislation, and battled each other in the press and on the Congressional floor. In particular, FASB was pushed back into the middle of the debate, with Senator Levin and his supporters agitating for mandatory changes to stock option valuation for financial accounting (and public disclosure) purposes. However, despite pressure from Senator Levin's committee, the SEC refused to cooperate in imposing standards on FASB. As noted in chapter 10, in 1995 FASB adopted FAS 123, requiring only that a reasonable value for outstanding options be disclosed in the footnotes to the issuer's financial statements.

11.1.2 End of the Century: 1997 to 2000

With the adoption of FAS 123 and the new securities disclosure rules (both effective for 1996), practitioners assumed that the roller coaster ride had ended. The combination of disclosure rules seemingly addressed public concern that stock options were devices for "stealth compensation." Nevertheless, in April 1997 Senator Levin revived the issue and introduced S. 576, the "Ending Double Standards for Stock Options Act." The proposed legislation looked to the Code to require any company that took a deduction for stock options under Section 83(h) to reflect the same expense for financial accounting purposes. An exception would have been made for certain broad-based plans.

A flurry of attention and rumored amendments followed the introduction of S. 576, but by the summer of 1997 the Senate had referred the bill to Senate Finance Committee, passing a "Sense of the Senate" that the Finance Committee and the Joint Tax Committee should hold additional hearings. In fall 1997, the Finance Committee staff stated that it had "committed" to Senator Levin to hold hearings in 1997. However, no such hearings were ever scheduled. Moreover, previous co-sponsors (most notably, Senator John McCain, R-Arizona) moved on to other issues, and momentum to reopen stock option accounting from the congressional side stalled as the FASB's initiative with respect to APB 25 gained momentum. On the Treasury side, while stock options were still on the agenda, projects related to the overhaul of the IRS took precedence over option reform.

In 1999, congressional attention was drawn to stock options by the actions of yet another government player: the Department of Labor (DOL). On February 12, 1999, the DOL issued an advisory letter stating that profits from the exercise of stock options must be counted as regular pay for purposes of computing overtime under the Fair Labor Standards Act (FLSA). The business community responded immediately and decisively to this latest threat to equity compensation, arguing that the administration of such a rule would be both expensive and unduly burdensome on employers. Congress moved quickly to enact legislation reversing the letter and passed P.L. 106-202, the "Worker Economic Opportunity Act," which amended the FLSA to expressly exclude amounts attributable to the exercise of most employee stock options from income taken into account for purposes of computing overtime. President Clinton signed the act into law on May 18, 2000.

11.1.3 Twenty-first Century Initiatives

The year 2000 was a fairly quiet one for stock option proponents. In the fall of 2001, however, the public outrage accompanying the Enron debacle spurred a new barrage of anti-equity propaganda and proposals. Chief among these proposals was the recycled Levin-McCain bill (S. 1940), this time dubbed the "Ending the Double Standard for Stock Options Act."[2] Once again, the bill sought to make accounting policy by limiting corporate tax deductions through the Code, an approach vigorously opposed by the Bush administration and numerous industry and accounting groups.[3] The Levin-McCain bill was too contentious to become law, and ultimately the adoption of FAS 123(R) by FASB ended the debate for all but the most interested parties.[4] Although no other option-related bills have been successfully introduced since that time,[5] both the Sarbanes-Oxley Act of 2002 and the American Jobs Creation Act of 2004 raise issues with respect to equity compensation, as further described below.

11.2 Recent Legislation Affecting Stock Options

Neither of the two pieces of federal legislation discussed herein are aimed specifically at stock options, but both have an impact on their use. We have summarized the equity compensation-related provisions of these laws below.[6]

11.2.1 Sarbanes-Oxley Act of 2002

The Sarbanes-Oxley Act of 2002, which amended both the Securities Exchange Act of 1934 and the Securities Act of 1933, was enacted on July 30, 2002.[7] Sarbanes-Oxley was intended to combat corporate fraud by imposing rigorous new obligations for public company disclosure, reporting, and compliance with respect to financial matters and executive compensation. The law has a reach far beyond the scope of this text. For purposes of equity compensation, it is most relevant to public company insiders as a result of the following provisions:

Loans to Executive Officers and Directors Are Prohibited

A company many not extend, arrange for, or renew credit in the form of a personal loan to its executive or directors. This has effectively curtailed the common practice of permitting executives to exercise stock options with promissory notes. In addition, because the concept of "arranging credit" is so broad, it has raised issues concerning the use of same-day sales by insiders. While many law firms and practitioners have weighed in on this question, the SEC has not yet formally addressed it.[8]

Accelerated SEC Reporting on Form 8-K[9]

Companies are required to promptly report changes in top management and directors, adoption or amendment of employment contracts and other material executive compensation or benefits arrangements. Section 1 of Form 8-K requires the company to report when it enters into or terminates "material definitive agreements," including employment agreements, compensation and retirement plans and agreements, and deferred compensation plans covering executive officers and directors. Equity arrangements with insiders are covered by Section 1 of Form 8-K.[10]

Under the SEC rules, the Form 8-K must be filed within four business days of the reportable event. Prior to Sarbanes-Oxley, most of these events were reported periodically (e.g., on a Form 10-Q or 10-K) rather than at the time of occurrence.

Forfeiture of Compensation

If an issuer is required to restate its financial statements due to its failure to comply with the nondisclosure requirements as a result of misconduct by the CEO or CFO, that executive must reimburse the company for any bonuses, and incentive-based or equity-based compensation (including profits realized from sale of company stock) received within the year following the first filling or issuance of the noncompliant statement. "Misconduct" is not defined in the statute.

11.2.2 American Jobs Creation Act of 2004

With the American Jobs Creation Act of 2004 (AJCA), Congress added new Section 409A to the Code, thus adopting sweeping changes to the tax treatment of deferred compensation. The impetus for Section 409A came from perceived abuses of deferred compensation by top executives in large companies. Over the years, such companies had developed many techniques for all but guaranteeing deferred compensation payments (using trusts and similar vehicles) while still remaining within the technical rules exempting such funds from immediate taxation to the executive. In effect, these techniques provided executives with interest-free loans of the tax money that would otherwise have been due, while at the same time postponing the company's tax deduction (until actual payment) and making the fund assets unavailable to the company in the interim.

Under the new law, those halcyon days of discretionary deferral are essentially over. As of January 1, 2005, any compensation deferred under a "nonqualified deferred compensation plan" (NDCP) is currently taxable unless it is subject to a substantial risk of forfeiture (i.e., using the principles of Section 83 of the Code) or satisfies the rigorous requirements of Section 409A summarized below. For purposes of Section 409A, nonqualified deferred compensation generally does *not* include: (1) qualified benefit plans, such as ESOPs or 401(k) plans; (2) sick leave, death benefits, or similar arrangements; (3) statutory stock options (i.e., ISOs and ESPPs qualified under Section 423 of the Code); (4) NSOs granted at fair market value (subject to certain limitations); (5) non-discounted restricted stock awards; and (6) non-discounted SARs. All other forms of nonqualified deferred compensation can be assumed to be deferred under a NDCP, *including:* (1) nonqualified employee stock purchase plans that include a discount feature; (2) nonstatutory options and stock appreciation rights that include a deferral feature (i.e., allowing an employee to defer receipt of the award after it has already been exercised); and (3) phantom stock, restricted stock units, performance shares, and similar plans.

Transition guidance to Section 409A was initially issued by the IRS in Notice 2005-1 (December 2004, as revised in January 2005). Proposed regulations were issued on September 29, 2005. The following overview incorporates both the transition guidance and the proposed regulations, as applicable (together, the "Section 409A rules").

General Application of the New Rules

If compensation deferred under a NDCP is not otherwise subject to a substantial risk of forfeiture, it will be taxed at the time of deferral unless the following conditions are satisfied:

1. The initial election to defer (including form of payment) is made before the start of the year in which the compensation is earned. An election to defer "performance-based" compensation may be made up to six months before the end of the performance period.

2. Any additional elections must be made at least 12 months before the date the deferred compensation would otherwise have been received, and in most cases deferral must be for at least five years after the original payment date.

3. Distributions may be permitted only upon separation from service (for certain "key employees" of public companies, this includes a six-month waiting period); at a specified date or dates (under a fixed schedule); or upon disability, death, change in control, and unforeseeable emergency, in each case as such terms are defined by Section 409A and its regulations.

4. No acceleration of payments is permissible, except as the IRS may provide in future regulations.

Note that short-term deferrals (i.e., no later than 2½ months after the close of the year the substantial risk of forfeiture lapses) will not run afoul of Section 409A.

Section 409A and the Section 409A rules are extremely complicated. Many issues (including issues affecting stock options) remain to
be resolved during the regulatory process and in years to come. Failure
to comply with these rules triggers severe and adverse tax consequences.
As noted above, the participant's total deferrals under the NDCP are
immediately taxed as income except to the extent not subject to a substantial risk of forfeiture (and not previously taxed). In addition, there
is a 20% penalty tax on the amount of the deferral and any earnings
attributable to it, plus cumulative interest at the underpayment rate
plus 1% on the tax that should have been paid on the original deferral
and any related earnings.

Specific Application of the New Rules to Equity Awards

As we have noted, many equity and equity-based awards are exempted
from the Section 409A definition of NDCP, either as a result of the
statutory language or the Section 409A rules. The following discussion
summarizes the IRS interpretation of Section 409A as it applies to SARs,
restricted stock, and NSOs granted after October 3, 2004. Note that
awards granted before that date that were earned and vested as of December 31, 2004, are exempt from Section 409A regardless of their
terms (so long as such terms are not materially modified after October
3, 2004).

Nonqualified Stock Options (NSOs) and Stock Appreciation Rights (SARs)

The Section 409A rules clarify that both NSOs and SARs[11] ("stock rights")
will be exempt from Section 409A so long as (1) the exercise price can
never be less than the fair market value of the underlying stock on the
date of grant; (2) the stock right is exercisable for "service recipient"
stock[12]; (3) the stock right includes no deferral features other than
deferral of income until exercise; and (4) the stock right is not modified
in a way that would otherwise subject it to Section 409A.[13] As with the
other exempt forms of compensation, stock rights may be thrown into

the purview of Section 409A if they are coupled with features that would otherwise be classified as payments under a NDCP. Note that generally, NSOs transferred in a merger or acquisition will not trigger deferred compensation treatment if they meet the 2004 regulations governing transfer of statutory options in a corporate transaction.

For purposes of setting the exercise price, Section 409A provides that fair market value may be determined using "any reasonable valuation method" and the proposed regulations elaborate on this concept. With publicly traded companies, this is never a problem. However, with the stakes now raised for stock rights, privately held companies must pay special attention to the hurdles inherent in setting fair market value so as to avoid inadvertently granting NSOs or SARs at a discount.[14]

Restricted Stock

Generally, grants of restricted stock (whether or not unvested at grant) will be subject to Section 83 of the Code rather than to Section 409A. However, the Section 409A rules note that a plan under which a service provider obtains a legally binding right to receive property in a future year may provide for the deferral of compensation and thus become a NDCP. A restricted stock unit, for example, will fall into Section 409A and accordingly must satisfy the general requirements to avoid early taxation (i.e., no deferral of delivery after vesting).

Transitional Relief

Under the proposed regulations, exercise of a discount stock right during the 2005 calendar year will be treated as a permitted cancellation of the deferred compensation element of the grant and will not be subject to penalties under Section 409A. This relief terminated as of December 31, 2005. If the discount stock right was not exercised prior to 2006, it may be amended on or before December 31, 2006, to increase the exercise price to equal the fair market value at the original date of grant. These rules terminate as of January 1, 2007.

11.3 Regulatory Developments Regarding Stock Options

11.3.1 Final Statutory Stock Option Regulations

In proposed final regulations published June 9, 2003, the IRS proposed an update, reorganization, and elaboration of existing rules governing statutory stock options (i.e., ISOs and ESPP options). After an extended comment period, the final regulations to Sections 421–424 of the Code went into effect on August 3, 2004. The 2004 regulations do not make dramatic changes to the originally proposed final regulations, although a number of technical uncertainties have been resolved. Note that the 2004 regulations replace proposed regulations existing since February 7, 1984.[15]

Generally, the new rules are effective August 3, 2004, but options granted before June 9, 2003, could rely on the 1984 regulations, the proposed final regulations, or the 2004 regulations until January 1, 2006, or the first regularly scheduled shareholder meeting occurring with six months of that date. Options issued in the interim period could rely on the proposed or 2004 regulations.

The very detailed regulations cover a variety of issues, but most simply restate, reorganize, and renumber existing regulations. The following summarizes the significant substantive changes between the old rules and the 2004 regulations:

Section 83(b) Elections

Under Section 83 of the Code, the optionee must pay ordinary income tax on the difference between the purchase price and the fair market value of the shares (the "spread") on the later of the date of exercise or the date of vesting. The Section 83(b) election is a technical device that allows the optionee to gamble that the spread will be greater on the date of vesting than on the date of exercise. Filing the election within 30 days of exercise "freezes" the spread and limits the optionee's ordinary income tax to the value at the date of exercise. Any additional gain is treated as capital gain (and any loss is a capital loss).

As a general rule, ISOs are not subject to Section 83 of the Code. However, there are two situations where Section 83 might apply to an ISO that is exercised for unvested stock: (1) if the ISO is later disqualified and thus becomes an NSO, and (2) for purposes of computing the alternative minimum tax (AMT). To anticipate the disqualification situation, practitioners sometimes suggested that optionees file a "prophylactic Section 83(b) election" when exercising an ISO for unvested shares. The theory was that at the time of a disqualification, the taxpayer could take the position that an 83(b) election to freeze the spread had already been filed, and thus his or her ordinary income would be limited to the spread at exercise. The 2004 regulations reject the use of the prophylactic 83(b) election for ISOs.

In the second situation, the optionee files a Section 83(b) election for AMT purposes only—i.e., to freeze the gain includible in the AMT computation to the spread on exercise. This makes sense because for AMT purposes, an ISO is treated as if it were an NSO. The 2004 regulations permit taxpayers to use a Section 83(b) election for AMT.

$100,000 Rule

One of the rules for an ISO is that not more than $100,000 in options, measured by taking the number of options times the fair market value of the stock at grant, can first become exercisable in any one year. The regulations expand on and incorporate IRS Notice 87-49 on this issue. For purposes of the rule, options are taken into account in the order they are issued. Options that are not ISOs when issued are disregarded. "First exercisable" is defined to mean the calendar year in which the option can first be exercised (normally, but not always, the year of vesting). This can get tricky if there is a change of control trigger or performance trigger that allows exercise if a change of control occurs before vesting or disallows exercise until a performance target is met. Under the regulations, if there is such an acceleration provision, then options first exercised during a calendar year pursuant to an acceleration clause do not affect the application of the $100,000 rule for options exercised before the acceleration provision. All of these prior options can be exercised, up to the $100,000 limit, even if the accelerated options are exercised in the same year. However, any options from the accelerated group that are in excess of $100,000 minus the fair market value at grant of the previously exercised options that year are disqualified as ISOs and must be treated as NSOs.

The regulations provide that an option is "disregarded for purposes of the $100,000 limit if, prior to the calendar year during which it would otherwise become exercisable for the first time, the option is modified and thereafter ceases to be an incentive stock option." Similar treatment applies to an ISO that is disqualified by being transferred or cancelled. Otherwise, modified, transferred, or cancelled options are considered outstanding until the end of the calendar year during which these awards would be first exercisable. Disqualifying dispositions also have no effect on the $100,000 determination.

Note that Treas. Reg. § 1.422-3(e) states that calculation of fair market value for these purposes may be made by any "reasonable method," including independent appraisals and valuation in accordance with the gift tax rules.[16]

Brokerage Fees

An optionee who disqualifies an ISO by selling the underlying shares before the end of the statutory holding period must pay ordinary income tax on the spread at exercise or the gain on sale, whichever is less. In the past, companies have reduced net income for optionees by deducting brokerage fees from the reportable spread; the 2004 regulations disallow such deductions.

Corporate Consolidations

Under the 2004 regulations, the requirement for shareholder approval of the plan will be satisfied in a corporate consolidation if the merger agreement fully describes the assumption of the plan. Separate shareholder approval will not be required for assumption or substitution of statutory options in connection with a merger if such options were already granted under an approved plan.

Definition of "Employee"

In the case of an assumption or substitution of an ISO, an option will be treated as granted to an employee if the optionee is in the three-month period following the end of employment, as well as to currently employed individuals. Optionees on leave pursuant to a statute (such as the Family Medical Leave Act) or contract that provides for continuing rights of re-employment continue to be considered employees for these purposes.

Definition of "Corporation"

Corporations are now defined to include not just C corporations but also any entity choosing to be taxed as a corporation under federal income tax rules, including S corporations, foreign corporations, and limited liability corporations (LLCs). Corporations electing to be taxed as partnerships, including LLCs, limited liability partnerships, and limited partnerships, would not be defined as a corporation. This definition makes it clear, for instance, that an employee of an LLC taxed as a corporation can receive a statutory option.

Definition of "Option"

The definition of an option is expanded to include warrants if the warrants meet other qualifications of the regulations. Warrants, like options, are financial instruments allowing the purchaser to buy shares at a fixed price for a defined period of time. Warrants are not usually issued specifically in return for service to the employer and usually carry a price at grant or purchase greater than fair market value. If a warrant otherwise meets the rules for an incentive option, the regulations would allow it to be defined as an option.

Definition of "Stock"

Stock is defined to include capital stock of any class and with any combination of voting rights or no voting rights. Preferred stock and special classes of stock authorized only to be issued to employees also qualify (tracking stock in a division issued just to employees, for instance, would presumably be an example of this), provided that this stock has the same rights and characteristics of capital stock.

Electronic Forms Allowed

Existing rules require options and option plans to be in writing; the new regulations allow electronic forms to be used as well, provided they meet regulatory requirements for such forms.

Maximum Number of Shares

Code Section 422(b)(1) requires that companies provide shareholders with information about the total number of shares subject to option under an ISO plan. The 2004 regulations clarify that this requirement applies for purposes of ISOs only. Companies may meet the requirement in a variety of ways, including by: (1) a number certain; (2) a percentage of shares outstanding at the date of adoption; or (3) an increase in shares relative to the number of shares outstanding at adoption based on a defined ratio. Note that for purposes of share counting, if outstanding shares are used to exercise an option, only the net number of shares issued to the optionee after the exercise is considered for purposes of calculating the maximum number of shares.

Modification of Options

Under Code Section 424(h)(1), modifications, extensions, and renewals of options are treated as the grant of a new option. Generally, an option will be "modified" only if the change results in an increase in benefits to the optionee. The 2004 regulations reiterate that a change in option terms by virtue of a "corporate transaction" will not be treated as a modification for these purposes. "Corporate transactions" include mergers, consolidations, reorganizations, and liquidations; changes in the corporate name; and other changes as may be prescribed by the Internal Revenue commissioner. Stock splits and dividends will not be modifications so long as they are proportionate and do not result in more than minor changes to the value of the awards. The 2004 regulations eliminate the earlier requirement that the transaction result in a significant number of employees "being transferred to a new employer or discharged or in the creation or severance of a parent-subsidiary relationship."

Certain exercises of discretion will not be treated as modifications so long as such discretion has been previously authorized, including the exercise of corporate discretion to (1) modify an option with respect to the payment of employment or withholding taxes, and (2) pay a bonus, make a loan, or offer the right to tender previously owned stock when an option is exercised. Note that if such discretion has not been previously authorized, the exercise of such discretion will be treated as a modification.

Shareholder Approval

In general, shareholder approval for statutory options is required if there is a change in the aggregate number of shares or in the employees (or class or classes of employees) eligible for the options. The 2004 regulations expand on these issues and specifically include a change in the shares to which the option applies, as well as a change in the issuing corporation. For instance, if a plan provides that a subsidiary's employees receive statutory options in the subsidiary and it is subsequently amended to permit grants from the parent, shareholder approval will be required within 12 months of the amendment. As noted above, additional shareholder approval is not required for validly granted ISOs assumed in a corporate transaction.

One final point with regard to shareholder approval: the 2004 regulations provide that an ISO plan adopted by the board of directors "subject to shareholder approval" *will be adopted on the date the plan is approved by shareholders.* If the board of directors stipulates a condition for adoption, the deemed adoption date is when that condition is satisfied. The 2004 regulations raise issues, yet to be resolved, as to whether ISO grants made before shareholder approval will ever be valid. Note that this rule does not apply to Section 423 ESPPs.

Treatment of Transferred Options

This has been an area of some uncertainty for some time. Under the 2004 regulations, an option that is transferred to a trust in a manner such that the option holder is considered the beneficiary of the trust still qualifies as a statutory option. Options transferred pursuant to a divorce, however, now lose their status as statutory options as of the date of transfer.[17]

Wash Sales

On a disqualifying disposition of an ISO, the optionee pays ordinary income tax on the lesser of the spread at exercise or the actual gain on sale. In a declining market, such a disqualification could offer a better tax benefit than holding for the full statutory holding period: e.g., if the spread on exercise was $100 and the gain on sale was only $50, it might be better to sell and pay tax on $50 than hold and pay AMT on $100. A recent strategy to take advantage of this anomalous result was to sell in a disqualification, pay ordinary income tax on the gain, and then get back into the market shortly thereafter. The new regulations clarify that this transaction qualifies as a "wash sale" under Section 1091 of the Code. Accordingly, the sale is treated as never having occurred, and the optionee will be required to pay tax on the full spread at exercise (in the example, $100).

11.3.2 Final Regulations on Option Transfers to Related Parties

Final regulations governing transfers of compensatory stock options between optionees and related persons under Section 83 of the Code were published on August 10, 2004. New Treas. Reg. § 1.83-7 excludes certain family members and control group members from favorable tax treatment under the "arm's length disposition" rules otherwise set out in the regulations to Section 83.[18]

In general, Section 83 permits a taxpayer who disposes of an option to a third party to close the compensatory portion of the transaction at the time of transfer rather than at the time of exercise. Treas. Reg.

§ 1.83-7 is intended to address a tax-avoidance scheme that allowed optionees to take advantage of the arm's length disposition rules for options while still retaining control of the ultimate exercise. Under the terms of the scheme, the optionee would sell an unexercised NSO to a relative or family limited partnership in which the optionee had a substantial interest (and implicit control). In exchange, the optionee accepted a long-term unsecured note that would come due only when the buyer exercised the option and sold the stock. This resulted in no tax to the optionee until the note was paid off, and no tax (or note payments) to the buyer until the stock was sold. In essence, the transaction created ISO deferral treatment for an NSO, minus the alternative minimum tax problem.[19]

Notes

1. Most major newspapers, including the *New York Times* and the *Washington Post*, ran articles on the perceived abuses of stock options in the early 1990s. The *Wall Street Journal* has published an annual insert tracking executive pay since 1990. These articles are far too numerous to list here. For a sense of the end-of-century views on this issue, see for example, "Stock Options Are Diluting Future Earnings," which ran as the cover story in the May 18, 1998, issue of *Forbes*; and "Taking Stock: Extending Employee Ownership Through Options," *ACA Journal* (Spring 1998) (entire issue).

2. Introduced by Senators Levin and McCain as S. 1940 on February 13, 2002; parallel H.R. 4075 introduced in the House by Rep. Pete Stark, D-California, on March 20, 2002.

3. Lobbying groups with names like the International Employee Stock Option Coalition (comprising 70 signatories, including the U.S. Chamber of Commerce) and the Coalition to Preserve and Protect Stock Options issued press releases, met with congressional leaders, and published position papers defending the status quo. See also, e.g., updated material available at *www.nceo.org*, *www.naspp.com*, *www.itaa.org*, *www.fwcook.com*, and *www.deloitte.com*. However, many articles in mainstream publications (*BusinessWeek*, the *New York Times*, the *Washington Post*, the *Wall Street Journal* and *Fortune*, to name but a few) supported Sen. Levin's bill.

4. See chapter 10. The intervention of the International Accounting Standards Board (IASB), which is engaged in promoting global accounting standards, also provided pressure to back off legislative efforts to control accounting.

The FASB announced in March 2003 that it had added a project on stock-based compensation for the purposes of achieving "convergence" with the anticipated International Financial Reporting Standard (IFRS) that would require all share-based compensation transactions to be recognized on corporate financial statements, including employee stock options. As of 2005, the convergence project is ongoing. For more information, see www.fasb.org.

5. One exception was the proposed "Broad-Based Stock Option Plan Transparency Act" (introduced March 20, 2003, as H.R. 1372 and S. 979), which would have delayed implementation of any new accounting rules for stock-based compensation for three years, pending study by the SEC and the Commerce Department. The bill ultimately passed the House, but died in the Senate.

6. The summaries are intended to provide general guidance only.

7. Sarbanes-Oxley Act of 2002, P.L. 107-204, 116 Stat. 745 (July 30, 2002).

8. Section 402 of the Act. Most law firms have concluded that a broker-assisted same-day sale (i.e., a margin loan), in which the company's only participation is to facilitate access to the broker, does not run afoul of Section 402. For more on this issue, see section 5.4 of chapter 5. Note that although a loan is not available, an outright cash bonus is acceptable under Sarbanes-Oxley (although it will trigger disclosure on Form 8-K, below).

9. The SEC finalized rules regarding Form 8-K effective August 23, 2004. A supplemental FAQ was published on November 23, 2004. For an additional discussion, see section 7.4.3 of chapter 7.

10. Note that in accordance with the FAQ, changes to equity compensation plans that include executive officers but are not material as to the individual officer need not be disclosed prior to the time the plan would normally be filed.

11. Under the transition guidance, SARs were subject to far more restrictions than NSOs, including limitations on their availability to private companies. These restrictions were dropped in the proposed regulations.

12. The proposed regulations limit service recipient stock to *common stock* of the employer or its parent or subsidiary.

13. Modifications are treated as the grant of a new stock right, which will result in a discount if the fair market value of the underlying stock has increased since the original date of grant. Moreover, even when there is no increase in price, many common modifications will now be viewed as adding a feature providing for additional deferrals for purposes of Section 409A (i.e., an extension of the post-termination exercise period).

14. See section 2.2 of chapter 2 for more details on setting fair market value under Section 409A.

15. See chapter 3 for an in-depth analysis of the application of the 2004 regulations.

16. See section 3.2.5 of chapter 3.

17. See chapter 16.

18. The new rules are effective for transactions after July 2, 2003.

19. For an extensive discussion of the IRS's view on Treas. Reg. § 1.83-7, see its Coordinated Issues Paper titled "Transfer or Sale of Compensatory Stock Options or Restricted Stock to Unrelated Persons," effective October 15, 2004, and posted on the IRS website at *www.irs.gov/pub/irs-utl/ compensatory_final.pdf.*

CHAPTER 12

Recent Cases Affecting Equity Compensation: 2004 and 2005

Contents

As the use of equity to compensate employees has increased, so have the number of court and agency actions with respect to it. This chapter summarizes some of the key *case* law developments and agency rulings that arose during 2004 and 2005. Although this review of cases and rulings is not necessarily comprehensive, it gives an indication of the direction of the law and the various approaches being taken by the courts (and litigants) to resolving disputes involving equity compensation. Please be aware that the following summaries are no more than that; they should not be relied upon without first consulting primary sources for details.

12.1 Tax Cases and Rulings

Tax issues can come up for resolution in a variety of settings. Most litigation arises out of a tax audit (either federal or state) that is ultimately appealed to the court.[1] At the federal agency level, the IRS has the authority to issue rulings at both public and private determinations in writing. Public determinations are called "revenue rulings" (Rev. Rul.) and they state the IRS position on the interpretation of the Code and its regulations. They are frequently accompanied by IRS notices, announcements, or other interpretive documents.[2] Revenue rulings are citable as precedent and may accordingly be relied upon by taxpayers. Private written determinations are directed at an individual taxpayer (or IRS field agent auditing a taxpayer) and as such may be relied upon only by that individual.[3] Although such private rulings are available to the public, they are intended only to serve as an indication of the IRS position on any issue and may not be cited or relied upon as precedent.[4]

Please note that recent tax-related legislation and regulations are discussed in chapter 11.

12.1.1 Tax Decisions in the Courts

U.S. Tax Court: Blackout Trading Period Not Substantial Risk of Forfeiture

In *Merlo v. Commissioner*, T.C.M. 2005-178 (July 20, 2005), the U.S. Tax Court ruled against petitioner Robert Merlo on summary judgment, holding that there was no issue of material fact as to whether petitioner's rights to shares were subject to a substantial risk of forfeiture when the only limitation on his sale of previously acquired ISO stock was the issuer's blackout period. Merlo had exercised his ISO at the end of 2000 (at the time of his termination), but failed to take into account the AMT preference on his tax return. On audit, he claimed that the preference was inapplicable because the shares were subject to a substantial risk of forfeiture under Section 83 in the form of the blackout period. Because ISOs are treated as NSOs for purposes of the AMT, Merlo argued that no AMT preference could arise until the blackout period was lifted.

He relied on *Robinson v. Commissioner* (substantial risk of forfeiture arises when company has a one-year call on the shares post-termination) in making his argument. The Tax Court noted that Merlo was neither a Section 16 insider (which could raise 83(c) arguments in favor of forfeiture) nor did the issuer have the ability to compel him to return his shares if he traded during the blackout period. Without more, there was no indication that he had a "substantial risk of losing the rights to his shares." Summary judgment was granted in favor of the government. For a similar development, see the discussion of Rev. Rul. 2005-48, below.

California: Taxes Must Be Paid by Non-Resident on Exercised Options

In *In re Randall*, No. 260104, California State Board of Equalization (March 22, 2005), the board ruled that a nonresident individual must pay taxes on the exercise of stock options earned while he was a resident of California. The individual involved earned the options while serving as the CEO of a California company. The options were ISOs, but were exercised before the required holding period elapsed. The taxpayer had moved out of state by the time of exercise, but the state ruled that income earned in the state is taxable because under California law income earned "is sourced to the state or states where the compensation was earned." Note that this is the standard rule for sourcing option income in many states. For a similar discussion, see *In Matter of the Petition of E. Randall Stuckless and Jennifer Olson*, below.

California: Stock Transfer Occurs Notwithstanding Margin Loan

In *Miller v. United States*, No. C 04-0511 JSW (N.D. Cal. Nov. 22, 2004), the U.S. District Court for the Northern District of California ruled against the taxpayer on a motion for summary judgment on his tax refund claim. Miller was a Microsoft employee who in 2000 did a cashless exercise for vested options with a margin loan from PaineWebber and paid taxes on the spread at exercise. By 2003, the stock price had fallen sufficiently to result in a margin call, and PaineWebber sold the shares. Proving hope and bad legal advice spring eternal, Miller filed for a tax refund, essentially arguing that the margin feature prevented the original transaction from closing for purposes of Section 83 of the Code. Under this novel argument (which the court duly noted as "a case of first impression"), Miller claimed that his exercise was actually deferred until the date sale—i.e., the stock was transferred to PaineWebber but not to him on the original exercise. Because the stock had lost its original value at the time of the margin call, Miller contended that there was no gain on exercise and accordingly his original tax payment should be refunded in full.

The court reviewed the established law and regulations with respect to Section 83 transfers (including transferability and substantial risk of forfeiture principles), and concluded that beneficial ownership in the shares was clearly transferred to Miller at the time of his exercise in 2000. Among other things, the court noted that the shares carried voting and dividend rights and that Miller had been able to make other investments based on the collateral in the margin account. Moreover, the regulations clearly indicate that the ability to pledge shares (e.g., for a margin loan) does not undermine beneficial ownership. Finally, the court noted that regardless of who actually wrote the check for the shares (i.e., Miller or PaineWebber) at the time of exercise, Microsoft received the exercise price and transferred the shares on Miller's behalf.

New York: Gain on Stock Options Must Be Allocated Between New York and Washington

In *In the Matter of the Petition of E. Randall Stuckless and Jennifer Olson,* DTA 819319 (N.Y. Div. of Tax App. July 8, 2004), the New York State Division of Tax Appeals upheld a state tax determination that a portion of the income received by a taxpayer from the exercise of stock options granted during his New York employment was subject to tax as New York source income, even though the exercise occurred while the taxpayer was a nonresident. Taxpayer Stuckless had appealed a New York state tax assessment on income earned from options granted to him while he was a New York resident but exercised while he was resident in Washington state. Stuckless was a New York Microsoft employee who was granted ISOs in 1991 and 1992. He transferred to Washington state in 1996 and exercised most of his previously granted (and fully vested) options between 1996 and 1998 while resident in Washington. He moved back to New York in mid-1998.

Stuckless tried a number of arguments on appeal (including that, notwithstanding federal tax precedent, the options were investment vehicles rather than compensatory options). His most important argument was that option income should be sourced to the state where the exercise occurred regardless of whether services were rendered elsewhere. However, the court looked to Sections 83 and 422 of the Code for the principle that income received on the exercise of vested options represents compensation for services rendered. In Stuckless's case, the court agreed with the New York Division of Taxation that Stuckless owed New York state taxes on the percentage of income allocable to his performance of services for Microsoft while a New York resident: i.e., the number of days worked while resident in New York over the total number of days worked. (Note: this is the same formula used by the IRS when allocating option gain between U.S. and foreign source income.)

12.1.2 IRS Rulings and Announcements

Rev. Rul. 2005-48: Income from Options Must Be Recognized Despite Stock Sale Restrictions

In Rev. Rul. 2005-48 (August 8, 2005), the IRS ruled that an employee could not delay taxation on the exercise of NSOs even though the options were subject to a six-month lockup period before the employee could sell the shares under company rules limiting insider trading, and (prior to exercise) a risk of lawsuit under Section 16 for any potential violation of securities laws. The employee was granted options in January 2005. In May, the company went public. Pursuant to an underwriting agreement, the employee could not sell the shares until the end of November. An insider trading compliance policy established by the company allowed insiders, such as this employee, to trade company shares only between November 5 and November 30.

In August, the employee exercised the options and paid cash for the shares. In addition to the lockup period rules, as an insider the

employee was subject to insider trading rules under Section 10b-5 of
the 1934 Securities Exchange Act. The employee contended that taxes
should not be due on the options exercise because of the various restrictions on selling the shares. Under Code Section 83(c)(3), taxes are
not due on the receipt of an award such as an option as long as the
award is subject to a substantial risk of forfeiture, including the risk of
a taxpayer lawsuit under Section 16(b) of the Securities Exchange Act
of 1934 for violation of insider trading rules.

In *Robinson v. Commissioner,* 44 T.C. 20 (1965), the First Circuit
Court of Appeals concluded that such risks as apply in this case were
sufficient to delay taxation until they lapse. The IRS, however, rejected
that reasoning here and (in information with the release of the ruling)
said it would rely on it only for cases with the jurisdiction of the first
circuit. In requiring taxation, the IRS argued that the period of risk for
a lawsuit under Section 16 applies to the six-month period from the
grant of the option, not the exercise. That period could be even shorter
if there is some other available exemption from the rules during the six-
month period. Because the employee exercised in August, eight months
after grant, the IRS concluded that there was no substantial remaining
risk. The risks of any further securities lawsuits and/or the decline in
value, the IRS concluded, were not sufficient to cause a significant risk
of forfeiture under Section 83. Moreover, the restrictions imposed for
compliance with insider trading rules and the lockup provisions were
"non-lapse" restrictions that do not affect the taxability of the award
under Section 83.

Rev. Rul. 2004-60: Transfer of Options in Divorce

In Rev. Rul. 2004-60 (June 14, 2004) the IRS provided guidance on
withholding, reporting, and tax issues in a situation where NSOs were
transferred incident to a divorce. In that situation, an employee spouse
transferred one-third of the total option grant to the nonemployee
former spouse (NEFS). The IRS ruled on the following points:

- *For purposes of FICA (Social Security and Medicare) and FUTA (unemployment) taxes,* the transfer of the options in and of itself is not

a compensation event for the NEFS. At the date of exercise by the NEFS, however, the spread is subject to FICA just as it would be if exercised by the employee spouse: i.e., "as and when the wages are taken into account for FICA tax purposes." This means that if the employee spouse has already exceeded the FICA limit, the exercise by the NEFS will not result in additional FICA withholding. The employee portion of FICA will be deducted from payments to the NEFS (not from payments to the employee spouse). Because the employer pays all of the FUTA tax, the NEFS obviously has no responsibility for FUTA.

- *For purposes of federal income tax,* the withholding obligation also arises at the time of exercise by the NEFS. The supplemental wage flat rate (currently 25% of amounts of $1 million or less, and 35% of amounts in excess of $1 million) may be used for this withholding. The NEFS is entitled to use this amount as a credit when computing income taxes.

- *For reporting purposes,* FICA tax withholding (including Social Security tax and Medicare) is reported on form W-2 using the employee spouse's name, address, and Social Security number. However, no income is included in Box 1 or Box 2 with respect to these taxes. Instead, income received by the NEFS is reported in Box 3 on a Form 1099-MISC as "other income," and income tax withheld is reported in Box 4. The employer files a Form 945 to record income tax withholding for the NEFS, while FICA is reported on the employer's Form 941 and FUTA on form 940.

Rev. Rul. 2004-37: IRS Shuts Down Purchase Price Adjustment Scheme

In Rev. Rul. 2004-37 (March 15, 2004), the IRS shut down an aggressive strategy whereby taxpayers took the position that certain forms of compensation-related loan forgiveness could result in nontaxable purchase price adjustments. The strategy revolved around the following scenario: (1) taxpayer receives a loan from his employer to exercise an option; (2) the loan requires only interest payments to be made, with principal due at the end of the term; (3) when the stock value drops while the loan is outstanding, principal is reduced ("adjusted") to reflect the new value; (4) loan forgiveness is *not* recorded for the adjustment. The ruling summarized the fact pattern as follows:

> In Year 1, Employer, a corporation, grants a nontransferable, nonstatutory option to its Employee to purchase 1,000 shares of Employer common stock at an exercise price of $75 per share, the fair market value of a share of Employer stock at the time the option is granted. Employee may exercise the option only during employment with Employer or within 90 days after cessation of employment.

> On January 1 of Year 2, when the fair market value of 1,000 shares of Employer stock is $100,000, Employee exercises the option and purchases 1,000 shares of Employer stock in exchange for a nontransferable recourse note ("Note") secured by the stock Employee receives on the exercise of the option. The Note has a stated principal amount of $75,000, which is payable at maturity on December 31 of Year 11. The Note also provides for payments of interest on December 31 of each year the Note is outstanding. The interest rate is one-year LIBOR (determined as of January 1 of each year the Note is outstanding) plus 25 basis points. The interest rate on the Note is not less than the appropriate applicable Federal rate (AFR) on the date the Note is issued. The stock is not subject to a substantial risk of forfeiture within the meaning of § 83(c).

> In Year 2, Employee includes $25,000 as compensation income under § 83(a). Employer reports $25,000 of compensation income on the Form W-2 issued to Employee for Year 2 and claims a corresponding deduction in Year 2 under § 83(h).

> In Years 2 and 3, Employee makes the required interest payments under the Note. On January 1 of Year 4, the fair market value of the Employer stock has declined to $50,000 and Employer and Employee agree to reduce the stated principal amount of the Note from $75,000 to $50,000. The interest rate on the Note is not less than the appropriate AFR on the date the Note is modified.

The IRS ruled that the normal analysis under Treas. Reg. § 1.83-4(c) applies to this fact setting. Thus, cancellation of a portion of indebtedness—no matter what the reason—constitutes compensation. The use of a note does not change the original purchase price, and fluctuations in value go only to the ultimate capital gain or loss on the stock. Any subsequent reduction in the purchase price by the service recipient is simply additional compensation to the service provider—i.e., taxable as wages and thus also subject to payroll taxes. The IRS noted that the same rules will apply to a reduction in interest or a change in the terms of the note from recourse to nonrecourse.

Announcement 2005-19: Settlement Initiative for Stock Option Tax Shelter Scheme

In Announcement 2005-19, later modified by Announcement 2005-39, the IRS issued settlement guidance on a stock option tax avoidance scheme used by a number of executives (49 PBD, March 15, 2005; 32 BPR 645, March 22, 2005).

The history of this ruling goes back to 2004, when the IRS issued final regulations on a tax avoidance scheme in which an option holder would sell an unexercised nonqualified option to a relative or family limited partnership in which the seller had a substantial interest. In exchange, the seller would receive a long-term unsecured note. The new holder of the option would exercise the option later and not recognize gain until sale. Meanwhile, the seller paid no tax on the note until payments were made. In effect, the scheme was used to give NSOs the tax treatment of ISOs, minus the alternative minimum tax problem. But the seller would actually retain control over the option through the relationship with the related party. The IRS ruled that transfers can only close the tax element under Code Section 83 if the transfer is the equivalent of an arm's-length sale; these clearly were not. The IRS also said the transactions would be considered listed transactions. On October 15, 2004, the IRS posted to its Web site an issue paper that described its views on this matter in more detail. The paper looked at a specific variant of this transaction in which an executive would transfer an option to a related party, such as a relative or family limited partnership. In exchange, the executive would get an unfunded promise of a balloon payment, meaning no payments would be made to the executive in the interim. Payment was not made for 15 to 30 years. The effect would have been to delay the tax payment until the balloon payment was made. The issue paper argued this was a sham transaction because its intention was simply to avoid taxes. The executive would retain actual control, even if this was not specified in the agreement, because of the family relationship.

In the 2005 announcements, the IRS detailed a settlement proposal for those using this scheme. Taxpayers had until May 23, 2005, to agree to the settlement; if not, the IRS would pursue a claim. Taxpayers who resolved their tax issues under 2005-19 do not have to disclose these deals under Section 6011 of the Code for taxable years ending in 2004 or any subsequent years.

PLR 200513012: Incentive Stock Option Plan with ESPP-Like Features Qualifies

In PLR 200513012 (April 1, 2005), the IRS ruled that a company's ISO plan qualified under Section 422. The plan was structured more like a Section 423 plan than a traditional option plan. Employees could enroll in the plan during a one-month enrollment period, during which time they could decide how much of the after-tax payroll they wanted to set aside on a regular basis to acquire shares later. The first day of the enrollment period was the grant date, which set the exercise price. The purchase price was the price at the end of the offering period, and the options had a one-year term. Employees could exercise at the end of one year, but then had to transfer the shares to a bank-operated nominee account for at least one more year (which would allow them to meet ISO holding period requirements).

PLR 200418020: Reduction in Offering Period Not a "Modification"

In PLR 200418020 (April 30, 2004), the IRS ruled on a shareholder approval issue for an ESPP plan in which the taxpayer company amended its plan because it failed to file a timely S-8 registration. The taxpayer company offered a conventional Section 423 ESPP with a 15% discount, a six-month offering period, and a look-back feature. It was required to register its ESPP stock on a Form S-8, but it missed the applicable deadline. Because the options issued under the plan must be covered by a registration statement, the company had to suspend the plan until the new statement was filed. The company thus amended its plan to extend the offering period that was under way for an additional quarter while suspending the purchase period until the registration was effective. The plan also was amended to require employees to notify the company of any disqualifying dispositions of stock acquired through the plan, and provided that the gain would be subject to withholding.

Under ESPP rules, a "material modification" to a Section 423 ESPP must be approved by shareholders. Because the modification at issue simply exchanged the right to exercise in the current quarter for a right to exercise in a later quarter, the IRS ruled that the amendment did not increase benefits and therefore was not a material modification for shareholder approval purposes. The changes related to disqualifying dispositions were simply minor technical changes and also did not rise to the level of material modification.

12.2 SEC Rulings and No-Action Letters

Microsoft Employee Wins Case Against UBS

On January 27, 2005, a Microsoft employee won a judgment from a National Association of Securities Dealers arbitration panel against UBS for urging him to exercise his stock options with a margin loan (NASD Case No. 03-00703, unpublished). UBS and a number of brokerage firms (against whom actions were still pending as of this ruling) actively promoted a strategy in which employees would use margin loans to exercise their ISOs. The employees would then try to hold on to the stock for at least one year to benefit from lower ISO tax treatment. Unfortunately, in the post-market-boom crash, their stock often fell quickly, especially in technology companies. When the stock price fell below the margin call requirement, employees had to sell, triggering ordinary income tax if the stock had not been held for at least one year from exercise and two years from the grant of the option. The employees were left in a net loss position. Not only had they sold their stock at what often was a price lower than they bought it for, but they also had to pay taxes on the difference between the exercise price and price at purchase, often a very large number.

Employees alleged both that the margin loan approach induced them to take excessive risk and that the brokerages should have used a risk management strategy, such as a stop-loss sale price that would have covered the taxes and the loan or a hedging strategy using put and call options to create a "zero cost collar." The employee in this case received $237,338, the amount such a hedging strategy would have saved.

Google, SEC Settle over pre-IPO Options

In *In re Google Inc.*, SEC, No. 3-11759, settled January 2005, Google settled SEC and state charges concerning its alleged failure to register options issued prior to its initial public offering (IPO) in 2004. At issue was $80 million in options Google issued in the two years prior to the IPO. The SEC said Google failed to register the securities, as required by federal and state law absent a specific exemption (such as Rule 701[5]), and to provide financial disclosure, as required by both federal and state (California) law.

Google had stated that it believed it could rely on an exemption from the requirements. Under federal law, offers to a company's employees, directors, general partners, trustees, officers, or certain consultants (those providing services to a company similar to what an employer might hire someone to do, but not consultants who help raise capital) can be made under a written compensation agreement. For total sales under $5 million during a 12-month period to the specified class of people above, companies must comply with anti-fraud disclosure rules; for sales of more than this amount, companies must disclose additional information, including risk factors, copies of the plans under which the offerings are made, and certain financial statements. These disclosures must be made to all shareholders. Optionees are included under this requirement. Google could have been exempted under this section, but the SEC found that it did not comply with the rules. In addition, securities laws also require public disclosure of relevant financial issues and risks for any issuance of options of more than $5 million in a year. Google did not make such disclosures, fearing that the information would put the company at a competitive disadvantage. Google had previously addressed the situation by offering employees the right to have their options repurchased at varying prices, all of which were far below what Google's stock eventually opened at in its IPO. There were few takers.

SEC Rules Performance-Based Options May Not Be Excluded from Shareholder Ballot

In *Crescent Real Estate Equities Co.*, SEC no-action letter (available April 5, 2004), the SEC ruled that a shareholder proposal that a significant portion of future stock option grants to senior executives be performance-based could not be excluded from a shareholder ballot. The company argued the proposal was too vague and contained misleading statements. The SEC said the statement did need to be amended to correct the errors but that the proposal could go forward.

The proposal was submitted by the board of trustees of the International Brotherhood of Electrical Workers Pension Benefit Fund. The proposal urged that a significant portion of future options be indexed options, premium-priced options, or performance-vested options. Counsel for the company argued that the proposal could be excluded under the 1934 Securities Exchange Act Rule 14a-8(j)(i)(3) because it was too vague. It did not name which specific officers would be covered, what "significant" meant, or whether the grant of such options should affect cash compensation. Counsel argued the company already based executive compensation on performance. The SEC staff agreed that some of the proposal had inaccuracies and some was too vague but said that if it were amended to correct these problems, the proposal could go forward.

SEC Counsel's Office Allows Options Proposal to Be Excluded

Shareholder Gerald English submitted a proposal to Woodward Governor Company to eliminate all option programs. Relying on Rule 14a-8(i)(7), on September 29, 2004, SEC Special Counsel Heather Maples signed a staff decision that the proposal could be excluded because the option program did not just cover senior executives and directors but also extended to "key management worker members as potential recipients." The company had provided options to 20 employees who were not officers or directors.

Comcast Option Liquidity Program Cleared by SEC Staff

In 2004, Comcast became the first company to adopt the model created by Microsoft and JPMorgan more than a year earlier to provide liquidity for underwater stock options. Under the arrangement, employees could tender their options to Comcast. JPMorgan purchased the options from Comcast at an arm's-length value (computed over an averaging period), and Comcast paid the JPMorgan price over to employees. The SEC staff, pursuant to Rule 13-e-4(f)(2)(ii), allowed Comcast to terminate the withdrawal rights to tendered options at the end of the employees' election period and, under Rule 13-e-4(f)(8)(i), permitted Comcast to exclude some options and optionees from the program. The staff said it would not object to the pricing structure.

The approach allowed Comcast employees with underwater options to get some (albeit usually small) value for them. Comcast, meanwhile, benefited from having fewer options outstanding, options that really had little incentive or compensation benefit. That gave Comcast more flexibility in creating a more effective equity program. JPMorgan, of course, hoped that it would be able to buy the options at a price that would make them profitable in the long run. To read the full letter, see *www.sec.gov/divisions/corpfin/cf-noaction/comcast100704.htm.*

12.3 Contract Cases Related to Stock Options

Delaware: Ex-CEO Can Prove Reliance on General Counsel's Advice Contrary to Plan Document

In *Vague v. Bank One Corp.*, No. 511, 2003 (Del. Sup. Ct. May 20, 2004), the Delaware Supreme Court reversed a summary judgment against Richard Vague, former CEO of First USA Inc., holding that Vague was entitled to prove at trial that he reasonably relied on the advice of in-house counsel regarding the deadline for exercise of $5 million in NSOs. Vague was CEO of First USA from 1992 to 1999, when Bank One acquired First USA. At that time, Vague was advised by Bank One's general counsel that he had a period of three to five years to exercise his stock options. Bank One's human resources department sent him an incorrect notice saying the same thing. In March and June 2000, however, Bank One sent correct summaries of his options, stating they had to be exercised by August 21 of that year. Vague contends he never reviewed these summaries (they were sent as part of quarterly statements) and learned only later that the options had expired.

Delaware: Sale of Bankrupt Company's Assets Triggers Change in Control

In *Fix v. Quantum Industrial Partners LDC,* No. 03-3698 (7th Cir. July 6, 2004), the U.S. Court of Appeals for the Seventh Circuit affirmed the trial court's holding that upon the bankruptcy and asset sale of Quantum's controlled corporation, Outboard Marine Corporation (OMC), Quantum owed $5 million to Roger Fix, OMC's former CEO. Fix was hired by Quantum in 2000 as a turnaround specialist under an employment agreement that, among other things, provided that Fix would receive $5 million less the value of his stock options at the time of a change in control (CIC). For these purposes, CIC was defined to include a sale of all or substantially all the assets of OMC; this definition did not contain a bankruptcy exception. Quantum had purchased the troubled OMC in 2000, but by the end of the year decided not to invest any more in the company. OMC filed for bankruptcy in December 2000, and after Fix arranged for the sale of its assets, Quantum fired him and refused to honor the contract.

Although Quantum argued that Fix was due compensation only if he created value at OMC by helping the company grow, the court held that under Delaware law Fix's contract unambiguously provided for the CIC payment on an asset sale. In addition, the court noted that the many lawyers and sophisticated investors who negotiated the employment contract could easily have excluded bankruptcy from the CIC definition if Quantum had intended that result, but they did not.

Delaware: Failed Merger Precludes Acceleration of Options

In *Bohan v. Honeywell International Inc.,* No. 03-1098 (8th Cir. May 30, 2004), the U.S. Court of Appeals for the Eighth Circuit affirmed the trial court's holding (applying Delaware law) that under Honeywell's stock plan, options would not accelerate before the completion of a merger. The plaintiffs in this case argued that they were entitled to full acceleration of vesting on their stock options because Honeywell and General Electric had executed a merger agreement and received shareholder approval for it, even though it ultimately failed to close because European regulators blocked it. Plaintiffs contended that the plan could be read to trigger acceleration on shareholder approval alone, but the

U.S. District Court for the District of Minnesota held that the plan's language that a merger had to be "completed" meant that approval was not enough. "To trigger acceleration," the court wrote, "the merger must result in Honeywell no longer existing as an independent, publicly owned corporation." The plan language specifically stated that "the Company will no longer survive as an independent publicly held corporation" and provided that option vesting would accelerate "on or following . . . a merger." There was no actual merger here. Although the plaintiffs argued that the third clause of the stock plan referred to approval by shareholders, courts at both levels ruled it was a dependent clause that could be effective only when read in tandem with the other merger requirements.

Idaho: Court Must Rule on Whether Effort to Exercise Options Can Be Cause for Firing

In *Paolini v. Albertson's Inc.*, No. 03-35724 (9th Cir., August 10, 2005), the U.S. Court of Appeals for the Ninth Circuit returned a case to the Idaho Supreme Court in which an executive claimed that he had been fired, in part, because he tried to exercise his options. Paolini was a 17-year executive at Albertson's. In 2001, he attempted to exercise his options because he believed there had been a change in control at the company (a matter in dispute but not relevant to the court's findings). Paolini believed that the change in control triggered plan provisions for accelerated vesting of his remaining options. He subsequently left the company, also for reasons in dispute. The company claimed he quit; he claimed he was fired for trying to exercise his options

A district court granted summary judgment to the company; Paolini appealed. The appeals court concluded there was evidence that Paolini was fired because of his effort to exercise the options. It said the Idaho court must decide if options can be wages under Idaho law. Different states have different rules on this, and Idaho has no clear legal precedent. In this case, the plan's administrator and some of the material describing the plan called options "compensation," although this in itself is not enough to establish that they are compensation for wage purposes. Second, if they are wages, then the Idaho Supreme Court must decide if Paolini's firing was a public-policy violation of Idaho's at-will employment laws. If so, then Paolini can sue based on Idaho employment law for wrongful dismissal; if not, then he has no case. The appeals court concluded that this too is a matter of triable fact as well as Idaho state policy.

Illinois: No Employer Obligation to Warn Employee of Stock's Future Outlook

In *Bors v. Duberstein*, No. 03 C 4636 (N.D. Ill. July 1, 2004), the U.S. District Court for the Northern District of Illinois held that executives did not have an obligation to tell an employee about the company's future outlook when it persuaded her to trade her phantom stock for restricted stock, even though the company later went bankrupt.

Kimberly Bors worked for Outboard Marine (OMC) from 1995 until 2000. In 1996, she received 10,000 units of phantom stock that would vest and be paid out on a change in control. In 1997, Greenmarine Acquisition Corp. (GMC) acquired OMC, then merged into the company. When Bors and other employees asserted their rights under the phantom plan, OMC executives persuaded them to exchange the phantom units for restricted stock in a tax-free exchange, predicting that OMC stock could reach $50 per share (it had been $18 at acquisition). Bors agreed to the exchange, but in 2000 OMC went bankrupt. Bors then sued four former executives of OMC, saying they should have warned her about the risks involved. The court held that the executives did not have a fiduciary relationship with Bors or the other employees. Illinois law specifies fraud only if a defendant's acts contribute to a plaintiff's misunderstanding of a material fact, and the defendant then fails to correct it. While the defendants made erroneous claims about the company's future stock price, under Illinois law claims for fraud cannot be sustained based on statements about future events. The court further noted that at the time of the exchange, Bors signed an agreement that specifically stated that OMC executives had no duty to disclose any information concerning OMC stock.

Iowa: Former Employee Who Agreed to Take Options in Lieu of Severance Pay Cannot Complain After Stock Price Declines

In *Martino-Catt v. E.I. DuPont de Nemours and Co.*, No. 4:02-cv-90500 (S.D. Iowa April 29, 2004) the U.S. District Court for the Southern District of Iowa dismissed a lawsuit against DuPont filed by a former employee whose stock options had declined in value. Susan Martino-Catt was an employee of Pioneer Hi-Bred International, which DuPont acquired in 1999. Pioneer established a change-in-control severance pay plan (a CIC) prior to the acquisition. Following initiation of class action litigation over the CIC by former Pioneer employees, DuPont offered a retention agreement to certain CIC participants. The retention agreement provided for a grant of DuPont stock options in exchange for waiver of the CIC. There was no obligation to take the retention agreement, however; employees were free to continue under the terms of the CIC.

Martino-Catt knew about the issues surrounding the CIC and the retention agreement and initially rejected the DuPont agreement. However, after reconsideration, she decided to accept the offer because she believed that DuPont intended to fire employees who did not waive the CIC. The stock value subsequently declined, and Martino-Catt claimed (among other things) that she had been coerced into accepting options that were not worth as much as the CIC benefits.

The court granted DuPont's motion to dismiss the case, agreeing that Martino-Catt had voluntarily agreed to the offer and that she had the needed information and skills to do so appropriately. The language of the release she signed was, in the court's view, "abundantly clear." Martino-Catt was a highly educated employee and had discussed this matter with counsel prior to her waiver.

Minnesota: Lock-Up Agreement Does Not Provide a Basis for Fraud Claim

In *Syverson v. FirePond Inc.*, No. 03-2410 (8th Cir. September 9, 2004), the U.S. Court of Appeals for the Eighth Circuit held that two employee/contractor optionees could not sustain a claim that defendant

FirePond and its underwriters had defrauded them by requiring a pre-IPO lockup agreement. Because of the lockup, the optionees were unable to sell their stock for six months after the IPO, during which time the share value rose from $3 to $100, and then fell to $1.

Syverson and the other employee/contractor, Flora, each alleged that they signed the lockup only because they were told that unless all optionees and pre-IPO investors agreed to the restrictions, the IPO would not go forward. After the IPO, they discovered that certain non-optionee investors had shorter (or no) lockup restrictions. Nonetheless, the Eighth Circuit affirmed the trial court's holding that Syverson and Flora were not defrauded because the terms of the lockup agreement expressly included a provision allowing the underwriters to waive the restriction for any third party. In addition, the court rejected Flora's argument that his original option agreement was oral and did not require a lockup since such an option (if it existed) was superseded by the written documents.

Tennessee: Employment Offer Letter Sufficient to Prove Mutual Assent on Phantom Stock Plan Terms

In *Hopmayer v. Aladdin Indus., LLC,* No. M2003-01583-COA-R3-DV (Tenn. Ct. App. June 9, 2004), a Tennessee appeals court affirmed the trial court's holding that an employment offer letter promising phantom stock was sufficient grounds to establish mutually agreed contractual terms on a phantom stock plan. Aladdin hired Jeffrey Hopmayer in 1999. The company's CEO mailed an employment offer letter to Hopmayer stating that, in addition to base pay, the company would adopt a phantom stock plan granting him 4,000 phantom units at $40 per unit. Hopmayer signed the agreement and went to work; 11 months later, he was fired. The company told him in writing that he would not get his phantom units because they had not vested. Aladdin said there had been no mutual assent to specific terms on the units, and that plan details were to be worked out later. An existing plan for other employees required three years of vesting and treated the units not as phantom stock but as stock appreciation rights (even though it called them phantom units).

Unfortunately for Aladdin, it never specified any of this in writing to Hopmayer, nor did he ever agree to any of it in writing. All he agreed to was the employment letter, which said he would get the phantom units. Nothing in that letter referred to vesting or to the idea that Hopmayer would only get the increase in value, not the total value of the units. There was no other evidence that Hopmayer knew these were the terms. Under Tennessee law, there is "assumed mutual assent" in contractual matters if there is evidence both parties came to an outward expression of agreement. Although Aladdin claimed the letter was insufficient as a contract because its definition of the phantom unit plan was vague as to the terms of the plan, the court held that the drafter's unstated intent was insufficient to void the contract.

Texas: Executive Must Repay Option Profits to Former Employer

In a bizarre case based on Texas employment law, *Olander v. Compass Bank*, No. 03-20048 (5th Cir. April 6, 2004), the U.S. Fifth Circuit Court of Appeals held that (1) a noncompete clause contained in a former executive's employment agreement was unenforceable and (2) because the noncompete was unenforceable, a "clawback provision" in the same contract requiring the executive to repay profits earned from exercising options was effective.

The noncompete purported to broadly bar the executive, Olander, from associating with interests contrary to his employer, Compass Bank. However, the contract also stated that if the clause were ruled invalid or unenforceable, then the clawback would kick in: e.g., Compass would be entitled to claim any profits from option exercises, plus any common stock held by Olander. Olander left Compass Bank to work for another bank in 2001, violating the terms of the agreement, but he won a declaratory judgment from the U.S. District Court (S.D. Texas) that the noncompete was unenforceable. Compass then filed an action for restoration of profits under the clawback, which it lost at the trial level. Ultimately, however, the Fifth Circuit agreed with Compass. Calling Olander's victory "pyrrhic," the court noted that the noncompete was unenforceable because the options were valuable only while Olander remained an employee of Compass (an "illusory" promise because Compass could terminate him at will). Nonetheless, the agreement clearly provided that if Olander won on the noncompete issue, he would lose on the option issue.

Texas: Executive Need Not Repay Option Profits to Former Employer

In *Dell Computer Corp. v. Rodriguez*, No. 03-50866 (5th. Cir. November 8, 2004), the Fifth Circuit Court of Appeals applied Texas law to invalidate a clawback provision that would have required a former Dell executive to pay back gains realized under a golden parachute and stock option agreement. In this very complicated case, Dell accused the executive, Sixto Rodriguez, of breaching his contract by engaging in unethical business practices after he was fired from Dell but while he still had a consulting contract with the company.

Rodriguez was given a severance package and a "penny stock arrangement" (PSA) when he was hired by Dell to head its Spanish operations in 1991. The PSA allowed Rodriguez to buy Dell shares for one penny per share, no matter what their value. Dell, however, kept a right to retain 60% of the stock for two years after the options vested. A clawback provision stipulated that if Rodriguez violated the terms of his employment contract or the PSA agreement, he would have to pay the gains back.

In 1998, Rodriguez and Dell negotiated a separation agreement, but he was allowed to stay on as a consultant for 16 months in order for his remaining options to vest. Three months later, a Dell internal investigation revealed financial irregularities at the Spanish division and sought to recapture the options gains and severance payment. Rodriguez immediately exercised his remaining options, gaining $1.08 million in value. Over the next month, he exercised more options, bringing the total to $2.7 million. Dell filed criminal and civil charges in Spain, but those cases were dismissed, and Dell ultimately filed an action in Texas. The U.S. District Court for the Western District of Texas held for Dell, but the Court of Appeals reversed on a technicality: by the time the lawsuit was filed, the statute of limitations under Texas law for claims under Rodriquez's employment contract had expired.

12.4 State Divorce Cases Related to Options

Arkansas: Income from Future Stock Options Includable in Alimony Settlement

In *Heitt v. Heitt*, No. 03-812 (Ark. Ct. App. April 14, 2004), an Arkansas appeals court held that a former spouse's future stock options may be treated as income for purposes of alimony. At trial, the defendant argued that unvested stock options were necessarily excluded from inclusion in divorce settlements by Arkansas law. The trial court, however, determined that the Heitts' divorce settlement had anticipated basing alimony on all future sources of income, specifically including vested and exercised options as reported on the employee's tax forms for a particular year.

Missouri: Stock Options Granted Day After Divorce Becomes Final Not Subject to Division in Divorce Settlement

In *Clance v. Clance*, No. WD62273 (Mo. Ct. App. March 2, 2004), a Missouri appeals court held that a trial court did not have jurisdiction to divide stock options a husband received the day after the divorce settlement became final. The divorce was granted December 12, 2000. The next day, the husband received options on 2,500 shares of this employer. The trial court decided that the options were granted, in part, for prior performance and thus were marital property. The husband appealed, saying that the options did not exist until after the marriage was dissolved.

Missouri law provides that property "acquired" by either spouse after a marriage but before dissolution is marital property. While the court agreed that an argument could be made that the options at issue were earned during the marriage, it ultimately held that there was no legal basis for the trial court's decision. Although the circumstances presented an extreme case, the court noted that current law did not set out a safe harbor for considering post-dissolution grants. Absent such guidance, permitting judicial discretion could cause innumerable existing cases to be reopened.

New Jersey: Stock Options Granted After Divorce Excludable from Child Support Calculation

In *Heller-Loren v. Appuzio,* No. A-0494-2T3 (N.J. App. Div. August 3, 2004), a New Jersey appeals court reversed a trial court and held that a non-custodial parent did not have an obligation to include stock options awarded after the divorce in his calculation of income for child support purposes. Both former spouses received options during the marriage, and those options were expressly included in calculating their proportionate share of income at the time of settlement. Under New Jersey law, future earnings from options could certainly have been included in income for all purposes. However, the couple's property settlement agreement set out a specific list of items that would be included in "income" for purposes of computing future child support, and stock options were not on that list. Given the specificity of the contract, the custodial spouse could not now complain that the omission was inadvertent.

12.5 Miscellaneous

The following cases, while of general interest to practitioners, are unpublished and therefore (like IRS private letter rulings) cannot be cited as precedent.

Third Circuit: Forfeiture of Restricted Stock Upheld

In *Schunkewitz v. Prudential Securities Inc.,* No. 03-1181 (3rd Cir. April 27, 2004), the U.S. Court of Appeals for the Third Circuit upheld the forfeiture provisions in Prudential's deferred compensation plan. Under the plan, employees could defer up to 25% of their compensation into the plan to be credited against shares of Prudential stock. The shares were restricted for three years, however, and would be forfeited if the employee left before the restrictions were lifted. Schunkewitz, as required by the plan, signed documents stating that he had read, understood, and agreed to these provisions.

Third Circuit: Former Executive Forfeited Options When Employment Agreement Expired

In *Moses v. Corning Inc.*, No. 03-3003 (3rd Cir. July 16, 2004), the U.S. Court of Appeals for the Third Circuit held that a former Corning executive's options were forfeited when his subsidiary was spun off into an independent company. But the court ruled that there was still an issue of whether Corning was equitably estopped from denying the employee's attempt to exercise his options after the spinoff based on oral representations from a Corning employee.

Thomas Moses was CEO of Clinical Pathology Facility, Inc., when Corning acquired it. Two years later, he was given options in Corning stock. The grant provided the options would expire when Moses' employment relationship with Corning was terminated. Moses' subsidiary was spun off as Quest Diagnostics in 1996 as an independent company, but Corning sent two letters to employees saying they could still exercise their options if their employment with the now-independent Quest was terminated. Moses' employment agreement expired a year later. Two years later, he tried to exercise his options. Corning said no, and Moses sued. The district court ruled, and the appeals court affirmed, that the plan's language was unambiguous as to termination, as was the language of the letters. There remained a question, however, of whether Moses had been told by a Corning legal representative that he could exercise his options until December 1997.

Third Circuit: ERISA Does Not Cover Stock Option Plans

In *Houston v. Aramark Corp.*, No. 04-1103 (3rd. Cir. October 1, 2004), the U.S. Court of Appeals for the Third Circuit held that a former executive's stock option plan was not subject to the Employee Retirement Income Security Act (ERISA). ERISA governs qualified retirement plans, such as pension and 401(k) plans. A plan can be subject to ERISA even if it is not explicitly subject to qualified plan rules if the plan effectively is a retirement plan that extends beyond a limited number of a company's employees.

In this case, former Aramark executive Peter Houston had two stock option agreements with the company. Aramark was a privately held company during that time. Houston retired before the company went public. Aramark called Houston's options shortly after he retired, paying him $2.4 million. One month later, the company announced its IPO. Had Houston held the shares until then, he would have had $5.4 million in stock. When Houston met with company officials shortly before retirement to discuss his stock programs, he was not informed the company was about to go public. Houston subsequently contended that ERISA required that he be informed of the impending development.

The Third Circuit affirmed the ruling of the U.S. District Court for the Western District of Pennsylvania that ERISA did not apply, stating that option plans are not covered by ERISA because they are designed to provide current income, not retirement income. While Houston exercised his options at retirement, that was his choice. The plan did not require this kind of deferral. The court also ruled that Aramark had no obligation under common law to inform him of the IPO because Houston had signed a stockholder agreement waiving the right to be so informed.

Fourth Circuit: Earnings from Options Excluded from Retirement Benefit Calculation

In *Scipio v. United Bankshares Inc.*, No. 03-2282 (4th Cir. December 22, 2004), the U.S. Court of Appeals for the Fourth Circuit affirmed the trial court's dismissal of Scipio's claim that exercised stock options should be included when calculating payments due under a nonqualified retirement plan sponsored by his employer, United Bankshares. The plan computed benefits based on 70% of an employee's final average earnings over the five consecutive years with the highest average earnings over the preceding 10 years. When Scipio retired, he contended that his earnings (which never exceeded $101,000 in a year) should include an additional $408,000 attributable to exercise of options during the five-year period. United argued that the definition of earnings in the plan was not intended to encompass the spread on exercise of an option, and the company demonstrated that in addition to its longstanding policy of not including the option spread, it had hired outside counsel and a compensation consultant, contacted the former CEO and chairman of the acquired bank, and talked with other employees before making a decision on Scipio's claim. They all concluded options were not normally included in retirement pay calculations.

Fifth Circuit: Jury Verdict Reversed in Change of Control Case

In *Sanchez v. Verio, Inc.*, No. 01-11341 (5th Cir. December 27, 2004), the Fifth Circuit Court of Appeals reversed a jury verdict entitling Rhonda Sanchez to have her options vested on her termination. Verio employed Sanchez from 1998 to 2000, and she received four option grants during that period. The options vested at 25% per year as long as Sanchez was still employed. Under the plan, options would fully vest if Sanchez were "terminated by the company or related entity without cause or by the optionee with good reason within 12 months of a change in control." When Sanchez was terminated, Verio was in discussions to merge, but the merger was not completed until four months after Sanchez left. Sanchez then attempted to exercise her 300,000 unvested options, claiming that the merger occurred within 12 months of her termination, but the company refused, saying that the merger occurred after termination and thus the change in control provision did not apply. A jury agreed with Sanchez, saying the contract was ambiguous. On appeal, the court held that Verio's interpretation of the plan was correct: for accelerated vesting, termination must occur within the 12-month period following the change in control, not vice versa.

California: 3Com Board Covered by Business Judgment Rule in Stock Options Split

In *Shaev v. Claflin*, No. H026204 (Cal. Ct. App. June 21, 2004), the California Court of Appeal affirmed the trial court's dismissal of the plaintiff's derivative shareholder action over 3Com's splitting of its options after its 2000 spinoff of Palm Inc. Palm had been a wholly owned subsidiary; it was spun off by 3Com in an IPO in which it sold 23 million shares and distributed 532 million shares to 3Com shareholders. After the spinoff (although not simply as a consequence of it), 3Com stock dropped by about 80%. To preserve the value of its stock options, 3Com adjusted the options to give each holder 4.8 options for each option held. 3Com's board justified the move as necessitated by a "change in capital structure" of the company. 3Com's option plans did not specifically authorize the board to make such an adjustment in reaction to a spinoff, but a catch-all phrase allowed the board to make adjustments for changes in capital structure.

David Shaev, a 3Com shareholder, filed a derivative class action suit alleging that 3Com's board did not have the authority to make such a change, resulting in greater ownership for the board and employees at the cost of shareholders. Shaev argued the board's action was self-serving and unauthorized by the plan. However, the court held that in making stock option adjustments the 3Com directors acted in accordance with stock option plans approved by the shareholders, that the adjustments did not amount to corporate waste, and that accordingly the actions were protected by the business judgment rule.

Notes

1. At the federal level, cases are appealed to the U.S. Tax Court, and then to the U.S. Supreme Court. Each state has its own system, which may or may not involve specialized review boards and tax courts.

2. Another form of public ruling is known as a "revenue procedure," or Rev. Proc. These rulings give technical guidance to taxpayers on the application of regulations or revenue rulings.

3. Private rulings may, among other things, take the form of a private letter ruling (PLR) to an individual taxpayer, a technical advice memorandum (TAM) to a field agent, or an Advice from the Office of the IRS Chief Counsel. See Section 6110 of the Code.

4. Section 6110(k)(3) of the Code provides that written determinations may not be used or cited as precedent unless otherwise established in regulations.

5. For a description of this rule, see section 7.3.3 of chapter 7.

CHAPTER 13

Shareholder Approval Considerations for Option Plans

Contents

Through the mid-1980s, boards adopted resolutions to add shares to employee plans and subsequently obtained shareholder approval for such additions at the closest subsequent annual meeting of shareholders. Management rarely confronted issues with obtaining such approval and therefore it became common practice to authorize additional shares for Section 423 plans mid-offering period, relying on the expectation that shareholder approval would be obtained before the next exercise date under the offering period.

In recent years, however, the hurdles for obtaining shareholder approval for transactions under option plans have become higher and higher. In addition, accounting rules regarding Section 423 plan share additions are more carefully enforced than in earlier years. Plan sponsors would be well-advised to think carefully about strategies for obtaining approval before embarking on any major changes to an employee plan.

13.1 When Is Shareholder Approval Required?

Authorization of shares for an ESPP or employee stock option plan may be subject to shareholder approval under tax, corporate, and stock exchange rules.[1]

The Code requires that shareholder approval of statutory option plans (both ISO plans and Section 423 plans) be obtained within 12 months of the date the board of directors authorizes the allocation.[2] Corporate law generally requires initial plan approval, and, depending on the state, also may require approval of additions to the pool.[3] Finally, each stock exchange has its own rules regarding shareholder approval, and the degree to which it must be obtained, for employee option plans. This means that shareholder approval may be necessary for nonstatutory as well as statutory plans and it is always necessary for ISO and Section 423 plans.

A further point with regard to shareholder approval: as of 2004, the final ISO regulations provide that an ISO plan adopted by a company's board of directors "subject to shareholder approval" *will be considered adopted on the date the plan is approved by shareholders, e.g.,* if the board stipulates an adoption condition, then the deemed adoption date is when that condition is satisfied. The regulation raises issues, yet to be resolved, as to whether ISO grants made prior to shareholder approval will ever be valid. Note that this rule does not apply to 423 plans.

13.1.1 Stock Exchange Rules

Effective June 30, 2003, companies listed on the New York Stock Exchange and the NASDAQ must receive shareholder approval for all equity compensation plans, with certain very narrow exceptions.

For the NYSE, the new rules are Section 303A(8) of the Listed Company Manual. For the NASDAQ, the new rules are NASD Rules 4310(c)(17)(a) and 4320(e)(15)(A). The rules are very similar to each other. The most significant exception is that the NYSE rules prohibit broker voting on these issues; NASDAQ already did not allow broker voting on any issue. In effect, therefore, the two sets of rules are the same for broker voting as to shareholder approval of equity plans.

Other inconsistencies are minor; probably the most significant is that the NYSE rules require the company to submit in writing to the SEC reasons why it is relying on one of the material modification exemptions; the NASDAQ is considering adding such a rule. A summary of the rules is as follows.

1. Scope: All equity compensation plans, and any material revisions to these plans, must be approved by shareholders, with certain narrow exceptions, as outlined below.

2. Equity compensation plans defined: An equity compensation plan includes any plan or other arrangement to deliver securities to employees, including options. The term does not include dividend reinvestment plans, or plans that allow employees, directors, or other service providers to buy shares on the open market for current fair market value.

3. Material modification: "Material" is not defined by these rules, although it specifically does not include the limitation of rights and benefits associated with a plan; only modifications expanding employee rights and benefits are covered. The list of covered modifications includes:

    a. A material increase in the number of shares available, other than for stock splits, corporate reorganizations, and similar arrangements. Evergreen plans require approval for each increase unless the plan has a term of not more than 10 years. If the increase is not pursuant to a formula, then each increase must be approved by shareholders. A requirement that grants be made out of treasury or repurchased shares will not, in itself, be considered a formula.

    b. An expansion of the types of awards available under the plan or of the class of employees, directors, or other service providers eligible to participate.

    c. A material extension of the term of the plan.

    d. A material change in the method of determining the strike price of options, such as changing the fair market value from the closing date on grant to the average of the high and low price on the date of grant.

e. The deletion or limitation of any provision prohibiting re-pricing.

4. Repricings: Under the NYSE requirements only, a plan that does not specifically permit repricing is considered to prohibit it. Any actual repricing other than an exchange offer that started before the effective date of these rules is thus considered a material modification. Cancellation of an option and substitution for a new award pursuant to a merger, acquisition, spin-off, or similar transaction is not included.

5. Employment inducement awards: If the company's independent compensation committee approves them, inducement awards to new hires may be made without shareholder approval. Companies must disclose in a press release, and in written material for the NYSE, a description of the award, its terms, the number of shares and its recipient. The term "new hires" includes rehires of previous employees following a "bona fide" period of non-employment.

6. Mergers and acquisitions: Shareholder approval is not required to replace options or other awards in a transaction. Shares available for award of a closely held company that is acquired may be used in post-acquisition grants provided the plan existed prior to the merger or acquisition being contemplated. The time the shares are available cannot be extended after the transaction.

7. Qualified plans: Employee stock ownership plans, other Section 401 plans invested in company stock (401(k), profit sharing, and stock bonus plans), and Section 423 employee stock purchase plans do not require approval.

8. Parallel excess plans: These are plans that provide additional company contributions or employee deferrals into qualified plans that limit the total amount of compensation that can be considered or place ceilings on the total amounts that can be contributed. Companies sometimes make up the difference that would be allowed

if these ceilings did not exist; the contributions or deferrals are not tax favored. Investments in equity in these plans would be exempted from shareholder approval requirements. The plan must cover all or substantially all affected employees, its terms must be the same for those covered, it must parallel the terms for the qualified plans, and no one can receive compensation in excess of 25% of cash compensation.

9. Transition rules: Plans adopted prior to the SEC's approval of these rules are not subject to shareholder approval requirements unless and until they are materially revised. Discretionary plans can issue additional awards only for a limited time, specifically until 1) the next annual meetings at which directors are elected that occurs 180 days after the effective date of these rules; 2) the first anniversary of these rules; 3) the expiration of the plan, whichever comes first. Similarly, formula plans that have not been previously approved by shareholders and do not have a term of 10 years or less could make additional grants after these rules become effective but only within the transition period limits. Formula plans approved after the rules became effective can continue to be used longer than the transition period if amended to provide for a term of 10 years or less, or if the grants are made only from shares immediately available after the effective date.

10. Broker voting: In what may be the most significant hurdle of the new rules, broker-held shares ("street name" shares) cannot be voted by proxy by brokers unless the beneficial owner provides specific instructions. This new rule became effective 90 days after the effective date of the rules.

13.2 Responding to the Issue

Most plans contain language providing that if the share pool is depleted before the end of an offering (or exercise) period, participants will receive a pro-rata allocation rather than their full allotment of option shares on the exercise date. While following through on pro-rata allocation language is certainly legal, it is likely to produce employee-relations problems, particularly in a bull market. Most companies would prefer to come up with alternative solutions to this problem, and practitioners are testing a number of possibilities.

One alternative is to use omnibus pools and/or evergreen provisions to protect against delayed shareholder approval problems. Under an omnibus pool, shareholders are asked to approve a pool of shares that could be freely allocated by the board of directors between all of the company's plans. If a Section 423 plan ran out of shares mid-offering, the board would be able to shift shares from an underused or more predictable plan (such as an option plan) to the Section 423 plan.[4]

Another device, and one that can be combined with the omnibus pool or separately added to each plan, is an "evergreen" provision that provides that a certain number of shares (or percentage of outstanding shares) be added annually to the plan.[5] Like the omnibus plan, the evergreen provision would be approved by the shareholders on a prospective basis.

A key advantage of an evergreen provision is that once approved, it reduces both the technical issues and the pragmatic issues involved with going back to the shareholders for approval. As an initial matter, the board of directors must be encouraged to use special vigilance in computing the number of shares necessary to fund its plans for a foreseeable period. In recent years, companies have noticed an increased reluctance among shareholders (particularly institutional shareholders) to automatically approve authorizations for employee stock plans. If the board can propose a reasonable pool (with an evergreen) early in the life of the plan, it can effectively protect its equity incentive programs.

Unfortunately, as further discussed in chapter 15, companies should expect shareholder approval of special features for employee stock plans to be highly political and somewhat elusive, notwithstanding the practical benefits of such features. In addition, the application of new stock exchange shareholder approval rules may limit the use of evergreen options for practical purposes.

Notes

1. In the rare case that a private company sponsors an ESPP, it should check state securities laws to determine whether a blue sky requirement of shareholder approval will still govern plans. See, e.g., California Securities Act, Section 25100 et al.

2. Section 422(b)(1) (ISOs); 423(b)(2) (ESPPs). See also PLR 9312035 (approving an increase of the ESPP share limit in the middle of the offering period).

3. California is a notable example of a state that requires shareholder approval on both plan adoption and addition of shares. See California Commissioner's Rules § 260.140.41–45.

4. Note that for statutory option purposes, the total number of shares in the pool would have to be stated as a maximum in the plan itself, regardless of whether any reallocation occurred. This is because under tax regulations, shareholder approval is valid only if a concrete number of shares (or a formula that produces a concrete number as of the date of approval) is approved.

5. Again, a certain number of shares must be known as of the date of approval. Accordingly, an evergreen provision for a 423 plan (or an ISO plan) might say "the lesser of 200,000 shares or 1% of shares outstanding on January 1."

CHAPTER 14

Transferable Options

Contents

In the late 1990s, transferable employee stock options (TSOs) generated a great deal of interest and activity, particularly among estate planners. This section briefly summarizes the various issues raised by their use.

14.1 Why the Interest in TSOs?

TSOs are primarily interesting because of their estate tax implications. Before the 1996 SEC rules, neither the Code nor the Exchange Act permitted lifetime transfers of options. In fact, special benefits were conferred on nontransferable options. This changed with the 1996 SEC Rules, however, and TSOs are now eligible for exemption from the short-swing profit rules under the Act.[1]

Because options can now be transferred without securities law penalties, TSOs offer the executive the ability to transfer high-worth options out of his or her taxable estate before death. Such a transfer has the dual benefit of reducing the total value of the estate *and* providing already taxed cash outside the estate with which to pay estate taxes.[2]

However, one should not be deceived into believing that TSOs are a panacea. As more fully explained below, statutory options will never be transferable under the Code. Moreover, employee stock option plans typically reward employees for past services, provide incentive for current services, and encourage retention for future services. Accordingly, it is logical that such stock plans will continue to place limits on who can receive the benefits of an option.

14.2 Limits on TSOs

Attractive as the benefits of TSOs may be, there are many factors limiting their use. At a minimum, the following considerations apply:

1. *Appropriate Transferees.* Under the Exchange Act, there are no limits on who may be the recipient of a transferred option, and Rule 16b-5 specifically exempts gift transfers. However, for practical purposes, companies will be unlikely to permit sales of untradable options to third parties. Instead, most practitioners advise companies to use this as an estate planning tool, contractually limiting option transfers to gift transfers to a family member or trust. In fact, companies may wish to further narrow eligible transferees so as to retain better control over option exercises. Limited transferability is particularly important with respect to employee options because taxation and exercisability of the option are generally conditioned upon the employment status of the optionee. Note that this issue frequently arises in the context of options that are divided pursuant to a divorce decree. Depending on the property (or community property) laws of the governing state, such division may not be considered to be a transfer.[3]

2. *Statutory Stock Options.* Under the Code, ISOs and options granted under a tax-qualified ESPP (e.g., a Section 423 plan) must be non-transferable during the lifetime of the optionee. Upon the optionee's death, the option may be exercised by the estate. Any lifetime transfer will disqualify the option for tax purposes unless it is to a grantor trust controlled by the optionee and the optionee is the sole beneficial owner while the option is held in trust. Except in this narrow instance, only an NSO may be a TSO.[4]

3. *Gift Tax Valuation.* The transfer of a TSO as a gift (whether to an individual or a trust) is subject to gift tax. For these purposes, the TSO will be valued as of the date of transfer. Because employee

stock options are generally not tradable, there is little guidance (and much argument!) on how such options should be valued.[5] Additional complications attach if the TSO is for both vested and unvested stock.[6]

4. *Income Tax Issues.* Neither the donee nor the donor is taxed on the transfer of the TSO. Exercise by the transferee will result in income to the employee/donor (or to the employee/donor's estate, if he or she is deceased). All of the normal tax rules regarding vesting and income tax withholding will apply to the donor and the company. The donee takes a stepped-up basis in the stock (equal to the exercise price plus the ordinary income realized by and taxed to the donor on exercise).[7] Effective as of July 2, 2003, the IRS in TD 9067 clarified that transfers of compensatory stock options to related persons (including family members) are not dispositions of such options: i.e., the transferor may not argue that for purposes of Section 83, the ordinary income component of the transaction "closed" at the date of the transfer. This is not really a change to the long-standing interpretation of Section 83. However, it appears that as transferable options have become more common, taxpayers have attempted to treat transfers to related parties as if they were transfers to unrelated parties for purposes of Section 83. The changes to Treas. Reg. § 1.83-7 are intended to prevent this result.

5. *Language of the Plan.* Most stock option plans contain language requiring all options to be nontransferable. Before granting TSOs, the plan should be reviewed and amended if necessary. State securities and/or corporate laws may also require nontransferability and should be double-checked for exemptions.[8] Amendments to permit transferability (to either the plan or an NSO) do not require shareholder approval for tax, accounting, or securities purposes. For accounting purposes, plan amendments should not have adverse consequences; however, adding a TSO feature to an already-existing option grant may result in a new measurement date and/or variable award accounting treatment.

6. *Tradability of TSO Stock.* The current Form S-8 rules permit regis-
    tration of option exercises by family members of an issuer's em-
    ployees who have received options through a gift or domestic re-
    lations order.[9] Issuers should note, however, that stock exchange
    requirements may still call for nontransferability. Until the 1999
    revision of the SEC rules for registration on Form S-8, shares trans-
    ferred to a family member or trust pursuant to a TSO were re-
    stricted stock subject to Rule 144 resale limitations (unless regis-
    tered on a Form S-3 by the company).

7. *Tracking.* The holder of the TSO must understand any plan and
    statutory limits on exercise and tradability. In addition, the com-
    pany needs to be aware of issues related to the nonemployee
    optionee's lack of access to material information at the time of
    exercise.

14.3 Recommendations

While TSOs may offer opportunities for executive planning, companies
need to be careful to consider all of the issues attendant to amending
old options (or granting new ones) to include transferability features.

Notes

1. Before and through the 1996 SEC rules, nontransferability was a require-
    ment for the Rule 16b-3 exemption.

2. The exercised TSO will have already been taxed for both gift and income tax
    purposes. A complete discussion of the estate and gift tax consequences of a
    TSO is beyond the scope of this chapter.

3. See chapter 16.

4. See Sections 422(b) and 423(b) of the Code, and Treas. Reg. § 1.421-1(b)(2).

5. The gift tax regulations provide a general standard for valuation of property,
    with no specific guidance as to stock options. In addition, throughout the
    1990s employee options have been the subject of a heated debate among
    practitioners, legislators, and the SEC regarding the appropriate methodol-
    ogy for valuation. See also Rev. Proc. 98-34 (valuation safe harbor for gifted
    stock options requires nondiscounted, recognized pricing model).

6. The gift must be "complete" or the transfer will be ineffective. The IRS ruled in Rev. Rul. 98-21 that transfers of unvested options are not completed gifts for these purposes. Accordingly, if a TSO is considered to be a grant of a future interest, it will not be eligible for the annual gift tax exclusion. For a thoughtful discussion of transferable options in estate planning, see P. Melcher and W. Rosenbloom, "Transferable Options: When They Work, When They Don't," *Practical Tax Lawyer* 15, no.1 (fall 2000): 5.

7. See Section 83 of the Code. If the exercise is by the estate, the spread will be subject to income tax reporting but not to withholding, although depending on timing, FICA/FUTA withholding may be required. Rev. Rul. 86-109.

8. For example, the California Corporate Securities Act previously required that options granted by privately held companies be nontransferable. This provision was amended in 2001 to allow transferability similar (but not identical) to that permitted under the federal rules, including lifetime transfers to "immediate family." California Commissioner's Rules § 260.140.41(d).

9. SEC Release No. 33-7646 (Apr. 7, 1999). On the same date, the SEC also finalized parallel changes to Rule 701. See SEC Release No. 33-7645 (Apr. 7, 1999).

CHAPTER 15

Reloads, Evergreens, Repricings, and Exchanges

Contents

Over the years, issuers have developed certain plan features to encourage employees to continue investing in the company's stock. The techniques described briefly below are lightning rods for opposing philosophies on equity compensation. On the one hand, the techniques ensure that shares of stock will be available for use as employee incentives on an ongoing basis. Companies generally view this as a positive long-term compensation tool. On the other hand, these techniques are currently viewed with suspicion by institutional shareholders and the public at large. Such critics view reloads, evergreen provisions, and repricings as dilutive devices that inappropriately compensate executives at the expense of shareholders.[1]

15.1 Reloads

A reload grant is intended to provide the optionee with a continuing option grant while he or she remains an employee of the company. Typically, the optionee's grant will provide that, upon exercise of an option with stock (a "stock swap"), the optionee will receive an additional option for the same number of shares that were purchased under the original option.[2] The reload option will be priced at the fair market value of the stock on the date of its grant. Other terms—such as vesting restrictions, exercise schedule, and term—may be exactly the same as the original grant, or may be on an accelerated (or shorter term) basis. Reload grants are subject to the same tax, accounting, and securities rules as are any ISO or NSO. In addition, for purposes of Section 162(m) of the Code, each reload grant will count against the annual "performance-based" limit on the date of grant. For accounting purposes, under FAS 123(R) a reload provision does not factor into the determination of grant date fair value. When a reload option is actually granted, it is accounted for as a separate award.

Companies may provide for automatic reloads for all employees or for a class of employees such as top executives, make automatic reloads a feature of specific grants, or award reload grants at the board's discretion only. In designing reload provisions, however, it is important to note that the addition of automatic reloads may be instantly rejected by institutional shareholders. This is a matter of the current climate rather than logic: reloads actually are not particularly dilutive because the new grant serves only to replace already outstanding (swapped) stock.[3]

15.2 Evergreen Provisions

In a sense, an evergreen provision is a reload for the issuer's plan rather than for an individual grant. Evergreen provisions permit an annual increase in the number of shares available under the plan with a one-time shareholder approval (i.e., at the time the evergreen provision is approved). The evergreen provision may be for a specific number of additional shares or may be a percentage increase based on outstanding shares at a designated date, and it may continue for the life of the plan or for a limited period of years (i.e., five years).

15.2.1 Tax Limitations

The statutory option rules require that a plan (whether an ISO plan or an ESPP) state at the time of shareholder approval the maximum aggregate number of shares that may be issued under the plan as statutory stock options. Such number may be either a stated number or a definite number arrived at by a percentage or formula calculation based on the number of outstanding, issued or authorized shares at the time the plan is adopted.[4] Thus, if an evergreen provision is intended to apply to ISOs or ESPP options, that portion of the evergreen applicable to such options must comply with the tax rules, including the 2004 regulations. For example, a workable evergreen provision could use the following language: "1% of all shares outstanding on January 1 of each year will be added to the plan; provided that with respect to ISOs, the addition shall be 200,000 shares per year."[5]

15.2.2 Nonapproved Plans

In the past, commentators encouraged public companies to deal with the issue of additional shares by side-stepping the shareholder approval requirements entirely. Such "nonapproved plans" could be adopted for NSO grants that were intended primarily (or entirely) for awards to individuals who are not insiders. So long as neither statutory options nor insider grants were within the purview of the plan, neither the securities nor tax laws require shareholder approval, and genuinely broad-based plans were exempt from the shareholder approval requirements of the major stock exchanges. However, as noted in chapter 13, both the securities laws and stock exchange rules have recently changed to seriously limit the availability of nonapproved plans.

Moreover, we can assume that institutional shareholders will have the same issues with nonapproved plans as with approved plans, i.e., the dilutive effect of such plans. If shareholders are unhappy with the overall stock plan strategy, they may be loath to approve additions to the plans that require shareholder approval. For this reason, companies that decide to use nonapproved plans should take care to establish sufficient limitations to allay shareholder fears about overuse of equity compensation. For example, nonapproved plans might be used solely for defined performance rewards or divisional merit grants for non-officers. Alternatively, they might serve as a limited stopgap measure to avoid accounting charges on ordinary grants if the company runs out of shares before an opportunity to obtain shareholder approval.

15.3 Repricing Programs

Much has been said and written over the years about how to deal with options in a down-market scenario, such as those that occurred in the late 1980s and early years of the 21st century. When the market falls and anxiety over employee retention rises, companies may rush to reprice or exchange "underwater" employee stock options (options that have an exercise price above the fair market value of the underlying stock). Repricing was particularly popular—and egregious—in the months following the stock market drop in 1987 and in the panic of 2000–2001. Experience shows that despite the issues associated with adjusting option pricing, it is inevitable that issuers will wish to reassess options that are no longer "in the money" (e.g., options that no long have an exercise price that is below the fair market value of the underlying stock) any time the market is poised for a downward correction. From the employer perspective, if employee options (unlike investor warrants) are intended to serve as a key element of the compensation package, they lose their attractiveness once they are underwater.[6]

Typically, in a repricing program the board of directors will set a repricing date and invite employees to trade underwater options for new options priced as of that date. As a general rule, the repriced options will require employees to give up some of the benefits of the original grants: for example, the repriced options may be for fewer shares (i.e., one new share for two old shares) or may have a different vesting schedule from the original options. Other typical conditions are blackout periods and vesting schedule set-backs. For example, the new grant may require that the optionee (1) accept an extended vesting period and (2) agree to a six-month blackout period during which he or she may not exercise for otherwise vested shares.

15.3.1 Corporate Considerations

Before adopting a repricing program, the board of directors should carefully consider the ramifications to the shareholders and make a determination as to the overall value of repricing to the company. The courts have long considered the issue of whether inappropriate repricing might involve corporate waste. Generally, lawyers advise that when the board of directors reprices options (particularly on a large scale), it should include new conditions on the repriced grants so as to ensure sufficient consideration to counter a shareholder challenge based on corporate waste.[7]

Companies should use this technique sparingly and only after careful consultation with legal counsel and accounting advisors. Although the accounting consequences that dissuaded repricing have largely disappeared under FAS 123(R), the technique frequently involves real economic costs to the company. Moreover, there may be costs in terms of perception, as shareholders—particularly institutional investors—often have serious issues with the philosophy inherent to pricing adjustments. In particular, opponents argue that options are not a guarantee of income but rather are intended to reflect the fortunes of the company and the employee's contribution to those fortunes. From the investor perspective, programs that adjust pricing offer downside protection to employees that is not otherwise available to shareholders.

Companies need to be aware that such concerns may give rise to litigation, particularly if there is a perception of wide-scale dilution as a result of the price adjustment. To this end, before adopting a protection program, the board of directors should carefully consider the ramifications to the shareholders in making a determination as to the overall value to the company. The company is best advised to ensure that the program is approved by a majority of its independent "disinterested" directors, so as to counter shareholder lawsuits based on self dealing or breach of fiduciary duty. In fact, in view of the governance concerns expressed by the Sarbanes-Oxley Act of 2002, boards may wish to consider retaining independent counsel to advise the compensation committee with respect to any potential large-scale option offers.[8]

15.3.2 Tax Considerations

If the repricing affects NSOs only, there will be limited adverse tax consequences to the optionee or to the company.[9] However, before the 2004 regulations, ISO repricings were trickier. Repricing constitutes a modification of the outstanding options for tax purposes.[10] When repricing underwater ISOs, the repricing itself was not the issue: the regulations require only that a modified option be repriced to current fair market value, which is the very point of the repricing.[11] The problem was a more subtle one: what if the optionee, when offered the opportunity for the repricing, declined to accept it, perhaps because he or she intended to terminate employment before the end of the blackout period? Had the optionee's old option been modified anyway? The 2004 regulations answered this question for us: a repricing offer will not result in a modification unless the offer remains outstanding for more than 30 days or is accepted.[12]

15.3.3 Securities Law Issues

After the 1996 SEC rules, there are no special shareholder approval requirements connected with repricings for securities law purposes. However, the employer has many other obligations under the Exchange Act with respect to a repricing. First, any participation in the repricing by Section 16 insiders will need to be disclosed in the company's proxy statements, and repriced grants will be reportable events under Section 16(a).[13] Second, in the early 21st century, the SEC focused on the application of the "tender offer rule" to employee repricings and exchange offers, reasoning that such exchanges (unlike normal option grants) require optionees to make individual investment decisions.[14] Under the Exchange Act, an issuer making a tender offer must comply with a variety of complex substantive and procedural rules relating to nondiscrimination and disclosure with respect the terms of the offer.[15] In 2001, the SEC issued an exemptive order for issuer exchange offers that are conducted for compensatory purposes, exempting such issuers from compliance with the nondiscrimination requirements of Rule 13e-4.[16] Notwithstanding the exemption, however, the issuer must still satisfy a number of hurdles to effect a valid exchange offer, including providing certain financial materials to both employees and the SEC, making various SEC filings, holding analyst calls (where appropriate), and providing a withdrawal period to offerees.[17]

15.3.4 Accounting Issues

For companies that have experienced a decline in stock price, FAS 123(R) may make repricing a viable alternative once again. Under APB 25, repricing an underwater stock option triggered variable plan accounting, which could ultimately be very costly for the granting corporation. Under FAS 123(R), however, repricings and other option modifications are accounted for using the same general principles that apply under FAS 123.

Under FAS 123(R), a repricing or other modification is viewed as a cancellation of the original option and the grant of a replacement option. None of the expense previously recorded for the cancelled option is reversed and, if the option is not yet fully vested, the company continues to record the remaining unamortized expense along with the additional expense for the replacement option. The expense for the replacement option is equal to its fair value less the fair value of the cancelled option at the time of the cancellation.

For example, assume that options having a fair value of $1 million are granted on January 1, 2006. The options vest as to 100% of the underlying shares approximately three years after the date of grant, on December 31, 2008. On June 30, 2007, the company's stock price has declined and the options are underwater. The company reprices the underwater options by canceling the existing options (assuming that none of the options have been exercised) and immediately grants re-placement options with a price equal to the current market value of the stock.

Under APB 25, the repricing would trigger variable plan account-ing. From June 30, 2007, forward, the company would estimate ex-pense for the replacement options based on the current intrinsic value of the options. The estimated expense would be adjusted each account-ing period until the options were exercised or expired unexercised. This results in an expense that varies from period to period and increases as the company's stock price recovers. Depending on when employees choose to exercise and the term of the replacement options, the com-pany could still be estimating and adjusting the expense many years after the repricing (possibly even five to 10 years later).

Under FAS 123(R), while the repricing is likely to result in addi-tional expense, the amount of the expense is fixed as of the date the replacement options are granted and is not subsequently adjusted (except possibly for forfeitures). At the time of the repricing, the com-pany has already recorded approximately $500,000 worth of expense for the underwater options (the repricing occurs exactly halfway through the three-year service period). None of this expense is reversed and the company must continue to record the remaining $500,000 of expense associated with the underwater options. The company must also com-pute incremental expense for the replacement options. Assume that the fair value of the replacement options is $400,000 and the fair value of the underwater options at the time they are cancelled is just $100,000. The incremental expense for the replacement options is $300,000. As a result, the total expense the company will record for the options is $1.3 million. This includes the expense of $1 million associated with the original options and the incremental expense of $300,000 associ-ated the replacement options. Since $500,000 of the original expense has been recorded prior to the repricing, the expense that is recorded over the service period of the replacement options is $800,000. But the company was already planning to accrue $500,000 of this amount, so the additional cost of the repricing is only $300,000. While, from a financial standpoint, the company would certainly prefer not to have any additional expense, a fixed amount of additional expense is generally preferable to the variable plan accounting that the repricing would trigger under APB 25. With a relatively fixed cost associated with the repricing, the company can more easily evaluate the benefits of repricing against the financial cost.

For simplification purposes, the above example does not address the impact of estimated and actual forfeitures on expense associated with the repricing. The standard includes specific and complex guidance on how forfeitures of modified options and awards are accounted for, particularly where the modification results in a change in the vesting conditions applicable to the arrangement. In some cases, a portion of the expense associated with a modified option or award is not reversed upon forfeiture if the original (pre-modification) vesting conditions are met. Always consult your accounting advisors before initiating any modifications of outstanding options and awards. This applies not only to repricings but to other types of modifications as well, including acceleration of vesting, extension of the period in which the arrangement can be exercised, and other modifications to the terms of the arrangement.

15.3.5 NYSE Listing Requirements

Under 2003 NYSE rules governing shareholder approval, a plan that does not specifically permit repricing is considered to prohibit it. Any actual repricing other than an exchange offer that started before the effective date of the rules is thus considered a material modification that requires shareholder approval. Canceling an option and substituting a new award pursuant to a merger, acquisition, spin-off, or similar transaction does not require shareholder approval under these rules.

15.4 Option Exchange Programs

Until FAS 123(R) went into effect, companies that wished to cancel underwater options and grant new fair market value options often would replace the canceled options six months and one day later—the minimum amount of time required to avoid treatment as a repricing under APB 25. While this technique permitted repricing, it got mixed reviews from both shareholders and employees: on the one hand, employees might be encouraged to stay at the company through the waiting period to make sure that their grants were reinstated;[18] on the other hand, they could be equally incentivized to try to keep the stock price artificially low so as to make sure their ultimate exercise price was a low as possible. Moreover, if the company underwent merger and acquisition activity during the waiting period, employees who agreed to the option exchange could be shut out of the benefits of a transaction.

For reasons described above in section 15.3.4, six months and one day exchanges no longer allow companies to avoid showing stock options related accounting expense on their income statements. Given that the basic tax, accounting, and securities law considerations outlined above for repricings also apply to option exchange programs,[19] and in view of the very real downside perceived by employees, there no longer appears to be any particular advantage to using an option exchange program post FAS 123(R).

Notes

1. Some consulting firms and organizations (such as the Investor Responsibility Research Center) publish annual surveys tracking the attitudes of shareholders on option matters, and these surveys have reflected a growing concern among larger investors. See, e.g., Pearl Meyers & Partners, *2004 Equity Stake: Study of Management Equity Participation in the Top 200 Corporations*, updated annually; Investor Responsibility Research Center, *Stock Plan Dilution 2005: Overhang for Stock Plans at the S&P Super 1500 Companies*. In addition, Institutional Shareholder Services (ISS), a consulting company that advises institutional shareholders on proxy voting, is well known for its negative recommendations on stock pool increases.

2. For a detailed discussion of stock swaps, see section 5.2 of chapter 5.

3. For an overview of planning techniques using reload grants, see *The Corporate Executive*, November–December 1998. While some of the technical concerns discussed in this article are no longer relevant, the conceptual framework remains useful.

4. Treas. Reg. § 1.422-2(b)(3); Treas. Reg. § 1.423-2(c)(3).

5. Treas. Reg. § 1.422-2(b)(3). It would also be permissible to state that the ISO addition would be 1% of the outstanding shares on the date of adoption;

however, in most cases the issuer will know what that number is on the date of adoption. Note that this is a departure from the previous rules, which permitted a formula or percentage computation in the future as well as at the date of adoption. See PLR 9531031 (percentage increase to pool acceptable if number of shares measurable as of a date certain).

6. According to Institutional Shareholder Services (ISS), U.S. employers adopted 170 programs for adjusting underwater options in 2001 (of which 125 were 6 months + 1 day exchanges). See *www.issueatlas.com* ("22 for 2002"). See also "2001 Repricing Odyssey" in the January-February 2002 issue of *The Corporate Executive*; D. Delves, "Underwater Stock Options," in *Strategic Finance* (Dec. 2001) at 26–32; P. Sweeney, "Stock Option Pitfalls and Strategies Du Jour," *192 Journal of Accountancy Online* No. 4 (October 2001); "Down Market Scenarios," *The Corporate Executive* (March–April 2001) at 2–5; "Underwater Stock Options: Complexities Multiply, Bringing New Challenges," *Towers Perrin Perspectives* (January 2001).

7. Lawyers particularly look to Delaware law in this regard. See, e.g., *Michelson v. Duncan*, 407 A.2d 211 Del. 1979) (Supreme Court remanded repricing action to trial court for determination on corporate waste; under Delaware statute, repricing must be in exchange for sufficient consideration).

8. See, e.g., *Byrne v. Lord*, 1995 WL 684868 (Del. Ch. 1995) For an excellent discussion of the status of option litigation with respect to director and corporate waste issues, see Thomas J. St. Ville, *Stock Option Litigation Guide* (BNA:2002) at chapter 1.

9. A tax issue may arise in a repricing for top executives under the Section 162(m) "$1 million cap." Treas. Reg. § 1.162-27(e)(2)(vi)(B) provides that both the original option and the repriced replacement will be counted against the annual performance-based compensation limitation when computing the cap. See section 9.5 of chapter 9 for more on this issue.

10. Note also that for purposes of the "first exercisable rule" if old options remain outstanding after a repricing, the amount first exercisable in any given year must be computed with reference to both the pre- and post-repricing options, and in some cases exercisability under the repriced grant will need to be adjusted to maintain ISO status.

11. Of course, the grant date (and thus the statutory holding period) is also changed. See section 3.6 of chapter 3 for a discussion of the effect of ISO modifications.

12. Section 424(h)(3) of the Code; Treas. Reg. § 1.424-1(e)(4)(iii). This is a major improvement over past practice. Prior to the 2004 regulations, most practitioners were concerned that the offer itself could modify the option,

and thus counseled employers to take a safer route and issue an "invitation to receive an offer" to optionees. The company would advise the optionee of the potential repricing and require him to request, in writing, an offer to exchange old options for new, repriced options. If the optionee failed to request an offer by a designated date, he or she was never offered the right to a lower priced option. The 2004 regulations make this dance unnecessary.

13. See section 7.4 of chapter 7.

14. Rule 13e-4 of the Exchange Act. See, e.g., SEC No-Action Letters re: *Lante Corporation* (Feb. 9, 2001); *Amazon.com, Inc.* (Feb. 28, 2001); *Digimarc Corp.* (Mar. 16, 2001); *LookSmart Ltd* (Mar. 20, 2001) (granting exemptions from certain aspects of the tender offer rule for employee option exchanges).

15. The nondiscrimination rules are commonly referred to as the "all holders" and "best price" rules. See Rule 13e-4(f)(8)(i), (ii). In addition, Rule 13e-4 requires extensive disclosure on Schedule TO-1, which must be filed via EDGAR and distributed to optionees in accordance with specific notice periods. See discussion below.

16. "Repricing," issued March 21, 2001. For the text of the release, see SEC Division of Corporate Finance, "Current Issues and Rulemaking Projects Quarterly Update, March 31, 2001," Section II, available at *www.sec.gov/divisions/corpfin/cfcrq032001.htm*. An issuer may take advantage of the Exemptive Order if:

(a) it is eligible to use Form S-8, the options subject to the exchange offer were issued under an employee benefit plan as defined in Rule 405 of the Exchange Act, and the securities offered in the exchange offer will be issued under such employee benefit plan;

(b) the exchange offer is conducted for compensatory purposes;

(c) the issuer discloses in the offer to purchase the essential features and significance of the exchange offer, including the risks that optionees should consider in deciding whether to accept the offer; and

(d) it otherwise complies with Rule 13e-4.

In issuing the Exemptive Order, the SEC notes that it had previously granted relief from the Rule 13e-4(f)(8) "all holders" and "best price" rules for employee repricings on a case-by-case basis.

17. See generally Rule 13e-4; Schedule TO-1 and Item 10 to Schedule TO.

18. Of course, this could have wrongful termination repercussions if employees are laid off or otherwise terminated before the regrant date. For more on increasing option litigation in the wrongful termination context, see chapter 17.

19. Note that before issuing its March 21, 2001, exemptive order on repricings, the SEC issued no-action letters with respect to several 6+1 exchange offers, and the exemptive order indicates the SEC's position that such exchange offers are also subject to Rule 13e-4.

CHAPTER 16

Death and Divorce

Contents

Special rules apply for the tax treatment of options when disposition of the option or optioned stock occurs as a result of death or divorce. Please note that in addition to the income tax rules cited below, estate and gift tax implications will also arise for the individual or decedent's estate.

16.1 Death

The Code makes exceptions from the statutory stock option rules for dispositions and transfers with respect to death. However, plan administrators should be careful to require proof of death before applying the rules. The company should have a policy of requesting a death certificate and (where indicated by state law) appropriate testamentary documents supporting the transfer.

- *Statutory Stock Options.* Statutory options are nontransferable except to an optionee's estate or beneficiaries and, as described in chapter 3, are subject to strict rules governing exercise.[1] Ordinarily, the holders of ISOs and ESPP options must satisfy both holding period and employment requirements to remain eligible for preferential tax treatment under Sections 422 and 423 of the Code. However, the Code provides special exceptions to the rules when an employee dies while holding an unexercised statutory option. Under the regulations to Section 421(a) of the Code, neither of these requirements will apply in the case of statutory options held or exercised by an estate or beneficiary of the optionee. Moreover, stock acquired before death under an ESPP or ISO can be transferred to the optionee's estate (or beneficiary) without resulting in a disqualifying disposition. Note that because disqualifying dispositions do not occur in the case of post-death transfers, the company is relieved of its Section 6039 reporting requirement.[2] Unless otherwise stated in the company's option plan, there are no time limits on post-death exercise.[3]

- *NSOs.* If the company's plan permits transferable options, exercise by the estate (or beneficiary) will result in wages, which must be reported by the company on a Form 1099-MISC but are not subject to income tax withholding. FICA/FUTA withholding will be required only if the exercise occurs in the same calendar year as the employee's death.[4]

- *Tax Treatment for Disposition of Section 423 Stock by Estate:* Note that the tax treatment for disposition of Section 423 stock by an estate depends on whether the optionee or the estate purchased the shares. If the optionee purchased the stock and died before its disposition, the optionee will have ordinary income in the year of death equal to the lesser of the offering date discount and the difference between the purchase price and the market value of the stock at the date of death. Regardless of the amount of the inclusion, the estate will take a stepped-up basis in the shares equal to the market value at the date of death. If the estate both purchases and disposes of the shares after the employee's death, the disposition will be treated as a qualifying disposition—i.e., the estate or beneficiary will have ordinary income equal to the lesser of the offering date discount or the spread on the purchase date. The amount included in the gross income of the estate (or beneficiary) is allowed as an estate tax deduction to the estate as if it were an item of income in respect of a decedent within the meaning of Section 691 of the Code.[5]

16.2 Divorce

As with transfers due to death, the Code provides some special rules for transfers "incident to divorce." A transfer "incident to divorce" is defined as a transfer that occurs not more than one year after the date the marriage ceases or a transfer pursuant to a divorce decree and no more than six years after the date the marriage ceases.[6]

In many cases, state law dictates the application of the tax laws, so the plan administrator must take care to ascertain the residence of the divorced couple during their marriage (usually by court order or copy of the divorce decree). In addition, this can become particularly tricky when the parties have litigated over the division of vested and unvested options (including options earned after a divorce—an issue that has begun to come up with surprising frequency in state courts across the country).[7]

16.2.1 Basic Technical Issues upon Transfer

- *Option Transfers.* After a divorce, the employer company is frequently asked to split an outstanding option between its employee and a nonemployee former spouse (NEFS). The company's ability to effect a split depends on two things: the state the (ex-)couple lived in, and the type of option being split.

  In a community property state, the option is considered to belong to both spouses even though only one "earned" it. A division of the option between the employee and the NEFS is not considered to be a transfer, but rather just a re-registration of legal title. This means that any option can be split after a divorce in a community property state without running afoul of rules about nontransferability.[8] The company should be advised to require validating paperwork, however, to make sure that it is splitting between the right parties.

  In a separate property state, the limits are stricter—an option cannot be split unless it is a TSO.[9] Without specific authorization in the plan or option grant, the company cannot legally permit the transfer of a nontransferable option to the NEFS, even pursuant to a divorce decree. In that case, the ex-spouses must agree that the employee spouse will exercise on behalf of the NEFS, with a subsequent transfer of the stock (see below). The company should have the employee spouse execute authorization and transfer paperwork before exercise by the NEFS.

- *Tax Treatment on Option Exercise.* The NEFS is treated as if he or she were the employee for purposes of income tax withholding upon exercise of an option. With the finalization of new ISO regulations in 2004, the rules regarding transfer of unexercised ISOs incident to divorce changed. Whereas previously the NEFS could in some circumstances be treated as exercising an ISO for tax purposes, the regulations now provide that upon transfer of an ISO—whether incident to the divorce decree or pursuant to a domestic relations order—the option will automatically be disqualified and treated as an NSO. Accordingly, when a NEFS exercises any option, the company must treat the spread as federal income tax wages for the NEFS and as FICA/FUTA wages for the employee. This means that the company must make sure that the NEFS provides for income tax withholding at the time of exercise *and* must report the spread as wages (on a Form 1099-MISC, because it will not have a W-2 for the NEFS). In addition, the company has to impute "phantom wages" to the employee for FICA/FUTA purposes and withhold as appropriate.[10]

- *Transfers of Optioned Stock.* Transfers of stock between a spouse and a NEFS are nonevents under the Code, regardless of whether the stock was purchased pursuant to exercise of an ISO or an NSO. ISO stock continues to be eligible for preferential treatment in the hands of the NEFS, so long as the original exercise was by the employee spouse.

- *Securities Law Issues.* Note that the concerns highlighted under "Transferable Options" in chapter 14 with respect to TSOs apply to employee options transferred to or exercised by an NEFS or a beneficiary. In most cases, the Form S-8 is now available to register such options.

- *Practical Issues.* For practical purposes, these requirements can be perplexing. What happens if the NEFS refuses to provide for withholding on exercise or if the company has insufficient information to report appropriately? What if the court has ordered a split of ISOs in a separate property state? What if the employee spouse refuses to execute transfer authorizations? In each of these cases, the in-house plan administrator needs guidance from legal counsel to properly protect the company. The goal should be to do the right thing from a legal perspective but stay out of any arguments between the ex-spouses.

16.2.2 Post-2004 Tax Compliance

In Revenue Ruling 2004-60 (June 14, 2004), the IRS provided guidance on withholding, reporting, and tax issues relating to NSO transfers incident to a divorce. In the case at hand, an employee spouse transferred one-third of the total options grant to the NEFS. The IRS rules on the following points:

1. For FICA (Social Security and Medicare) and FUTA (unemployment) tax purposes, the transfer of the options in and of itself is not considered the payment of income to the NEFS. At the date of exercise by the NEFS, however, the spread is subject to FICA just as it would be if exercised by the employee spouse. This means that if the employee spouse has already exceeded the FICA withholding ceiling, then the exercise by the NEFS will not result in additional FICA withholding. The employee portion of FICA is actually deducted from the payments to the NEFS, not from payments to the employee spouse. Because the employer pays all of the FUTA tax, the NEFS obviously has no responsibility for FUTA.

2. For federal income tax purposes, when the NEFS exercises the options, the employer must withhold taxes. The supplemental wage flat rate (25% of amounts of $1 million or less, and 35% of amounts in excess of $1 million) may be used for this withholding. The NEFS is entitled to use this amount as a credit when computing income taxes.

3. For reporting purposes, any FICA tax withholding is reported on Form W-2 using the employee spouse's name, address, and Social Security number. However, no income is included in Box 1 or Box 2 with respect to these taxes. Instead, income received by the NEFS is reported in Box 3 on a Form 1099-MISC as "other income," and income tax withheld is reported in Box 4. The employer files a Form 945 to record income tax withholding for the NEFS, while FICA is reported on the employer's Form 941 and FUTA on form 940.

Notes

1. Section 422(b)(5) and 423(b)(9) of the Code.

2. Section 424(c)(1).

3. Generally, post-death exercise occurs only in the case of ISOs, as ESPP plans are usually designed to refund cash in the event of an employee termination (for any reason) before the plan's exercise date.

4. Rev. Rul. 86-109.

5. The Code sets out the rules for post-death dispositions in Sections 421(c), 423(c), and 424(c); see also Treas. Reg. § 1.423-2(k)(2).

6. See Section 1041 of the Code (transfers between spouses generally); Section 424(c) of the Code (ISOs).

7. See, e.g., *Heitt v. Heitt*, No. 03-812 (Ark. Ct. App. Apr. 14, 2004) (former spouse's future stock options may be treated as income for purposes of alimony); *Hill v. Hill*, 2003 Conn. Super. LEXIS 490 (Conn. Super. Ct. Feb. 21, 2003) (exercise of stock options after divorce increased income for purposes of child support when not specifically excluded in separation agreement); *Otley v. Otley*, 810 A.2d 1 (Ct. Spec. App. 2002) (unexercised and unvested options acquired during marriage may be marital property subject to division); *Jensen v. Jensen*, 824 So.2d 315 (Fla. Dist. Ct. 2002), *rev. den.* 842 So. 2d 844 (Fla. 2003) (unvested options are marital assets subject to equitable distribution); *Fox v. Fox*, 2002 Ohio 2010 (Ohio Ct. App. 2002) (options granted during marriage may be marital property); *Palin v. Palin*, 2002 Cal. App. Unpub. LEXIS 4318 (Cal. App. Jan. 31, 2002) (all or portion of options granted during marriage and before separation are community property); *Fisher v. Fisher*, 769 A.2d 1165 (Pa. 2001) (permitting distribution of proceeds rather than options); *Henry v. Henry*, 758 N.E.2d 991 (Ind. 2001) (vested options part of marital estate); *Hopfer v. Hopfer*, 757 A.2d 673 (Conn.

2000) (unvested options not part of marital estate). For an extensive overview of the law, see William Dunn and Donna Yip, "Stock Options in Divorce," in *Selected Issues in Equity Compensation, 3d Edition.* (Oakland, CA: NCEO, 2005.) See also Thomas J. St. Ville, *Stock Option Litigation Guide* (BNA, 2002), 47. Additional recent cases are discussed in chapter 12.

8. Rev. Rul. 76-83; PLRs 9433010, 8751029, and 8451031.

9. See chapter 14, "Transferable Options."

10. See Rev. Rul. 2002-22 (option transfers to NEFS generally); Rev. Rul. 2002-31 (instructions on reporting).

CHAPTER 17

Post-Termination Option Issues

Contents

When an employee leaves employment for a reason other than death or disability, a number of equity-related issues can arise. For example, a company may seek to use equity as a form of severance, either by accelerating vesting or by extending exercise terms. On the other end of the spectrum, a company may attempt to create an equity-based noncompete agreement by including (and enforcing) forfeiture clauses in all option grants. In any event, former employers need to look carefully at the whole picture before using equity as part of a termination strategy. Moreover, even when no special strategies are adopted, employers need to exercise care in administering the post-termination provisions of the plan or individual option grant. In recent years, allegations of unfair treatment with respect to options have increasingly formed the basis for claims in wrongful termination litigation. Litigation particularly arises with respect to disputes over vesting and exercise rights on termination. Such claims are governed by state law and generally turn on contract construction—a strong reason to draft plan documents clearly and follow them precisely.[1] Finally, the employer must always be aware that Section 409A of the Code may apply to treat payments made upon separation from employment as a deferral of compensation under a nonqualified deferred compensation plan. Any structuring of post-termination equity compensation will need to be done carefully so as to avoid Section 409A accelerated taxation and penalties.[2]

17.1 Using Equity as Severance

A common executive severance strategy is to allow options to continue to vest for a period of time after termination and also extend the exercise period past the normal post-termination window. There are two ways to approach additional vesting. The first is to simply accelerate vesting on the date of termination as to stock that would otherwise have vested during a specific period's worth of stock (the "severance period") as of his termination date. The second is to require the former employee to enter into a consulting agreement with the company for the severance period, with the shares continuing to vest over that period. In creating this type of package, the company should consider the following tax and accounting issues:

17.1.1 Acceleration

From the business perspective, acceleration provides a clean break with the former employee. However, such acceleration may change the tax character of the option if it is an ISO. Under Section 424(h) of the Code, acceleration of vesting will not, in and of itself, convert the ISO to an NSO. The problem is that in operation, such acceleration can easily run afoul of the "$100,000 first exercisable" rule in Section 422 of the Code. That rule states that an ISO may be first exercisable as to no more than $100,000 worth of stock (valued as of the date of grant) in any calendar year. If the former employee is at (or near) his or her

$100,000 limit on the date of termination, acceleration of vesting may exceed the limit. Under the Code, the excess options will be automatically converted from ISOs to NSOs, with the attendant tax consequences for the optionee. If termination is near the end of a calendar year, the best way around this result is to defer the termination date into the next year and accelerate exercisability only in the new calendar year. Generally, the accelerated installment would have been first exercisable in the new year anyway, and so acceleration should not have any new affect on tax status.

For accounting purposes, FASB Staff Position FAS 123(R)-1 provides that an outstanding option that is modified to accelerate vesting after termination will subject it to liability accounting under Statement of Financial Accounting Standards No. 150. Depending on the facts, this could be costly for the company.

17.1.2 Consulting Agreements

The consulting agreement alternative provides the company with continuing access to the former employee's knowledge base and may also be used to help negotiate a noncompete agreement or similar post-termination settlement. However, the technical tax and accounting analysis may be unattractive to both parties, particularly if the option is an ISO.

For tax purposes, the Code requires that ISOs may be granted only to employees and may be exercised only for a period of up to 90 days after termination of employment (more on this below). If vesting continues after the former employee is no longer an employee, the portion of the option that vests after the termination date must be treated as an NSO, although the portion of the option that has already vested on the termination date will still be an ISO.

17.1.3 Extension of Exercise Period

Any extension of the period within which the former employee may exercise the option will be a modification for both tax (ISO) and accounting purposes. As noted above, the Code allows a maximum 90-

day post-termination exercise period for ISOs, but if the plan or option agreement states a shorter period, that period will govern. ISO status on any portion of the option can be preserved only if that portion of the option is exercised during the stated post-termination period. Once the stated period has expired, there is an automatic modification, and the entire unexercised option will be treated as an NSO. Further, FAS 123(R)-1 provides that any extension of the exercise period will result in a modification for accounting purposes. As with the modifications described above, this changes the accounting for the award to liability accounting.

17.1.4 Limitations in the Document

In devising severance packages, employers should always check the plan document first for authority. Most plans have language that gives broad discretion to the board of directors to accelerate or otherwise amend options. However, planners should not take this for granted: companies should always review the sections governing the "powers of the administrator" and in the individual grant documents before making any changes. If the language is too restrictive, the plan may need to be amended before the option can be accelerated. The same issue applies to the post-termination exercise period: some plans limit such periods to 90 days. If the plan has this type of limitation, it will need to be amended before the board can extend the right to exercise the option.

17.1.5 Tax Deductions

Note that the above analysis assumes that the company wants to give the former employee a chance to retain ISOs and the preferential tax treatment accorded such ISOs. This may not, however, be the best choice for the company. As noted above, the company gets a tax deduction on the exercise of NSOs, but not on the exercise of ISOs (unless such ISOs are disposed of in a disqualifying disposition).[3] Further, if the former employee was one of the five named employees whose compensation falls under Section 162(m) of the Code, the company will need to double-check that all accelerated options are "performance-based options" that continue to fall outside the "$1 million cap" rule in order to preserve any available tax deduction.[4] Note also that in the event the acceleration and severance is part of a change of control package, both the company and the former employee must be alert to potential golden parachute issues under Sections 280G and 4999 of the Code as well.[5]

17.1.6 Inadvertent ERISA Severance Plans

It is important to make sure that any severance-based acceleration is limited to key employees on a case-by-case basis. If too many optionees receive acceleration on termination, and if such acceleration becomes known to employees in general, there may be an argument that acceleration is a severance benefit of the company for purposes of the Employee Retirement Income Security Act of 1974 (ERISA).

17.1.7 Related Change-in-Status Issues

As noted above, FAS 123(R) applies to changes in status from employee to consultant. Issues also arise when full-time employees become part-time employees. Is it permissible to adjust options to reduce vesting in accordance with the number of hours worked? Although few plans address this concern directly, the right answer is that changes in vesting for reduced hours should follow company policy. To avoid allegations that such adjustments unilaterally take away benefits from optionees, companies should amend their plans to refer to such policies (and ensure that the company actually adopts them!).

Another question that may arise is whether a change in status from employee to consultant will relieve the company of its withholding obligation on an option exercised by a former employee. If the former employee is granted a new option as a consultant at the time of the change, it is possible that there would be an argument that his services as an employee were unrelated to stock compensation earned under the consulting agreement. However, as a general rule if the terms of the option (for example, pricing or vesting) could only have been derived as a result of the employment relationship, the employer should assume that withholding will be required. Treas. Reg. § 31.3401(a)-

1(a)(5) specifically provides that remuneration for services, unless such remuneration is specifically excepted by statute, constitutes wages *even though at the time paid the relationship of employer and employee no longer exists* between the person in whose employ the services are performed and the individual who performed them. As a general rule, payroll tax obligations will also apply with respect to any payments that would have been paid if the former employee had remained employed. If the consulting agreement is really a form of severance (i.e., no real services are expected), the answer is even clearer, as there is extensive IRS authority indicating that severance payments are subject to withholding.[6]

17.1.8 Participating in a 423 Plan After Termination

As discussed in chapter 4, participants in a 423 plan must, at all times during the period beginning with the offering date and ending on the day three months before the exercise date, be employees of the sponsoring corporation (or its parent or subsidiary). Nonemployees are not eligible to participate in a 423 plan.

In theory, an employee who terminates employment less than three months before the end of an exercise period could be allowed to remain in the plan through the next exercise date. However, there are serious risks to this alternative. First, if the post-termination period is actually longer than three months, the offering period may be disqualified for all participants because of the participation of a nonemployee. Second, in order to comply with the "equal rights and benefits" requirements of Section 423, the right to exercise post-termination would need to be extended to all participants and could not be awarded on a case-by-case basis (as, for example, with a discretionary stock option). Failure to offer a benefit on a nondiscriminatory basis may also result in disqualification of the offering period or even the entire plan.

For obvious reasons, most Section 423 plans are designed to automatically withdraw former employees from participation on the date they terminate employment.

17.2 Forfeiture Clauses: A Note of Caution to Companies That Do Business in California

In recent years, certain commentators have aggressively argued that employers should include forfeiture provisions in their stock option grants as a method of ensuring that former employees refrain from competition during a post-termination period.[7] Forfeiture clauses have been used successfully by large companies (most notably IBM) to force former employees to disgorge option profits in the event a noncompete is violated.[8] Whether or not such clauses are advisable, they are clearly enforceable in most states.

Companies that employ California residents, however, need to be aware that it is generally illegal in California to require an employee to agree to a post-employment restraint on trade.[9] Although in *IBM v. Bajorek* the Ninth Circuit Court of Appeals upheld IBM's forfeiture clause as applied to a California resident, many California lawyers believe that the federal panel substantially misinterpreted California law in coming to its decision. The facts of the case are that the former employee, Dr. Bajorek, signed a boilerplate employment agreement with IBM that included (1) a forfeiture provision providing for disgorgement of any profits made on the exercise of options if Bajorek joined a competitor within six months of leaving IBM, and (2) a choice-of-law provision stipulating that New York law would apply in interpreting the agreement. Dr. Bajorek worked and lived entirely in California. Before terminating employment with IBM, he exercised his vested options and realized a spread of approximately $900,000. After leaving, he joined a company that IBM considered to be a competitor. IBM sued Bajorek for breach of contract and lost at the district court level. The U.S. District Court found in favor of Bajorek, holding that the IBM noncompete provision violated California's strong public policies against restraint of trade (and in favor of protecting employee wages). On appeal, a panel of the Ninth Circuit reversed and remanded for judgment under New York law, which has no such protective policies.[10]

A careful reading of the decision reveals that the Ninth Circuit made at least two serious errors. First, it ignored Bajorek's argument that the governing law provision was non-negotiable boilerplate and assumed that he willingly agreed to subject himself to New York law.[11] More importantly for our purposes, the Ninth Circuit completely misunderstood the nature of the amounts realized on exercise of the stock option. In his strangely reasoned opinion, Judge Andrew J. Kleinfeld, writing for the panel, made the following observation:

> The [California Labor Law] statute does not apply because its words read literally and in light of its purposes do not apply—stock options are not "wages." Wages are defined by the statute as "all amounts for labor performed by employees of every description, whether the amount is fixed or ascertained by the standard of time, task, piece, commission basis or another method of calculation." Stock options are not "amounts." They are not money at all. They are contractual rights to buy shares of stock. The purposes of … protecting employees' reliance interests in their expected wages do not apply to stock options.[12]

From there, the opinion goes on to state that the options cannot be treated as wages because "the value that Dr. Bajorek obtained from them depended largely on the vagaries of the stock market valuations on those dates." Because the ultimate value of the option is not fixed at time of grant, the employee may not claim that he has earned it. Despite the huge weight of tax, accounting, securities, and employment law to the contrary on this issue, Judge Kleinfeld cited no authorities for his conclusion that the proceeds from Bajorek's fully vested options were not wages protected by the law.

Since *IBM v. Bajorek*, California state courts have expressed disapproval of the Ninth Circuit's analysis of the California policy and statutory provision at issue. In *Walia v. Aetna*,[13] the First District Court of Appeal for California was presented with a challenge to a noncompete clause similar in scope to that in *Bajorek*. In finding for the employee, the court rejected Aetna's argument that the reasoning in *Bajorek* now authorizes the use of broad noncompete clauses in California. Instead, the opinion specifically states that *"IBM, in fact, is* contrary to California law because it is contradicted by [previous California Supreme Court cases]" (emphasis in original). The conflict between *Walia* and *Bajorek* highlights an ongoing "grey area" with respect to the status of option forfeitures under California employment law.

At first glance, forfeiture clauses may provide some level of comfort (and even a sense of justice) to companies that wish to send a message to employees that noncompetes are serious business. However, in the opinion of this writer, such clauses are ill-advised, particularly for California employees. Although stock options are now used to enhance compensation throughout the country, they have a particularly strong presence and visibility in California's Silicon Valley. In the competitive technology community, equity compensation is viewed by employees as a necessary component of the overall salary package. Employees historically view the standard vesting restrictions as a necessary evil to equate equity compensation to cash compensation: e.g., payment for services rendered. Forfeiture clauses circumvent this reasoning. Even if legally enforceable, such clauses are likely to undermine an employer's ability to recruit and retain top talent in the current job market. Given the suspect reasoning of the *Bajorek* opinion, reliance on this case in California as support for stock option forfeiture clauses is a risky proposition. Moreover, this problem will plague any employer that seeks candidates from the highly mobile talent pool—both inside and outside of California.

There are many lawful ways to enforce noncompetition clauses other than to require forfeiture of already-earned income. For example, companies routinely include specific, narrowly drawn noncompete/nonsolicitation provisions in employee confidentiality agreements. The California courts will, in fact, routinely uphold such provisions when they are based upon protection of trade secrets and not simply upon a desire to restrict post-termination competition. Severance and/or post-termination consulting agreements may also stipulate noncompete requirements in exchange for additional options or payments. Such techniques have the advantage of achieving their goal while respecting previous service rendered by the employee.

Notes

1. For just a few recent examples of situations giving rise to litigation, see, e.g., *Braun v. CMGI*, 64 Fed. Appx. 301(2d Cir. 2003) (oral promises to grant options); *Oracle Corp. v. Falotti*, 187 F. Supp. 2d 1184 (N.D. Cal 2001), *aff'd* 319 F.3d 1106 (9th Cir. 2003), *cert. den.* 72 USLW 3240 (2003) (termination

before vesting); *Alexander v. Codemasters Group Ltd.*, 104 Cal App. 4th 129 (2002) (oral promise regarding vesting); *Scully v. US Watts*, Inc., 238 F.3d 497 (3d Cir. 2001) (post-termination exercise); *Scribner v. Worldcom, Inc.* 249 F.3d 902 (9th Cir. 2001) (exercise post-sale of company); *Harrison v. Netcentric Corp*, 433 Mass. 465 (2001) (unvested options); *Richards v. Jain*, 168 F. Supp. 2d 1195 (W.D. Wash. 2001) (oral promises to grant options). Additional cases can be found in chapter 12.

2. Prop. Treas. Reg. § 1.409A-1(b)(9). See chapter 11 for a brief summary of Section 409A.

3. In order to take the deduction, the employer will be required to withhold on the former employee's exercise. Treas. Reg. § 1.83-6. See section 9.1 of chapter 9; Exhibit 9-1.

4. See section 9.5 of chapter 9.

5. See section 9.6 of chapter 9.

6. See generally Sections 3121(a)(13)(FICA); 3306(b)(10)(FUTA). See also Rev. Rul. 90-72, 1990-2 C.B. 211 (lump-sum payments for involuntary separation made under employer plan do not qualify as supplemental unemployment benefits and were "wages" for purposes of FICA, FUTA, and federal withholding income tax); Rev. Rul. 74- 252, 1974-1 C.B. 287 (involuntary separation from service payments were in the nature of dismissal payments and were "wages" for purposes of FICA, FUTA, and income tax withholding); Rev. Rul. 73-166, 1973-1 C.B. 411 (lost pay to striking employee not re-employed after settlement of strike were dismissal payments subject to FICA, FUTA, and income tax withholding); Rev. Rul. 72-572, 1972-2 C.B. 535 (payment made in settlement of a discrimination claim brought by employee whose services were involuntarily terminated constituted "wages" for purposes of FICA, FUTA, and income tax withholding); Rev. Rul. 71-408, 1971-2 C.B. 340 (dismissal payments made to employees whose services were terminated were "wages" for purposes of FICA, FUTA, and federal income tax withholding).

7. For an example of this argument, see the *Corporate Counsel*, September-October 1999.

8. See *IBM v. Martson*, 37 F. Supp. 2d 613 (S.D.N.Y. 1999); *IBM v. Bajorek*, 191 F.3d 1033 (9th Cir. 1999). The California decision was by a panel of the Ninth Circuit.

9. California Business and Professions Code § 16600.

10. For purposes of this discussion, it is not necessary to analyze California Business and Professions Code § 16600, which was the central provision at issue and governs restraint of trade in California. However, in this author's

opinion, the Ninth Circuit's discussion of what constitutes a competitor for these purposes is surprisingly glib.

11. As any employee (or lawyer) who has attempted to negotiate with IBM knows, no ordinary individual has bargaining power to change the IBM agreement. The very fact that California employees were required to sign away their state labor protections in order to work for IBM in California should indicate that they had no say in the matter. In fact, many employment lawyers would counsel an employee confronted with such boilerplate that regardless of the contract, no California court would permit a California employee to be subjected to the less protective employment laws of another state in which they neither resided nor worked.

12. *Bajorek,* 191 F.3d at 1039.

13. 93 Cal. App. 4th 1213 (Cal. Ct. App. 2001). The opinion was certified for partial publication only so its precedental value is not clear. However, *Walia* clearly shows us the thinking of the California courts on this issue.

CHAPTER 18

Using an Independent Compensation Committee to Validate Equity Compensation

Contents

As discussed throughout this book, with the passage of the Sarbanes-Oxley Act of 2002, Congress forcefully expressed its intent to hold public company directors to the highest standards of independence in fulfilling their oversight obligations, including obligations with respect to executive compensation. Although the act does not specifically require compensation committees to retain outside advisors (as it does audit committees), its legislative history and general tenor suggest that the best way for directors to demonstrate their independence from management will be to retain outside experts when reviewing compensation proposals and policies. Moreover, while the act does not apply to private companies, directors at any privately held company with aspirations to go public or engage in high-profile transactions should be scrupulous in their approach to independent decision-making.

18.1 Establishing the Compensation Committee's Independence

Experts believe that conflicts of interest at the board level influenced the executive compensation debacles in the early years of the century. Although equity compensation has come under particular fire, commentators agree that stock options and awards are not in and of themselves evil. It is the method by which such awards were granted that led to their (perceived) widespread abuse. Thus, the key to preserving independence is to establish a process that includes diligence, analysis, and conflict avoidance. Shareholders must be satisfied that the board has carefully reviewed any compensation proposals before accepting (or rejecting) them; even the appearance of a "rubber stamp" could trigger complaints and litigation.

One particularly sensitive area is equity compensation in general. In recent years, both public and privately held companies have reviewed their policies on granting options, considering how to amend or limit stock option plans, working with alternative forms of compensation (both equity and performance-based), and devising creative strategies for restricted stock and other vehicles. Once management has prepared a proposal for equity compensation at any level, the compensation committee must be prepared to do its own in-depth study before making its recommendation: what are the legal implications of the proposal? The accounting issues? Where do the shareholders stand? What are comparable companies proposing? The committee may need to engage both legal and compensation experts to guide it in decision-making for these purposes. The committee chair may also need to be prepared to discuss the committee's recommendations at a shareholder meeting and to field questions from the shareholders on the committee's decision-making process and result.

Another area requiring extreme care is individual executive compensation. Compensation committees cannot be too careful when it comes to reviewing specific bonus packages, incentive compensation, relocation awards, deferred compensation, and similar perks. Personal loans to top executives are, of course, no longer permissible under the act. However, boards may begin to see proposals for increased cash compensation or fringe benefits in place of proposals for favorable loan packages. Again, the compensation committee should neither approve nor reject these proposals out of hand. Instead, careful analysis will be the rule. What is the rationale for the package? Who is making the proposal and why? Is there significant relationship to performance? What are the tax and securities law implications? Are executives within the company compensated rationally when compared to one another ("internal pay equity")? How will the shareholders react to disclosure? What form should the disclosure of perks take in the proxy statement?

In 2003, the (privately held) New York Stock Exchange fired Richard Grasso, its CEO, in response to a wave of highly publicized shareholder concern over what was perceived to be an excessive compensation package. The package was approved by a committee that, while "independent," was largely comprised of representatives of member companies of the exchange—i.e., companies that would be profoundly affected by the CEO's regulatory decisions. Much of the published criticism was leveled not at Mr. Grasso, but at the independence (or lack thereof) of the company's compensation committee.[1]

18.2 Best Practices for Compensation Committees

Many observers and stakeholders have weighed in on best practices for board compensation committees after the Sarbanes-Oxley Act. This is truly an evolving area of governance. The most comprehensive early response to the issues was published by The Conference Board Commission on Public Trust and Private Enterprise in its September 17, 2002, report *"Executive Compensation: Principles, Recommendations and Specific Best Practice Suggestions."*[2] In its introduction to the report, the commission observed that: (1) some issues cannot be fully addressed by regulation and legislation, (2) there is a need for corporations to change their own governance practices, and (3) boards of directors must "step up to the problem" on both a corporate governance and personal responsibility level.

After noting the political and social context of current scrutiny, the commission made a series of suggestions regarding the compensation committee and its responsibilities, suggesting that the committee should:

- *Be composed of only independent members* ("directors free of any relationships with the company . . . and its management"), with a strong committee chair who actively takes a lead role and "ownership" of the committee's activities;

- *At its own discretion, retain outside consultants* who advise it, and provide that such consultants report solely and directly to the committee (and not to corporate management);

- *Vigorously exercise continuous oversight* regarding all matters of executive compensation policy, holding meetings as appropriate and responding directly to the shareholders regarding the same;

- *Be actively engaged in reviewing and approving all equity and other incentive programs, perks, and employment and employment-related agreements with senior management* (including senior management of subsidiaries, special purpose entities, and affiliates); and

- *Exercise independent judgment* in determining proper levels and types of compensation to be paid by the company, taking into account both industry comparables and past company practices, but not necessarily basing all decisions upon those factors.

Another far-reaching and interesting review of compensation committee responsibilities (including guidelines for executive compensation assessment) can be found in the lengthy report issued in August 2003 by Richard Breeden, former SEC chairman and court-appointed monitor charged with investigating corporate practices at WorldCom (now MCI) in response to the SEC's fraud complaint of 2002 (the "Breeden Report").[3]

The Breeden Report, which includes 10 sections and no less than 78 recommendations, takes a hard-line approach to governance issues, including those related to compensation committee practices. The recommendations reflect the overwhelming extent of the abuse at

WorldCom and most are far too harsh to merit wholesale adoption by companies other than MCI; for example, burdensome shareholder approvals are required for many day-to-day board and management activities that (in most companies) should clearly be left to the discretion of the directors. However, notwithstanding the severity of the recommendations, the in-depth analysis contained in the report has played a significant role to date in the national debate over what constitutes adequate corporate governance procedures.[4]

Since the publication of the Breeden Report, governance advisors have focused on developing practical approaches to resolving the issues raised by Congress and the commentators. In particular, some professionals have promoted the use of "tally sheets" to provide complete information on executive compensation packages prior to decision-making by compensation committees. We will undoubtedly see more creative thinking about compensation committee best practices as consulting firms devote time and attention to developing opportunities for advising in this field.[5]

18.3 Applying the Principles to Compensation Committee Review

In discussing the "breakdown of public trust which grew out of the scandals at Enron, WorldCom and other companies," the Conference Board went so far as to lay some of the blame on "professional advisors of companies, such as public auditors, compensation consultants, and law firms … [that] failed to provide truly independent advice and professional judgment as they came to view management as the 'client' instead of the corporation." In other words, independent "outside" advice must truly come from outside—it cannot come from the company's general corporate counsel or compensation consultants.

Not every compensation decision will require the committee to retain outside experts, but the more far-reaching the issue, the greater the need for independent advice. The kind of advice needed will vary with the proposal at hand. Quantitative surveys, competitive industry analyses, and current compensation practices are generally the domain of the consultant. Proposal and document review, legal analysis, and governance issues fall within the domain of legal counsel. Although case-by-case advice may be useful for specific problems, board committees will be best served by retaining experts on an ongoing basis, so that they may participate in meetings and help frame the issues as they arise. The relationship with outside advisors, like all other aspects of the process, needs to be carefully considered and resolved by the committee before conflicts arise.

18.4 Specific Guidelines

Both form and substance are at issue when formulating guidelines for any compensation committee. The committee's actions must both *be independent* and *appear independent*. Every company's needs are different, but generally the compensation committee should:

- Meet regularly at meetings called by the committee's chairman (i.e., not just when the regular board meets);

- Require advance notice of all management proposals regarding compensation and engage management in a substantive discussion of each proposal;

- Retain outside advisors to provide context and counsel to the committee on management proposals;

- Carefully document meetings and decisions in minutes and resolutions; and

- Use the annual compensation committee report to fully describe independent actions taken during the year.

The best recommendation is for the board to expressly adopt these guidelines as part of a compensation committee charter.[6] A written charter will serve the dual purposes of giving concrete guidance to the committee and demonstrating the board's good governance practice for the stockholders. Given the continuing attention to compensation by stockholders and their advisors, the board can only benefit from paying attention to these issues and responding transparently and actively to resolve them.[7]

Notes

1. See, e.g., K. Eichenwald, "In String of Corporate Troubles, Critics Focus on Boards' Failings," *New York Times*, September 21, 2003.

2. The commission's report (which can be downloaded from The Conference Board's Web site at *www.conference-board.org/knowledge/governCommission.cfm*) sets out six principles related to executive compensation, including various controversial suggestions on equity and performance compensation. "The Compensation Committee's Responsibilities" is Principle 1.

3. The Breeden Report (formally titled "Restoring Trust: Report on Corporate Governance for the Future of MCI, Inc.) can be downloaded in its entirety from *news.findlaw.com/usatoday/docs/worldcom/corpgov82603rpt.pdf*. As a condition of the settlement and emergence from bankruptcy, MCI was required to adopt all of the recommendations made in the report (or obtain a court exemption from adoption).

4. Leading the opposition to the Breeden Report is Martin Lipton of New York's Wachtell Lipton law firm, who published his own memorandum, "Restoring Trust or Losing Perspective" (August 27, 2003). The Lipton Memo (downloadable at *www.thecorporatelibrary.com/special/lipton/lipton_082803.pdf*) offers a scathing critique of the Breeden Report, calling it a "wanton piling on" of "counterproductive" restrictions and rules.

5. See, e.g., "Fred Cook Speaks to Directors About Executive Compensation," (June 21, 2005), available at *www.fwcook.com*. Interestingly, in November 2005 ISS announced that it would recommend withholding votes for directors who serve on compensation committees in companies that exhibit "poor" compensation practices. Further, while not recommending "withhold" votes for failure to use a tally sheet, ISS has indicated that it believes companies should use—and disclose—tally sheets when setting compensation for their CEOs. See "ISS 2005 U.S. Policy Update: Board, Compensation," available at *www.issproxy.com*.

6. Many companies, both public and private, have already taken this route. In addition, under the new stock exchange governance rules (approved by the SEC in August 2003), NYSE companies will be required to have a compensation committee charter under the proposed new NYSE governance rules.

7. See note 5 above.

Appendixes

Designing a Broad-Based Stock Option Plan

Corey Rosen

Corey Rosen is the executive director of the National Center for Employee Ownership (NCEO). He received his Ph.D. from Cornell University in political science in 1973, taught government at Ripon College until 1976, and then served as a Senate staff member until 1981, when he cofounded the NCEO. Mr. Rosen has authored or coauthored several books and written more than 100 articles on various aspects of employee ownership for a variety of professional, academic, and trade publications. He has lectured on the subject across the U.S. and abroad.

Many companies seeking to provide broad-based equity compensation to employees are attracted to stock options because within the applicable legal limitations, companies still have considerable discretion as to how to operate their plans. This advantage, however, means that designing these plans can be much more complex than, for instance, designing an employee stock ownership plan (ESOP), where decisions about many issues, such as eligibility and vesting, must occur within a narrow band of requirements. While stock option companies can look to surveys and peers for ideas on how similar companies set up their plans, each company needs to devise a plan that is adapted to its own particular circumstances. This chapter lays out the principal areas where decisions need to be made, suggesting some considerations about how to think about making them. Because every situation is so different, however, it does not attempt to provide any universal guidelines but rather is a checklist of things to consider.

How Much to Share

The first decision is how much ownership to share. This issue will differ for closely held companies and public companies, so considerations for each kind of company are discussed separately.

Closely Held Companies

The most typical way a decision is made about how much ownership to share in a closely held company is for the current owner or owners to set aside an amount of stock that is within the maximum dilution level with which they are comfortable. This approach can create problems, however.

Typically, once this number is set, a large portion of those shares is either optioned immediately to existing employees or allocated to employees over a certain number of years. The problem with this strategy is that if the company grows faster than anticipated, there are no or relatively few shares left to give to new employees. That can be a severe problem in attracting and retaining good people. It can also create two classes of employees, some with large option grants and some without them, within the company. Moreover, this model often does not create an explicit link between employee effort and the rewards of ownership.

A second approach focuses on what percentage of compensation in the form of options is necessary to attract, retain, and motivate people. While there is no "bright line" dividing point, studies of option and other ownership plans indicate that the median point for the value of ownership to employees is about 1.5 times one year's pay (in real dollars) at the end of 10 years of work and four times at the end of 20 years (these numbers are in real dollars and reflect the actual data from employee ownership companies). Based on an NCEO survey conducted in 2000, typical stock option plans are making annual grants with a face value of the option equal to about 10% to 20% of pay. In other words, if an employee makes $40,000, he or she would get options to buy $4,000 to $8,000 of stock annually. These numbers, of course, will vary considerably from company to company, often depending on the company's competitive labor market conditions, its expectations about growth, its corporate culture, and how well it is doing financially.

Rather than thinking about "how much" in terms of a total percentage of company shares or total compensation, it might make sense to use a more dynamic model based on performance. In this approach, the issue for existing owners is not "what percentage of the company do we own," but "how much is what we own worth?" Owners in this model would rather own 10% of a $10 million company than 90% of a $1 million company. Robert Beyster, retired CEO and founder of Science Applications International Corporation (SAIC), for instance, diluted his ownership to less than 10% in the first few years of the company's existence, and to less than 2% today, but the company he heads now employs more than 40,000 people and, in 2006, plans one of the largest IPOs ever. Beyster believes that by continually sharing ownership with employees, the company grew much faster than it could have otherwise.

This notion can be made into an explicit plan by telling employees that if the company meets or exceeds certain targets, they will get a percentage of the incremental value created by that performance in the form of options. If the company exceeds its goals, then, by definition, sharing part of the surplus value leaves both the employees and the existing owners better off than they would have been. The targets can be anything—sales, profits, market penetration, and so on—but perhaps the most useful way to create a target is to decide on a "critical number," the particular measurement that most drives the company. In a manufacturing company, it might be output; in an engineering company, it might be billable hours as a percentage of total hours worked. Managers almost always have these critical numbers in their heads. In the option model proposed here, this number is shared with employees as the goal whose achievement will target an option reward. Deciding how much of the increment to share can then be based on an assessment of what would be motivating to employees, an analysis along the same lines as the percentage of payroll calculations above. For instance, management might set a realistic goal that, if achieved, would provide a level of options consistent with the assumptions used in the percentage of compensation model. Unlike the pure compensation approach, however, what employees actually get could be higher or lower depending on whether performance falls above or below the goal.

Of course, this model is subject to some risk—indeed, every model is. For instance, if things go very well, a company might end up giving out a lot of options; then if things go poorly, new employees will see no ownership. But a fixed approach (x% of outstanding shares per year, up to x% of total shares available overall, or the gradual division of shares up to a maximum percentage, for instance) also has risks associated with unexpected growth or decline. The benefit of the model proposed here is that the risks are at least tied to specific measures of performance and the amount provided adjusts with the success or difficulties of the company.

This model will not work on its own for every company, however. In some labor markets, it may be necessary to *always* provide a certain amount of ownership, at least to some employees. Data on industry practices can be obtained from stock option-specific surveys, such as the NCEO's *Current Practices in Stock Option Plan Design*, as well as a number of general compensation analyses available for a fee (the Internet has a number of these sites that compare compensation). These issues apply mostly to more highly compensated employees, however. For the broader sector of the work force, options may be a benefit either never expected at all or, if they are, expectations about a specific level of rewards will usually not be so defined.

Publicly Traded Companies

Publicly traded companies face many of the same design issues as their closely held counterparts and may want to use some of the same decision guidelines. There are some significant differences in their investor and regulatory market environments, however, that can affect these decisions.

First, investors may object to "overhang" levels they view as excessively dilutive to outstanding shares. For broad-based plans, the NCEO's 2000 stock options survey discussed in *Current Practices in Stock Option Plan Design* found that the average overhang (meaning the total number of shares represented by outstanding, unexercised stock options plus the total shares available for grant divided by the total number of common shares outstanding) was 19.7%; this average was relatively consistent across categories of respondents. These percentages include options available to management and non-management groups; in general, about half the value of the options goes to management. Investors and stock market analysts seem less concerned about dilution resulting from options for rank-and-file employees than they do for dilution from management employees, but, ultimately, it is the total number that matters most. The tolerance for dilution will vary from industry to industry and company to company, depending on such factors as the investors' perceptions of what is necessary to compete in the labor market, how well the stock has performed, whether the company will issue new shares to satisfy the option exercises or will buy back existing shares (thus offsetting the dilution factor), and what impact the outstanding options will have on the company's financials. In any event, a public company will not have the same flexibility that a closely held company has. Robert Beyster could dilute his ownership dramatically, but if his company had been public, providing the amount of ownership he did to employees would almost certainly have resulted in shareholder desertion, lawsuits, or both.

A second consideration is the growth prospects of public companies. Because they are usually at a more mature stage of their growth cycle, public companies will have more modest expectations about how large a component of compensation options will play than will, for instance, a high-tech startup. Of course, the risk that the options will have no value is lower as well. Because of this risk/reward factor, public companies can usually afford to provide a smaller percentage of their total equity to employees while, on a risk-adjusted basis, providing comparable value. Of course, these issues will vary from company to company.

Finally, because a public company is public, it does not have to worry about issuing options to so many employees that it becomes a de facto public company, a consideration that might cause it to limit the number of option holders it would want to include.

What Kind of Options?

Most broad-based stock option plans use either incentive stock options (ISOs) or nonqualified options (NSOs), which are discussed in detail in the main part of this book.

Stock option plans may provide for only NSOs, only ISOs, or some of both. Most broad-based option plans provide NSOs for rank-and-file employees because few of these employees will be able or want to meet the buy-and-hold conditions of the ISO (most will want to use a form of cashless exercise, as described below, that allows them just to get the spread on the options without having to come up with cash to buy them). Many of those who do want to hold onto the shares, moreover, will not get a large benefit from being able to pay capital gains taxes rather than ordinary income tax rates. Because the employees will not use the benefits of an ISO anyway, companies reason they might as well get the tax benefit of an NSO.

On the other hand, many plans aimed at highly paid employees are ISOs because these employees can greatly benefit from capital gains treatment, and they may demand such options to come to work for or stay with a company.

Some people have argued that companies should structure their plans as ISOs for all employees regardless. Their argument is that if an employee fails to meet the ISO requirements, the tax treatment for the employee and the company defaults to NSO status. So if employees can use the ISO treatment, they get an advantage. Meanwhile, the company does not have to pay payroll taxes (Social Security and Medicare) or withhold on the spread, regardless of whether the employee gets NSO or ISO treatment. Instead, the spread becomes an item for employees to add into their annual tax returns.

The ISO approach puts an added reporting burden on employers, requires more complex administration by the company ("disqualifying dispositions," i.e., dispositions before the end of the one year/two year holding period required for ISOs, must be tracked), and could put some employees into an estimated income tax situation in which, if they do not anticipate the option spreads they will receive, could end up forcing them to pay tax penalties. Note, however, that ISOs could, under some circumstances, trigger the application of the alternative minimum tax for some highly paid employees.

Labor markets and the company's stage of development also are factors in choosing an ISO or NSO. A startup company, for instance, may not be able to hire the talent it needs without offering an ISO, especially if its cash flow makes higher salaries impractical. At the same time, it might not be worried too much about not having a tax deduction, even some years from now, if it foresees plowing all its profits into growth strategies anyway. An established, large company with substantial tax costs and attentive public shareholders, by contrast, may see NSOs as more practical.

Who Is Eligible and Who Will Actually Get Options?

It is first important to distinguish between theoretical and actual eligibility. Many public companies draft their plans so that everyone or most people are eligible, but state that who actually will get options, or whether any options will be granted to certain employee groups at all, is up to management's discretion. In part, companies draft plans this way to maximize their future flexibility. So a company might want to draft very broad eligibility rules into a plan even though it has no current plans to follow through on this approach. For the purposes of this paper, however, we are focusing on plans that are drafted with eligibility rules that are intended to be used in the near future.

In the past, the answer to the question of who is eligible for options was very simple for most companies: just the "key" people. In some ways, this is still how companies view options; it is just that their definition of "key" has changed. For many companies, everyone is a key person. When the receptionist answers the phone, that person is "the company" to whomever is calling. When the warehouse people fail to ship the right software (designed by all those key technical people), they represent the company to the customers. Moreover, many companies are pushing down more decision making to all levels of the company, asking employees to make business decisions on a regular basis. Management at these companies reasons that if it wants people to think and act like owners, it should make them owners. At the same time, for some companies in some labor markets, it is necessary to provide options at all levels just to attract and retain people.

For companies in these situations, the answer to "who's eligible?" is simple— everyone is. Other companies choose a more complex approach, however. There are several criteria that can be considered in making this decision.

Tenure

At the simplest level, companies can require that people only can get options after they have worked a minimum amount of time, often one year. This assures at least some commitment on the part of the employee to the company.

Full-Time/Part-Time

In the past, it was unusual to provide options to part-time employees. Innovators like Starbucks, however, have provided options to everyone, arguing that many of their part-time people would (or if properly rewarded could) be long-term employees. Changes in both the work force and the nature of some jobs, however, have made part-time workers more an integral and, in some cases, stable part of a company's total employment. Given the high cost of training and recruitment, providing an incentive for part-time people to stay makes sense for them. In making this decision, companies need to consider how important it is to retain part-time people, or whether these employees are more seasonal and short-term and thus very unlikely to stay with the company more than a short time under any circumstances.

When Options Will Be Granted

Options can be granted either according to some kind of merit judgment or on the basis of a universal rule, such as allocating options annually; on the date of hire or promotion; or upon the achievement of an individual, group, or corporate objective. These methods are not mutually exclusive; most companies use a combination of these techniques.

A typical merit-based plan would provide work unit managers (or a single manager in a smaller company) with a number of options that can be granted to employees in the group based on a performance appraisal. That appraisal might come from the manager or from an employee peer group. This approach has the advantages of flexibility and providing employees an incentive to perform, but the discretionary and individually based nature of the plan could cause some employees to see it as unfair and arbitrary. Moreover, unless the performance appraisal standards are set very clearly at the outset, employees won't know exactly what they need to do in order to achieve an option award. To resolve this, companies might set individual performance goals for each option period (that could be a set amount of time such as one or two years, or it could be whatever time is needed to achieve the goals). Setting so many personal goals, however, would be a very time-consuming process, and it could end up making employees focus too much on their personal targets at the expense of working collaboratively.

An alternative to individual merit judgments is to provide that a pool of options will be given to a work team on the achievement of their own goals. If the goals are met, the pool could then be divided equally, by salary, by a consensus of the group, at the discretion of the group leader, or according to some other formula.

At the other end of the spectrum is an automatic formula based on compensation, seniority, promotion, or some other work-related, measurable construct. For instance, a number of larger companies, such as Wendy's, provide all employees meeting basic service requirements with 10% of pay every year in stock options. The argument behind these formulas is that compensation reflects management's judgment of an employee's contribution to the company, and options are simply another form of compensation. Employees are more likely to see these plans as at least being equitable, if not necessarily fair (they may think the underlying compensation distribution is unfair).

Providing options on hiring, with additional grants on promotion or periodic refresher grants (commonly called "reload options"), is another common allocation rule. Linking additional option grants to promotion gives employees an incentive to improve their skills and rewards those people the organization believes are making greater contributions. On the other hand, it can lose the attention of employees who may be very good performers but who are not in jobs that can easily lead to a promotion. It is particularly a problem in very flat organizations in which relatively few people get promoted.

Refresher grants give employees additional options when they exercise some of the options they were previously granted. For instance, if an employee has 1,000 options and exercises 200, then he or she would be given new options on another 200 shares at exercise. The objective here is to maintain a constant level of equity interest in the company. Similarly, refresher options might be granted when the company issues additional shares so that an employee maintains the same percentage of potential ownership as was held before the dilution (this feature would be more common for executive plans). While these automatic additional grants help to keep the employee's equity interest high, shareholders might object to the ongoing dilution.

Finally, some companies provide one-time grants, often with an indication that additional grants might be forthcoming. The NCEO's *Current Practices in Stock Option Plan Design* study found that 14% of the respondents had plans with a single grant. For instance, a company might announce that all employees were receiving options on 100 shares to celebrate a milestone, such as an anniversary or the achievement of a corporate objective; other companies might announce that employees will get options if a certain objective is met. In most of these cases, management announces that it might provide additional grants in the future, but makes no commitment to do so.

The advantage and the disadvantage of a one-time grant is precisely that it does not commit the company to an ongoing program. This provides more management flexibility and may be less objectionable to shareholders, but it also may be seen by employees more as a reward for past behavior or an idiosyncratic occurrence than an expression of a corporate philosophy that ongoing employee ownership is an important part of the corporate culture. A one-time grant also runs the risk that the options will either never have any value or that they will do exceptionally well. Either way can create distorted perceptions should the company provide additional grants in the future. By contrast, regular grants let employees go through a number of ups and downs and thus educate them to have more realistic expectations.

When Will Employees Be Able to Profit from the Options?

There are two issues in deciding when employees will be able to convert their options into cash: vesting and exercise periods. Vesting provides that an employee accrues an increasing right to the options granted based on the number of years worked. The exercise period allows the employee to exercise a stock option for a defined number of years into the future.

Vesting patterns are fairly consistent across companies, with three- to five-year graduated vesting being the most common schedule. A more difficult decision is whether to provide for immediate vesting upon an event, such as going public or sale. This clearly provides a good benefit for employees, but it may make it more difficult to sell a company or take one public, especially if potential buyers perceive that employees will now have fully vested options that, if they can also then be exercised, may be valuable enough so that some essential employees will just walk away.

In public companies, by far the most common exercise period is 10 years. Some exercise periods are shorter, but they are rarely longer. There is nothing magical about 10 years for nonqualified options, but for incentive options, the exercise period cannot exceed 10 years. To simplify plan design, most companies coordinate the exercise periods of their ISOs and NSOs. The more volatile a company's stock, the more important a longer exercise period is so that employees can weather the downturns. Some public companies, however, do not allow employees to exercise their options until a defined event occurs, such as the achievement of a certain stock price or earnings goal. This accomplishes two things. First, it provides an incentive to meet the goal, and second, it reassures investors that option dilution will occur only if the company meets certain targets. Once these targets are met, employees would normally be given a certain amount of time after the event to exercise the options, anywhere from a few months to several years. Alternatively, a company could provide that options can be exercised upon the occurrence of an event or after *x* number of years pass, whichever comes first, and could continue to be exercised for *y* number of years into the future after that.

In closely held companies, allowing exercise only upon sale or going public is a very common approach. If a company allows exercise before then, employees end up owning stock and having a tax obligation if their options are NSOs; if they are ISOs, employees have no tax but are holding shares whose value could decline by the time they actually can sell them. Unless the company can provide a market for the shares (an issue discussed below), this combination may not seem like much of a reward. Consequently, many closely held companies restrict exercise until sale or an initial public offering. This can sound better than it is, however. Few companies actually go public (a few to several hundred per year in strong market years, many fewer in weak years). Finding a buyer is much more likely than doing an IPO, but most closely held companies will not be sold during anyone's foreseeable future. So providing for exercise only on these events should be carefully and realistically considered and other market-making alternatives weighed.

It is also important to consider, as with vesting, that if employees can exercise upon a sale or an IPO, buyers of the stock may not find the company so valuable. A minority of closely held companies are restrict exercise to some time after a sale or an IPO (in a sale situation, this would require the acquiring company to provide options in the new employer).

Finally, the plan design should be specific in its compliance with applicable securities laws and stock exchange rules that can restrict the exercise of options and/or the sale of shares acquired through options by certain employees for a specified period after an IPO.

Providing a Market for the Shares

For publicly traded companies, providing a market for shares obtained through stock option exercises is not an issue, but for employees of closely held companies, it is one of the most important of all design issues. The majority of closely held companies solve the problem by limiting the exercise of options to when the company is sold or goes public. This makes sense for companies that realistically see these alternatives likely to happen in the foreseeable future. Some company leaders who call us, however, assume that they can *only* provide for marketability upon these events because a closely held company, for one reason or another, cannot provide a market itself. These companies at least should be aware of the other alternatives. Moreover, some companies prefer to stay closely held. There are a variety of ways these companies can provide a market.

Purchases by Other Employees

Other employees can purchase the shares directly, although this is not likely to provide enough of a market for all the shares. When an employee purchases shares, the purchase is normally done with after-tax dollars. It can also be subject to securities laws (see the section below for more details). Companies can help employees buy the shares by loaning them the money, although the interest subsidy on loans that are on less than arm's-length terms could involve taxation to the employee. A few large closely held companies even provide their own internal stock markets, creating periodic trading days for the buying and selling of shares. This requires establishing in-house broker dealers and complying with complex securities rules in each state where the company does business.

One way employees can purchase shares with pretax dollars is through their 401(k) plans. Shares acquired through options could then be sold to employees in the 401(k) plan who wanted to purchase them. The plan would have to provide that employees can make this choice, which can add expense and complexity to the plan's administration. These purchases would also be subject to the same securities rules as any plan. (Note that employees cannot hold options themselves in the 401(k) plan; Travelers Corporation tried to do this but ultimately was prevented from doing so by government rulings.)

Company Redemption

For a closely held company, the most practical method in most cases is for the company to buy back the shares, either directly or through an ESOP or 401(k) plan. If the company redeems the shares, the redemption is not a tax-deductible expense. If the company sets up an ESOP, however, it can make tax-deductible cash contributions to the plan (within certain limits), which can then be used to buy back the shares. While sellers to an ESOP that owns 30% or more of a closely held company can normally defer taxation on the gain from the sale by reinvesting in qualified replacement securities, owners who hold their shares as a result of stock options cannot get this benefit. The sale of their shares to the ESOP would be treated in the same way as a sale to any other buyer.

Valuation of the Shares

Companies whose shares are "readily tradable on an established market" get off easy on this issue; the value of their shares is set every day by the market. Closely held companies, however, must determine how they will set a value for the shares subject to options. Until proposed regulations for the deferred compensation provisions of the 2004 American Jobs Creation Act (AJCA) were issued, it appeared that companies could use almost any method of setting a value without much risk of legal or tax problems. But under proposed Treasury regulations issued in 2005, rules for most kinds of equity valuations in closely held companies have become much stiffer. These rules state that stock options and SARs will be treated as deferred compensation—and thus be subject to steep taxes—if issued at less than fair market value. The regulations set out three alternatives for valuations that won't lead to deferred compensation treatment:

1. A valuation using the rules followed for ESOP valuations. These require an independent, annual appraisal to determine what a willing non-strategic buyer would pay a willing seller.

2. A formula valuation that establishes fair market value as part of a nonlapse restriction under Treas. Reg. § 1.83-5 and that is used on a consistent basis for other equity transactions.

3. In companies in their first 10 years, a formula that meets somewhat less rigorous guidelines, but is still applied on a consistent basis and that uses a well-established theory of valuation, not just a "back-of-the-envelope" or "what I heard at a conference" valuation.

Restricted stock is not specifically covered, but the prudent course would be to follow these rules. If the rules are not followed, the compensation could be considered deferred compensation subject to Section 409A of the Code, which was created by the AJCA. Section 409A and its proposed regulations require that any deferrals beyond the vesting date of an award be made not later than the end of the year prior to which the awards vest (so the end of 2008 for an award vesting in 2010, for instance), or, if performance based, six months before. Deferrals are considered to be short-term and thus not subject to 409A if the payout is made no later than 2½ months after the end of the service provider's taxable year or service recipient's taxable year in which the award ceases to be subject to a substantial risk of forfeiture, whichever is later. For first-time grants, the deferral must be made within 30 days in of the award. That takes away a lot of the advantage of most equity compensation programs. If the rules are violated, the tax penalties are significant.

The safest course is to value equity awards at grant and exercise using an independent appraiser. The technicalities of how shares are valued in closely held companies are beyond the scope of this chapter. Suffice it to say that a formal appraisal of a closely held company would first involve an estimate of what a willing buyer would pay a willing seller for the entire enterprise. These estimates are set primarily by looking at comparable companies, discounted earnings or cash flow, and book value. Discounts for the lack of marketability (shares of public companies are easier to sell and therefore worth more) and lack of control (the enterprise value assumes a buyer is purchasing control of a company, which is a valuable additional right not gained from holding shares that constitute a minority interest) are then applied to determine the value of an individual share.

Having a formal appraisal performed is clearly the best way to set a value. Nonetheless, most closely held companies will choose to set a value internally, usually by having the board rely on a formula, such as a multiple of earnings, book value, or some other rule of thumb. That formula, under the new rules, needs to be very carefully set, preferably with professional advice. Companies value stock in-house mostly to avoid the costs of an appraiser (typically $5,000 to $10,000 for this kind of assessment), but if their rule-of-thumb appraisal is off by just a small percentage, they could create at least two problems, aside from the deferred compensation issue. If the appraisal is too high, then when employees exercise the options, they will be getting more value than the shares are really worth. If the shares are valued too low, then the options could be considered deferred compensation for tax purposes and be subject to immediate taxes and penalties. While some might shrug off these problems, saying that one will offset the other, formula-based values can produce a value both too low at grant and too high at exercise if the essentials of the industry move in the right way for this to happen over time. As any appraiser would note, a formula that is appropriate in 2006 will probably not be appropriate a few years later. Moreover, appraisals that are off substantially could lead to tax problems or lawsuits by employees or other shareholders.

Finally, companies need to be careful that they do not grant options at too low a price and then go public. The closer to an IPO underpriced options are issued, the more of a potential problem they become. Because this so-called "cheap stock" can raise tax and securities law issues upon an IPO, companies at the very least should get an independent appraisal about 18 months before an IPO.

How Often Should Options Be Granted?

The stock market turmoil in the early 2000s brought into focus the importance of designing broad-based stock option plans in ways that work under the normal conditions of stock markets, rather than the extraordinary year-after-year growth of the preceding years. Stock options inherently involve risk, but the design of plans can accentuate that risk. Companies that provide one-time grants or grants on the occurrence of an event, such as hiring, promotion, or meeting some corporate target, base most or all of an employee's ownership interest in the company on the price of stock at a single point in time.

This practice accelerates the risk of options both for the employee and the company. Options granted at a high price may never be "in the money" (i.e., at a point where the market value exceeds the option price so that the employee can make a profit); those given at a low price may cost the company more than it ever intended when they are redeemed. Employees who happen to get their chunk of options at a good time end up doing very well, while those who have gotten their grants when the price was not so favorable don't do well at all. Creating an ownership culture of "we're all in this together" can be very difficult in these circumstances.

For many companies, the best way to deal with these potential problems is to provide option grants in smaller amounts but more frequently. This works best for companies using stock options as a compensation strategy. Start-ups whose stock value is close to zero anyway or who use large initial grants to attract people away from other opportunities may find this less appropriate. It also won't work for companies that want simply to make grants of options at the occasional discretion of the company, often on the attainment of some corporate milestone. These companies see options more as a symbolic reward than as ongoing ownership strategy.

Assume a company wants to give an employee options on 600 shares over the next few years of his or her employment. Rather than provide all 600 at once, the company could make grants in 100-share increments over a period of two or three years. Some companies even make grants monthly.

This is easiest to do in public companies where the share price is readily ascertainable and where share prices change continually. In a closely held company, there would be no point in granting options more frequently than the stock is valued. Giving an employee an option grant three times a year when the price per share is determined annually, for example, would give the employee three sets of options all at the same price.

This periodic allocation of options accomplishes a number of goals. First, it "dollar-cost averages" the options. Investors have long used dollar-cost averaging (periodically investing a set amount of money in the market so that fewer shares are bought when a stock price is higher and more shares are bought when it is lower) to smooth out the bumps in investing. If a small percentage of a portfolio is used to buy stock at a price that turns out to be near the investment's peak, not that much will be lost when it falls. Conversely, if shares are sold at what turns out to be a low point, many other shares will remain to take advantage of the higher prices later. The potential for outsized gains is diminished, but so is the possibility of large losses.

In the options context, this strategy works even better because employees usually have several years over which they can exercise their options. If they have been given their options in periodic grants, rather than all at once, the period of time during which they can exercise at least some of their options "in the money" is extended. Unless a company issues options at a historically high price over a long period of time, and they then fall and stay down for a long time, employees will find that (1) they are less likely to have most of their options underwater, and (2) they are more likely to be able to sell options when their share price is favorable.

Finally, this approach gives employees more of a long-term, ongoing stake in the company. If a large grant of options is substantially in the money, employees may be more tempted to cash in and leave than if they have continuing blocks of options remaining to be exercised at any time. They also have a continuing equity interest in the company as long as they work there. With the vesting schedules attached to the repeated grants of options, employees are provided an even longer-term interest in the company's performance. Finally, there will be fewer big winners and losers among employees with otherwise similar jobs.

Frequent grants are not all good news, of course. The more often options are granted, the more complex their administration becomes. Even with the best software, there will be much more data entry, many more forms to file and disseminate, and many more errors that can be made.

Securities Law Issues

The granting of options does not in itself raise federal securities law considerations (although it may raise securities law issues at the state level, as in California, for example), but when employees exercise their options, that is considered an offer to sell and hence is subject to securities laws. This chapter is not intended to provide a primer on the complicated issues involved with state and federal securities laws, but rather to describe briefly the general issues so that plan designs can be created that will not lead to unexpected regulatory burdens.

The two key elements of securities laws are registration and disclosure. Registration means the filing of documents with the state and/or federal securities agencies concerning the employer whose stock is being sold. There are registration procedures for small offerings of stock (under $1 million or $5 million, depending on the procedure) that can be done for relatively small legal fees (as little as $10,000 in some cases), but larger offerings require a lot of complex paperwork and fees often exceed $100,000. Registration requires the filing of audited financial statements and continuing reporting obligations to the federal Securities and Exchange Commission (SEC) and appropriate state agencies.

Disclosure refers to providing information to buyers about what they are getting, similar to, but frequently less detailed than what would be in a prospectus. At times, there are specific state and federal rules about what needs to go in these documents, including objective discussions of risks, the financial condition of the firm, officers' and directors' salaries, and other information. In the absence of requirements for the registration of the securities, disclosure is intended to satisfy the anti-fraud requirements of federal and state laws.

Generally, offers to sell securities (stocks, bonds, etc.) require registration of those securities unless there is a specific exemption. In addition, companies with 500 or more shareholders are considered public firms under federal law and must comply with the reporting requirements of the Securities Exchange Act of 1934 even if they do not have to register under the Securities Act of 1933. There are various exemptions from registration for privately held companies, listed below. Whenever stock is offered for sale, however, the company may still need to provide appropriate financial disclosure to satisfy anti-fraud rules.

Under Rule 701 of the Securities Act of 1933, offers to a company's employees, directors, general partners, trustees, officers, or consultants can be made under a written compensation agreement. The maximum amount that can be sold under Section 701 in a 12-month period cannot exceed the greater of (1) $1 million dollars; (2) 15% of the issuer's total assets; or (3) 15% of the outstanding securities of that class.

These rules, which went into effect on April 7, 1999, are considerably more flexible than prior rules. The offerings must be discrete (not included in any other offer, generally considered to be at least six months from the prior offer).

Another exemption is available under Section 4(2) of the Securities Act of 1933, which allows for exemptions from federal registrations in offerings of stock to a limited number of investors who have access to the same information normally provided in a public offering and who are accredited investors or sophisticated enough both to assess and bear the risks. This exemption has been interpreted in different ways by the courts. Whether it allows such approaches as offering stock to all of a company's "key employees" is unclear.

Another set of exemptions is available under Regulation D, issued by the Securities and Exchange Commission, which provides a number of exemptions for small offerings. The best known of these is Rule 505 and its related Rule 506, which provide an exemption to offerings of up to $5 million to as many as 35 non-accredited investors in any 12-month period. If every investor is sophisticated (Rule 505), however, there is no limit on the amount of the offering. Rule

504 allows offerings up to $500,000 (or $1 million if there is a registration for up to $500,000 with a state securities agency) to as many people as wanted, with no limits of their being sophisticated or accredited.

"Accredited investors" include directors, partners, or executives of the issuing company, anyone with a net worth (including that of their spouses) of over $1 million, and anyone with an income over $200,000 (or whose joint income with a spouse is $300,000) who has made that amount for the preceding two years and is likely to continue to make it. "Sophisticated investors" are people who, on their own or with the aid of a representative such as an accountant, are able to judge the risks, merits, and disadvantages of a particular investment. Finally, offerings that are made only to residents of the state in which the offering is made are exempt if the offeror has its principal office in that state, gets 80% of its gross revenue from business conducted in the state, and has 80% of its assets in the state.

These exemptions from registration are available under federal law. Some states track federal exemptions; some do not. Thirty-nine states have "blue sky laws" (the general name for state securities laws) that comply with the Uniform Securities Act, which is partly based on federal law. Perhaps most important for offerings to employees, however, states that have a specific exemption parallel to the federal Rule 701 exemption (for offerings to employees) are the exception rather than the rule. State registration for such offerings may be needed, therefore, unless other exemptions are met. Some states have limited offering exemptions for sales up to 35 non-accredited investors and an unlimited number of accredited investors. Unless the buyers are sophisticated investors, issuers must believe the offering is suitable for the purchasers in terms of the purchasers' financial condition, including other securities holdings. Note, however, that even if all these exemption requirements are met, some states require companies to pay filing fees to operate their plans.

Public Company Issues

Public companies cannot use Rule 701 for an exemption from securities law filings. Instead, most rely on Form S-8, a simplified registration form that can be used to comply with securities laws in conjunction with an offering of options. Public companies do not have to offer a formal prospectus to potential buyers, as closely held companies would. They are, however, required to provide information to employee stock purchasers about the company and its option plan. The Form S-8 registration statement allows that to be done by reference to already available public documents or the dissemination of the required information.

Public companies must also make sure their plan design complies with trading restrictions that apply to corporate insiders. This requires the filing of various reports and the restriction of some trading activity, among other things. These issues are too technical for adequate discussion here. Public companies should consult with their legal counsel on these matters before designing their plan.

Design Issues Raised by Securities Laws

Because of the expense and complexity of dealing with securities laws, some closely held companies prohibit the exercise of options until the company is sold or goes public, when either the acquirer must deal with these issues or the public offering will make most of them go away. (Note that this discussion does not include, however, a description of special rules that public companies must meet for the exercise of options that are primarily focused on "insiders," a term whose definition would almost always exclude rank-and-file workers.)

Most closely held companies, however, will be able to avoid securities registration requirements at the federal level even with a broad-based option plan; some will have to meet state requirements, but these are generally much less onerous. Anti-fraud disclosure statements will raise cost issues, however, and some companies may not want to divulge the required information. When designing a plan, therefore, these issues need to be considered carefully with qualified counsel to assure that the operation of the plan will not trigger requirements the company does not want to meet.

Methods of Exercising Options

There are a variety of ways employees can exercise their options. These must be specified in the plan's documents if employees are to be able to exercise their options. Some of these methods will work only for public companies, however.

Cash or Promissory Notes

The simplest approach is that the employee simply pays for the exercise of the option in cash. However, simplicity has its cost. If an employee is exercising a substantial amount of options, it could require a large amount of up-front cash that some people may not have. Companies can loan employees the funds for this purpose, but the plan document should spell out the terms under which such loans will occur.

Stock Swaps

If an employee already owns shares in the company, he or she can exchange those shares for the shares to be acquired by the exercise of the option. Some companies provide a "reload" option along with the stock swap. This approach provides that when an employee trades in stock to exercise an option, the employee gets an equivalent value in new options for the shares traded in. Stock swaps are generally useful only for more highly compensated employees who have significant amounts of company stock in their personal accounts; as a means to provide for exercise in a broad-based plan, they are not usually of much value. Another benefit of a stock swap is ability to purchase shares with pretax appreciation in already owned shares.

Same-Day Sale

This approach is intended for public companies. Its mechanics can be a bit complicated, but the concept is simple: an employee exercises options on a given number of shares, then has a broker (one working with the company) resell that number of shares the same day. The employee can pay with cash, but it is more common for the employee to execute a "cashless" exercise. This approach involves a simultaneous option exercise and stock sale, with the sale proceeds used to cover the exercise costs of the option. The broker buys the shares up front and the employee gets the spread between the exercise price, minus any applicable taxes, on the settlement of the trade. The spread could be delivered in shares or cash, although it normally would be cash.

Cashless Exercise in a Closely Held Company

A closely held company could arrange a transaction in which the employee only purchases the shares in the most technical sense. The employee buys the shares and the company immediately repurchases them, giving the employee the cash value of the difference, minus applicable taxes. A variation on this approach would give the employee shares equal to the value of the spread.

Note, however, that any form of exercise in which the employee sells shares sooner than one year after exercise will not qualify for incentive stock option treatment.

Accounting, Corporate, and Communications Issues

The discussion above focuses on matters that need to be addressed in a plan document. In designing a plan, however, it is important to consider a variety of other issues. For instance, the accounting treatment of stock options means they show up as an expense on the company's income statement. Will this cause adverse reactions from other owners? How will the present value of the options be determined for this disclosure? Are there corporate bylaws or other policies that need to be changed, aside from the mandatory shareholder approval requirements for ISOs? Finally, how will the company communicate how options work to employees, and, more importantly, what new roles will employees play as "owners-in-waiting?"

Conclusion

There is no single template for a broad-based stock option plan. Designing a plan that works for a company requires a careful assessment of at least the company's goals, culture, finances, corporate structure, demographics, and labor market situation, as well as consultation with peers and experienced advisors.

Primary Sources

Contents

This book makes use of many primary source materials, some of which are reproduced here for the reader's convenience. Readers are also encouraged to take advantage of the many Web sites that now offer free access to statutes, legislative history, and related authority online. To start your search, go to *www.firstgov.gov* (government materials only) or to any of the following sites:

- IRS Web site: *www.irs.gov*
- IRS Revenue Rulings: *www.taxlinks.com*
- FASB Web site: *www.fasb.org*
- IASB Web site: *www.iasb.org.uk*
- SEC Web site: *www.sec.gov*

Section 83 of the Internal Revenue Code
Property transferred in connection with performance of services

(a) **General rule.** If, in connection with the performance of services, property is transferred to any person other than the person for whom such services are performed, the excess of—

(1) the fair market value of such property (determined without regard to any restriction other than a restriction which by its terms will never lapse) at the first time the rights of the person having the beneficial interest in such property are transferable or are not subject to a substantial risk of forfeiture, whichever occurs earlier, over

(2) the amount (if any) paid for such property,

shall be included in the gross income of the person who performed such services in the first taxable year in which the rights of the person having the beneficial interest in such property are transferable or are not subject to a substantial risk of forfeiture, whichever is applicable. The preceding sentence shall not apply if such person sells or otherwise disposes of such property in an arm's length transaction before his rights in such property become transferable or not subject to a substantial risk of forfeiture.

(b) **Election to include in gross income in year of transfer.**

(1) **In general.** Any person who performs services in connection with which property is transferred to any person may elect to include in his gross income for the taxable year in which such property is transferred, the excess of—

(A) the fair market value of such property at the time of transfer (determined without regard to any restriction other than a restriction which by its terms will never lapse), over

(B) the amount (if any) paid for such property.

If such election is made, subsection (a) shall not apply with respect to the transfer of such property, and if such property is subsequently forfeited, no deduction shall be allowed in respect of such forfeiture.

(2) **Election.** An election under paragraph (1) with respect to any transfer of property shall be made in such manner as the Secretary prescribes and shall be made not later than 30 days after the date of such transfer. Such election may not be revoked except with the consent of the Secretary.

(c) **Special rules.** For purposes of this section—

(1) **Substantial risk of forfeiture.** The rights of a person in property are subject to a substantial risk of forfeiture if such person's rights to full enjoy-

ment of such property are conditioned upon the future performance of substantial services by any individual.

(2) Transferability of property. The rights of a person in property are transferable only if the rights in such property of any transferee are not subject to a substantial risk of forfeiture.

(3) Sales which may give rise to suit under section 16(b) of the Securities Exchange Act of 1934. So long as the sale of property at a profit could subject a person to suit under section 16(b) of the Securities Exchange Act of 1934, such person's rights in such property are—

(A) subject to a substantial risk of forfeiture, and

(B) not transferable.

(d) Certain restrictions which will never lapse.

(1) Valuation In the case of property subject to a restriction which by its terms will never lapse, and which allows the transferee to sell such property only at a price determined under a formula, the price so determined shall be deemed to be the fair market value of the property unless established to the contrary by the Secretary, and the burden of proof shall be on the Secretary with respect to such value.

(2) Cancellation If, in the case of property subject to a restriction which by its terms will never lapse, the restriction is canceled, then, unless the taxpayer establishes—

(A) that such cancellation was not compensatory, and

(B) that the person, if any, who would be allowed a deduction if the cancellation were treated as compensatory, will treat the transaction as not compensatory, as evidenced in such manner as the Secretary shall prescribe by regulations,

the excess of the fair market value of the property (computed without regard to the restrictions) at the time of cancellation over the sum of—

(C) the fair market value of such property (computed by taking the restriction into account) immediately before the cancellation, and

(D) the amount, if any, paid for the cancellation, shall be treated as compensation for the taxable year in which such cancellation occurs.

(e) Applicability of section. This section shall not apply to—

(1) a transaction to which section 421 applies,

(2) a transfer to or from a trust described in section 401(a) or a transfer under an annuity plan which meets the requirements of section 404(a)(2),

(3) the transfer of an option without a readily ascertainable fair market value,

(4) the transfer of property pursuant to the exercise of an option with a readily ascertainable fair market value at the date of grant, or

(5) group-term life insurance to which section 79 applies.

(f) Holding period. In determining the period for which the taxpayer has held property to which subsection (a) applies, there shall be included only the period beginning at the first time his rights in such property are transferable or are not subject to a substantial risk of forfeiture, whichever occurs earlier.

(g) Certain exchanges. If property to which subsection (a) applies is exchanged for property subject to restrictions and conditions substantially similar to those to which the property given in such exchange was subject, and if section 354, 355, 356, or 1036 (or so much of section 1031 as relates to section 1036) applied to such exchange, or if such exchange was pursuant to the exercise of a conversion privilege—

(1) such exchange shall be disregarded for purposes of subsection (a), and

(2) the property received shall be treated as property to which subsection (a) applies.

(h) Deduction by employer. In the case of a transfer of property to which this section applies or a cancellation of a restriction described in subsection (d), there shall be allowed as a deduction under section 162, to the person for whom were performed the services in connection with which such property was transferred, an amount equal to the amount included under subsection (a), (b), or (d)(2) in the gross income of the person who performed such services. Such deduction shall be allowed for the taxable year of such person in which or with which ends the taxable year in which such amount is included in the gross income of the person who performed such services.

Section 162 of the Internal Revenue Code

Trade or Business Expenses
Subsections (a) and (m) only

(a) In general. There shall be allowed as a deduction all the ordinary and necessary expenses paid or incurred during the taxable year in carrying on any trade or business, including-—

(1) a reasonable allowance for salaries or other compensation for personal services actually rendered;

(2) traveling expenses (including amounts expended for meals and lodging other than amounts which are lavish or extravagant under the circumstances) while away from home in the pursuit of a trade or business; and

(3) rentals or other payments required to be made as a condition to the continued use or possession, for purposes of the trade or business, of property to which the taxpayer has not taken or is not taking title or in which he has no equity.

For purposes of the preceding sentence, the place of residence of a Member of Congress (including any Delegate and Resident Commissioner) within the State, congressional district, or possession which he represents in Congress shall be considered his home, but amounts expended by such Members within each taxable year for living expenses shall not be deductible for income tax purposes in excess of $3,000. For purposes of paragraph (2), the taxpayer shall not be treated as being temporarily away from home during any period of employment if such period exceeds 1 year. The preceding sentence shall not apply to any Federal employee during any period for which such employee is certified by the Attorney General (or the designee thereof) as traveling on behalf of the United States in temporary duty status to investigate or prosecute, or provide support services for the investigation or prosecution of, a Federal crime.

* * *

(m) Certain excessive employee remuneration.

(1) **In general.** In the case of any publicly held corporation, no deduction shall be allowed under this chapter for applicable employee remuneration with respect to any covered employee to the extent that the amount of such remuneration for the taxable year with respect to such employee exceeds $1,000,000.

(2) **Publicly held corporation.** For purposes of this subsection, the term "publicly held corporation" means any corporation issuing any class of common equity securities required to be registered under section 12 of the Securities Exchange Act of 1934.

(3) **Covered employee.** For purposes of this subsection, the term "covered employee" means any employee of the taxpayer if—

(A) as of the close of the taxable year, such employee is the chief executive officer of the taxpayer or is an individual acting in such a capacity, or

(B) the total compensation of such employee for the taxable year is required to be reported to shareholders under the Securities Exchange Act of 1934 by reason of such employee being among the 4 highest compensated officers for the taxable year (other than the chief executive officer).

(4) **Applicable employee remuneration.** For purposes of this subsection—

(A) In general. Except as otherwise provided in this paragraph, the term "applicable employee remuneration" means, with respect to any covered employee for any taxable year, the aggregate amount allowable as a deduction under this chapter for such taxable year (determined without regard to this subsection) for remuneration for services performed by such employee (whether or not during the taxable year).

(B) Exception for remuneration payable on commission basis. The term "applicable employee remuneration" shall not include any remuneration payable on a commission basis solely on account of income generated directly by the individual performance of the individual to whom such remuneration is payable.

(C) Other performance-based compensation. The term "applicable employee remuneration" shall not include any remuneration payable solely on account of the attainment of one or more performance goals, but only if—

(i) the performance goals are determined by a compensation committee of the board of directors of the taxpayer which is comprised solely of 2 or more outside directors,

(ii) the material terms under which the remuneration is to be paid, including the performance goals, are disclosed to shareholders and approved by a majority of the vote in a separate shareholder vote before the payment of such remuneration, and

(iii) before any payment of such remuneration, the compensation committee referred to in clause (i) certifies that the performance goals and any other material terms were in fact satisfied.

(D) Exception for existing binding contracts. The term "applicable employee remuneration" shall not include any remuneration payable under a written binding contract which was in effect on February 17, 1993, and which was not modified thereafter in any material respect before such remuneration is paid.

(E) Remuneration. For purposes of this paragraph, the term "remuneration" includes any remuneration (including benefits) in any medium other than cash, but shall not include—

(i) any payment referred to in so much of section 3121(a)(5) as precedes subparagraph (E) thereof, and

(ii) any benefit provided to or on behalf of an employee if at the time such benefit is provided it is reasonable to believe that the employee will be able to exclude such benefit from gross income under this chapter.

For purposes of clause (i), section 3121(a)(5) shall be applied without regard to section 3121(v)(1).

(F) Coordination with disallowed golden parachute payments. The dollar limitation contained in paragraph (1) shall be reduced (but not below zero) by the amount (if any) which would have been included in the applicable employee remuneration of the covered employee for the taxable year but for being disallowed under section 280G.

Section 280G of the Internal Revenue Code

Golden parachute payments

(a) General rule. No deduction shall be allowed under this chapter for any excess parachute payment.

(b) Excess parachute payment. For purposes of this section—

(1) In general. The term "excess parachute payment" means an amount equal to the excess of any parachute payment over the portion of the base amount allocated to such payment.

(2) Parachute payment defined.

(A) In general. The term "parachute payment" means any payment in the nature of compensation to (or for the benefit of) a disqualified individual if—

(i) such payment is contingent on a change—

(I) in the ownership or effective control of the corporation, or

(II) in the ownership of a substantial portion of the assets of the corporation, and

(ii) the aggregate present value of the payments in the nature of compensation to (or for the benefit of) such individual which are contingent on such change equals or exceeds an amount equal to 3 times the base amount.

For purposes of clause (ii), payments not treated as parachute payments under paragraph (4)(A), (5), or (6) shall not be taken into account.

(B) Agreements. The term "parachute payment" shall also include any payment in the nature of compensation to (or for the benefit of) a disqualified individual if such payment is made pursuant to an agreement which violates any generally enforced securities laws or regulations. In any proceeding involving the issue of whether any payment made to a disqualified individual is a parachute payment on account of a violation of any generally enforced securities laws or regulations, the burden of proof with respect to establishing the occurrence of a violation of such a law or regulation shall be upon the Secretary.

(C) Treatment of certain agreements entered into within 1 year before change of ownership. For purposes of subparagraph (A)(i), any payment pursuant to—

> (i) an agreement entered into within 1 year before the change described in subparagraph (A)(i), or
>
> (ii) an amendment made within such 1-year period of a previous agreement,

shall be presumed to be contingent on such change unless the contrary is established by clear and convincing evidence.

(3) Base amount.

> (A) In general. The term "base amount" means the individual's annualized includible compensation for the base period.
>
> (B) Allocation. The portion of the base amount allocated to any parachute payment shall be an amount which bears the same ratio to the base amount as—
>
> > (i) the present value of such payment, bears to
> >
> > (ii) the aggregate present value of all such payments.

(4) Treatment of amounts which taxpayer establishes as reasonable compensation. In the case of any payment described in paragraph (2)(A)—

> (A) the amount treated as a parachute payment shall not include the portion of such payment which the taxpayer establishes by clear and convincing evidence is reasonable compensation for personal services to be rendered on or after the date of the change described in paragraph (2)(A)(i), and
>
> (B) the amount treated as an excess parachute payment shall be reduced by the portion of such payment which the taxpayer establishes by clear and convincing evidence is reasonable compensation for personal services actually rendered before the date of the change described in paragraph (2)(A)(i).

For purposes of subparagraph (B), reasonable compensation for services actually rendered before the date of the change described in paragraph (2)(A)(i) shall be first offset against the base amount.

(5) Exemption for small business corporations, etc.

> (A) In general. Notwithstanding paragraph (2), the term "parachute payment" does not include—

(i) any payment to a disqualified individual with respect to a corporation which (immediately before the change described in paragraph (2)(A)(i)) was a small business corporation (as defined in section 1361(b) but without regard to paragraph (1)(C) thereof), and

(ii) any payment to a disqualified individual with respect to a corporation (other than a corporation described in clause (i)) if—

(I) immediately before the change described in paragraph (2)(A)(i), no stock in such corporation was readily tradeable on an established securities market or otherwise, and

(II) the shareholder approval requirements of subparagraph (B) are met with respect to such payment.

The Secretary may, by regulations, prescribe that the requirements of subclause (I) of clause (ii) are not met where a substantial portion of the assets of any entity consists (directly or indirectly) of stock in such corporation and interests in such other entity are readily tradeable on an established securities market, or otherwise. Stock described in section 1504(a)(4) shall not be taken into account under clause (ii)(I) if the payment does not adversely affect the shareholder's redemption and liquidation rights.

(B) Shareholder approval requirements. The shareholder approval requirements of this subparagraph are met with respect to any payment if—

(i) such payment was approved by a vote of the persons who owned, immediately before the change described in paragraph (2)(A)(i), more than 75 percent of the voting power of all outstanding stock of the corporation, and

(ii) there was adequate disclosure to shareholders of all material facts concerning all payments which (but for this paragraph) would be parachute payments with respect to a disqualified individual.

The regulations prescribed under subsection (e) shall include regulations providing for the application of this subparagraph in the case of shareholders which are not individuals (including the treatment of nonvoting interests in an entity which is a shareholder) and where an entity holds a de minimis amount of stock in the corporation.

(6) Exemption for payments under qualified plans. Notwithstanding paragraph (2), the term "parachute payment" shall not include any payment to or from—

(A) a plan described in section 401(a) which includes a trust exempt from tax under section 501(a),

(B) an annuity plan described in section 403(a),

(C) a simplified employee pension (as defined in section 408(k)), or

(D) a simple retirement account described in section 408(p).

(c) Disqualified individuals. For purposes of this section, the term "disqualified individual" means any individual who is—

(1) an employee, independent contractor, or other person specified in regulations by the Secretary who performs personal services for any corporation, and

(2) is an officer, shareholder, or highly-compensated individual.

For purposes of this section, a personal service corporation (or similar entity) shall be treated as an individual. For purposes of paragraph (2), the term "highly-compensated individual" only includes an individual who is (or would be if the individual were an employee) a member of the group consisting of the highest paid 1 percent of the employees of the corporation or, if less, the highest paid 250 employees of the corporation.

(d) Other definitions and special rules. For purposes of this section—

(1) Annualized includible compensation for base period. The term "annualized includible compensation for the base period" means the average annual compensation which—

(A) was payable by the corporation with respect to which the change in ownership or control described in paragraph (2)(A) of subsection (b) occurs, and

(B) was includible in the gross income of the disqualified individual for taxable years in the base period.

(2) Base period. The term "base period" means the period consisting of the most recent 5 taxable years ending before the date on which the change in ownership or control described in paragraph (2)(A) of subsection (b) occurs (or such portion of such period during which the disqualified individual performed personal services for the corporation).

(3) Property transfers. Any transfer of property—

(A) shall be treated as a payment, and

(B) shall be taken into account as its fair market value.

(4) Present value. Present value shall be determined by using a discount rate equal to 120 percent of the applicable Federal rate (determined under section 1274(d)), compounded semiannually.

(5) Treatment of affiliated groups. Except as otherwise provided in regulations, all members of the same affiliated group (as defined in section 1504, determined without regard to section 1504(b)) shall be treated as 1 corporation for purposes of this section. Any person who is an officer of any member of such group shall be treated as an officer of such 1 corporation.

(e) Regulations. The Secretary shall prescribe such regulations as may be necessary or appropriate to carry out the purposes of this section (including regulations for the application of this section in the case of related corporations and in the case of personal service corporations).

Section 421 of the Internal Revenue Code

General rules [stock options]

(a) Effect of qualifying transfer. If a share of stock is transferred to an individual in a transfer in respect of which the requirements of section 422(a) or 423(a) are met—

(1) no income shall result at the time of the transfer of such share to the individual upon his exercise of the option with respect to such share;

(2) no deduction under section 162 (relating to trade or business expenses) shall be allowable at any time to the employer corporation, a parent or subsidiary corporation of such corporation, or a corporation issuing or assuming a stock option in a transaction to which section 424(a) applies, with respect to the share so transferred; and

(3) no amount other than the price paid under the option shall be considered as received by any of such corporations for the share so transferred.

(b) Effect of disqualifying disposition. If the transfer of a share of stock to an individual pursuant to his exercise of an option would otherwise meet the requirements of section 422(a) or 423(a) except that there is a failure to meet any of the holding period requirements of section 422(a)(1) or 423(a)(1), then any increase in the income of such individual or deduction from the income of his employer corporation for the taxable year in which such exercise occurred attributable to such disposition, shall be treated as an increase in income or a deduction from income in the taxable year of such individual or of such employer corporation in which such disposition occurred. No amount shall be required to be deducted and withheld under chapter 24 with respect to any increase in income attributable to a disposition described in the preceding sentence.

(c) Exercise by estate.

(1) In general. If an option to which this part applies is exercised after the death of the employee by the estate of the decedent, or by a person who acquired the right to exercise such option by bequest or inheritance or by reason of the death of the decedent, the provisions of subsection (a) shall apply to the same extent as if the option had been exercised by the decedent, except that—

(A) the holding period and employment requirements of sections 422(a) and 423(a) shall not apply, and

(B) any transfer by the estate of stock acquired shall be considered a disposition of such stock for purposes of section 423(c).

(2) Deduction for estate tax. If an amount is required to be included under section 423(c) in gross income of the estate of the deceased employee or of a person described in paragraph (1), there shall be allowed to the estate or such person a deduction with respect to the estate tax attributable to the inclusion in the taxable estate of the deceased employee of the net value for estate tax purposes of the option. For this purpose, the deduction shall be determined under section 691(c) as if the option acquired from the deceased employee were an item of gross income in respect of the decedent under section 691 and as if the amount includible in gross income under section 423(c) were an amount included in gross income under section 691 in respect of such item of gross income.

(3) Basis of shares acquired. In the case of a share of stock acquired by the exercise of an option to which paragraph (1) applies—

(A) the basis of such share shall include so much of the basis of the option as is attributable to such share; except that the basis of such share shall be reduced by the excess (if any) of (i) the amount which would have been includible in gross income under section 423(c) if the employee had exercised the option on the date of his death and had held the share acquired pursuant to such exercise at the time of his death, over (ii) the amount which is includible in gross income under such section; and

(B) the last sentence of section 423(c) shall apply only to the extent that the amount includible in gross income under such section exceeds so much of the basis of the option as is attributable to such share.

Section 422 of the Internal Revenue Code

Incentive stock options

(a) In general. Section 421(a) shall apply with respect to the transfer of a share of stock to an individual pursuant to his exercise of an incentive stock option if—

(1) no disposition of such share is made by him within 2 years from the date of the granting of the option nor within 1 year after the transfer of such share to him, and

(2) at all times during the period beginning on the date of the granting of the option and ending on the day 3 months before the date of such exercise, such individual was an employee of either the corporation granting such option, a parent or subsidiary corporation of such corporation, or a corporation or a parent or subsidiary corporation of such corporation issuing or assuming a stock option in a transaction to which section 424(a) applies.

(b) Incentive stock option. For purposes of this part, the term "incentive stock option" means an option granted to an individual for any reason connected with his employment by a corporation, if granted by the employer corporation or its parent or subsidiary corporation, to purchase stock of any of such corporations, but only if—

(1) the option is granted pursuant to a plan which includes the aggregate number of shares which may be issued under options and the employees (or class of employees) eligible to receive options, and which is approved by the stockholders of the granting corporation within 12 months before or after the date such plan is adopted;

(2) such option is granted within 10 years from the date such plan is adopted, or the date such plan is approved by the stockholders, whichever is earlier;

(3) such option by its terms is not exercisable after the expiration of 10 years from the date such option is granted;

(4) the option price is not less than the fair market value of the stock at the time such option is granted;

(5) such option by its terms is not transferable by such individual otherwise than by will or the laws of descent and distribution, and is exercisable, during his lifetime, only by him; and

(6) such individual, at the time the option is granted, does not own stock possessing more than 10 percent of the total combined voting power of all classes of stock of the employer corporation or of its parent or subsidiary corporation.

Such term shall not include any option if (as of the time the option is granted) the terms of such option provide that it will not be treated as an incentive stock option.

(c) Special rules.

(1) **Good faith efforts to value of stock.** If a share of stock is transferred pursuant to the exercise by an individual of an option which would fail to qualify as an incentive stock option under subsection (b) because there was a failure in an attempt, made in good faith, to meet the requirement of subsection (b)(4), the requirement of subsection (b)(4) shall be considered to

have been met. To the extent provided in regulations by the Secretary, a similar rule shall apply for purposes of subsection (d).

(2) Certain disqualifying dispositions where amount realized is less than value at exercise. If—

> (A) an individual who has acquired a share of stock by the exercise of an incentive stock option makes a disposition of such share within either of the periods described in subsection (a)(1), and

> (B) such disposition is a sale or exchange with respect to which a loss (if sustained) would be recognized to such individual,

then the amount which is includible in the gross income of such individual, and the amount which is deductible from the income of his employer corporation, as compensation attributable to the exercise of such option shall not exceed the excess (if any) of the amount realized on such sale or exchange over the adjusted basis of such share.

(3) Certain transfers by insolvent individuals. If an insolvent individual holds a share of stock acquired pursuant to his exercise of an incentive stock option, and if such share is transferred to a trustee, receiver, or other similar fiduciary in any proceeding under title 11 or any other similar insolvency proceeding, neither such transfer, nor any other transfer of such share for the benefit of his creditors in such proceeding, shall constitute a disposition of such share for purposes of subsection (a)(1).

(4) Permissible provisions. An option which meets the requirements of subsection (b) shall be treated as an incentive stock option even if—

> (A) the employee may pay for the stock with stock of the corporation granting the option,

> (B) the employee has a right to receive property at the time of exercise of the option, or

> (C) the option is subject to any condition not inconsistent with the provisions of subsection (b).

Subparagraph (B) shall apply to a transfer of property (other than cash) only if section 83 applies to the property so transferred.

(5) 10-percent shareholder rule. Subsection (b)(6) shall not apply if at the time such option is granted the option price is at least 110 percent of the fair market value of the stock subject to the option and such option by its terms is not exercisable after the expiration of 5 years from the date such option is granted.

(6) Special rule when disabled. For purposes of subsection (a)(2), in the case of an employee who is disabled (within the meaning of section 22(e)(3)), the 3-month period of subsection (a)(2) shall be 1 year.

(7) **Fair market value.** For purposes of this section, the fair market value of stock shall be determined without regard to any restriction other than a restriction which, by its terms, will never lapse.

(d) **$100,000 per year limitation.**

(1) **In general.** To the extent that the aggregate fair market value of stock with respect to which incentive stock options (determined without regard to this subsection) are exercisable for the 1st time by any individual during any calendar year (under all plans of the individual's employer corporation and its parent and subsidiary corporations) exceeds $100,000, such options shall be treated as options which are not incentive stock options.

(2) **Ordering rule.** Paragraph (1) shall be applied by taking options into account in the order in which they were granted.

(3) **Determination of fair market value.** For purposes of paragraph (1), the fair market value of any stock shall be determined as of the time the option with respect to such stock is granted.

Section 423 of the Internal Revenue Code

Employee stock purchase plans

(a) **General rule.** Section 421(a) shall apply with respect to the transfer of a share of stock to an individual pursuant to his exercise of an option granted after December 31, 1963, under an employee stock purchase plan (as defined in subsection (b)) if–

(1) no disposition of such share is made by him within 2 years after the date of the granting of the option nor within 1 year after the transfer of such share to him; and

(2) at all times during the period beginning with the date of the granting of the option and ending on the day 3 months before the date of such exercise, he is an employee of the corporation granting such option, a parent or subsidiary corporation of such corporation, or a corporation or a parent or subsidiary corporation of such corporation issuing or assuming a stock option in a transaction to which section 424(a) applies.

(b) **Employee stock purchase plan.** For purposes of this part, the term "employee stock purchase plan" means a plan which meets the following requirements:

(1) the plan provides that options are to be granted only to employees of the employer corporation or of its parent or subsidiary corporation to purchase stock in any such corporation;

(2) such plan is approved by the stockholders of the granting corporation within 12 months before or after the date such plan is adopted;

(3) under the terms of the plan, no employee can be granted an option if such employee, immediately after the option is granted, owns stock possessing 5 percent or more of the total combined voting power or value of all classes of stock of the employer corporation or of its parent or subsidiary corporation. For purposes of this paragraph, the rules of section 424(d) shall apply in determining the stock ownership of an individual, and stock which the employee may purchase under outstanding options shall be treated as stock owned by the employee;

(4) under the terms of the plan, options are to be granted to all employees of any corporation whose employees are granted any of such options by reason of their employment by such corporation, except that there may be excluded—

(A) employees who have been employed less than 2 years,

(B) employees whose customary employment is 20 hours or less per week,

(C) employees whose customary employment is for not more than 5 months in any calendar year, and

(D) highly compensated employees (within the meaning of section 414(q));

(5) under the terms of the plan, all employees granted such options shall have the same rights and privileges, except that the amount of stock which may be purchased by any employee under such option may bear a uniform relationship to the total compensation, or the basic or regular rate of compensation, of employees, and the plan may provide that no employee may purchase more than a maximum amount of stock fixed under the plan;

(6) under the terms of the plan, the option price is not less than the lesser of—

(A) an amount equal to 85 percent of the fair market value of the stock at the time such option is granted, or

(B) an amount which under the terms of the option may not be less than 85 percent of the fair market value of the stock at the time such option is exercised;

(7) under the terms of the plan, such option cannot be exercised after the expiration of—

(A) 5 years from the date such option is granted if, under the terms of such plan, the option price is to be not less than 85 percent of the fair market value of such stock at the time of the exercise of the option, or

(B) 27 months from the date such option is granted, if the option price is not determinable in the manner described in subparagraph (A)

(8) under the terms of the plan, no employee may be granted an option which permits his rights to purchase stock under all such plans of his employer corporation and its parent and subsidiary corporations to accrue at a rate which exceeds $25,000 of fair market value of such stock (determined at the time such option is granted) for each calendar year in which such option is outstanding at any time. For purposes of this paragraph—

(A) the right to purchase stock under an option accrues when the option (or any portion thereof) first becomes exercisable during the calendar year;

(B) the right to purchase stock under an option accrues at the rate provided in the option, but in no case may such rate exceed $25,000 of fair market value of such stock (determined at the time such option is granted) for any one calendar year; and

(C) a right to purchase stock which has accrued under one option granted pursuant to the plan may not be carried over to any other option; and

(9) under the terms of the plan, such option is not transferable by such individual otherwise than by will or the laws of descent and distribution, and is exercisable, during his lifetime, only by him.

For purposes of paragraphs (3) to (9), inclusive, where additional terms are contained in an offering made under a plan, such additional terms shall, with respect to options exercised under such offering, be treated as a part of the terms of such plan.

(c) Special rule where option price is between 85 percent and 100 percent of value of stock. If the option price of a share of stock acquired by an individual pursuant to a transfer to which subsection (a) applies was less than 100 percent of the fair market value of such share at the time such option was granted, then, in the event of any disposition of such share by him which meets the holding period requirements of subsection (a), or in the event of his death (whenever occurring) while owning such share, there shall be included as compensation (and not as gain upon the sale or exchange of a capital asset) in his gross income, for the taxable year in which falls the date of such disposition or for the taxable year closing with his death, whichever applies, an amount equal to the lesser of—

(1) the excess of the fair market value of the share at the time of such disposition or death over the amount paid for the share under the option, or

(2) the excess of the fair market value of the share at the time the option was granted over the option price.

If the option price is not fixed or determinable at the time the option is granted, then for purposes of this subsection, the option price shall be determined as if the option were exercised at such time. In the case of the disposition of such share by the individual, the basis of the share in his hands at the time of such disposition shall be increased by an amount equal to the amount so includible in his gross income. No amount shall be required to be deducted and withheld under chapter 24 with respect to any increase in income attributable to a disposition described in the preceding sentence.

Section 424 of the Internal Revenue Code
Definitions and special rules [stock options]

(a) Corporate reorganizations, liquidations, etc. For purposes of this part, the term "issuing or assuming a stock option in a transaction to which section 424(a) applies" means a substitution of a new option for the old option, or an assumption of the old option, by an employer corporation, or a parent or subsidiary of such corporation, by reason of a corporate merger, consolidation, acquisition of property or stock, separation, reorganization, or liquidation, if—

> **(1)** the excess of the aggregate fair market value of the shares subject to the option immediately after the substitution or assumption over the aggregate option price of such shares is not more than the excess of the aggregate fair market value of all shares subject to the option immediately before such substitution or assumption over the aggregate option price of such shares, and

> **(2)** the new option or the assumption of the old option does not give the employee additional benefits which he did not have under the old option.

For purposes of this subsection, the parent-subsidiary relationship shall be determined at the time of any such transaction under this subsection.

(b) Acquisition of new stock. For purposes of this part, if stock is received by an individual in a distribution to which section 305, 354, 355, 356, or 1036 (or so much of section 1031 as relates to section 1036) applies, and such distribution was made with respect to stock transferred to him upon his exercise of the option, such stock shall be considered as having been transferred to him on his exercise of such option. A similar rule shall be applied in the case of a series of such distributions.

(c) Disposition.

> **(1) In general.** Except as provided in paragraphs (2), (3), and (4), for purposes of this part, the term "disposition" includes a sale, exchange, gift, or a transfer of legal title, but does not include -

(A) a transfer from a decedent to an estate or a transfer by request or inheritance;

(B) an exchange to which section 354, 355, 356, or 1036 (or so much of section 1031 as relates to section 1036) applies; or

(C) a mere pledge or hypothecation.

(2) Joint tenancy. The acquisition of a share of stock in the name of the employee and another jointly with the right of survivorship or a subsequent transfer of a share of stock into such joint ownership shall not be deemed a disposition, but a termination of such joint tenancy (except to the extent such employee acquires ownership of such stock) shall be treated as a disposition by him occurring at the time such joint tenancy is terminated.

(3) Special rule where incentive stock is acquired through use of other statutory option stock.

(A) Nonrecognition sections not to apply. If—

(i) there is a transfer of statutory option stock in connection with the exercise of any incentive stock option, and

(ii) the applicable holding period requirements (under section 422(a)(1) or 423(a)(1)) are not met before such transfer,

then no section referred to in subparagraph (B) of paragraph (1) shall apply to such transfer.

(B) Statutory option stock. For purpose of subparagraph (A), the term "statutory option stock" means any stock acquired through the exercise of an incentive stock option or an option granted under an employee stock purchase plan.

(4) Transfers between spouses or incident to divorce. In the case of any transfer described in subsection (a) of section 1041—

(A) such transfer shall not be treated as a disposition for purposes of this part, and

(B) the same tax treatment under this part with respect to the transferred property shall apply to the transferee as would have applied to the transferor.

(d) Attribution of stock ownership. For purposes of this part, in applying the percentage limitations of sections 422(b)(6) and 423(b)(3)—

(1) the individual with respect to whom such limitation is being determined shall be considered as owning the stock owned, directly or indirectly, by or for his brothers and sisters (whether by the whole or half blood), spouse, ancestors, and lineal descendants; and

(2) stock owned, directly or indirectly, by or for a corporation, partnership, estate, or trust, shall be considered as being owned proportionately by or for its shareholders, partners, or beneficiaries.

(e) Parent corporation. For purposes of this part, the term "parent corporation" means any corporation (other than the employer corporation) in an unbroken chain of corporations ending with the employer corporation if, at the time of the granting of the option, each of the corporations other than the employer corporation owns stock possessing 50 percent or more of the total combined voting power of all classes of stock in one of the other corporations in such chain.

(f) Subsidiary corporation. For purposes of this part, the term "subsidiary corporation" means any corporation (other than the employer corporation) in an unbroken chain of corporations beginning with the employer corporation if, at the time of the granting of the option, each of the corporations other than the last corporation in the unbroken chain owns stock possessing 50 percent or more of the total combined voting power of all classes of stock in one of the other corporations in such chain.

(g) Special rule for applying subsections (e) and (f). In applying subsections (e) and (f) for purposes of section 422(a)(2) and 423(a)(2), there shall be substituted for the term "employer corporation" wherever it appears in subsection (e) and (f) the term "grantor corporation" or the term "corporation issuing or assuming a stock option in a transaction to which section 424(a) applies" as the case may be.

(h) Modification, extension, or renewal of option.

(1) In general. For purposes of this part, if the terms of any option to purchase stock are modified, extended, or renewed, such modification, extension, or renewal shall be considered as the granting of a new option.

(2) Special rule for section 423 options. In the case of the transfer of stock pursuant to the exercise of an option to which section 423 applies and which has been so modified, extended, or renewed, the fair market value of such stock at the time of the granting of the option shall be considered as whichever of the following is the highest—

(A) the fair market value of such stock on the date of the original granting of the option,

(B) the fair market value of such stock on the date of the making of such modification, extension, or renewal, or

(C) the fair market value of such stock at the time of the making of any intervening modification, extension, or renewal.

(3) Definition of modification. The term "modification" means any change in the terms of the option which gives the employee additional benefits under the option, but such term shall not include a change in the terms of the option—

> (A) attributable to the issuance or assumption of an option under subsection (a);

> (B) to permit the option to qualify under section 423(b)(9); or

> (C) in the case of an option not immediately exercisable in full, to accelerate the time at which the option may be exercised.

(i) Stockholder approval. For purposes of this part, if the grant of an option is subject to approval by stockholders, the date of grant of the option shall be determined as if the option had not been subject to such approval.

(j) Cross references. For provisions requiring the reporting of certain acts with respect to a qualified stock option, an incentive stock option, options granted under employer stock purchase plans, or a restricted stock option, see section 6039.

Section 6039 of the Internal Revenue Code
Information required in connection with certain options

(a) Furnishing of information. Every corporation—

> (1) which in any calendar year transfers to any person a share of stock pursuant to such person's exercise of an incentive stock option, or

> (2) which in any calendar year records (or has by its agent recorded) a transfer of the legal title of a share of stock acquired by the transferor pursuant to his exercise of an option described in section 423(c) (relating to special rule where option price is between 85 percent and 100 percent of value of stock),

shall (on or before January 31 of the following calendar year) furnish to such person a written statement in such manner and setting forth such information as the Secretary may by regulations prescribe.

(b) Special rules. For purposes of this section—

> **(1) Treatment by employer to be determinative.** Any option which the corporation treats as an incentive stock option or an option granted under an employee stock purchase plan shall be deemed to be such an option.

> **(2) Subsection (a)(2) applies only to first transfer described therein.** A statement is required by reason of a transfer described in subsection (a)(2) of a share only with respect to the first transfer of such share by the person who exercised the option.

> **(3) Identification of stock.** Any corporation which transfers any share of stock pursuant to the exercise of any option described in subsection (a)(2)

shall identify such stock in a manner adequate to carry out the purposes of this section.

(c) **Cross references.** For definition of—

(1) the term "incentive stock option", see section 422(b), and

(2) the term "employee stock purchase plan" see section 423(b).

Section 16 of the Securities Exchange Act of 1934
Directors, Officers, and Principal Stockholders

(a) **Disclosures required.—**

(1) **Directors, officers, and principal stockholders required to file.**—Every person who is directly or indirectly the beneficial owner of more than 10 percent of any class of any equity security (other than an exempted security) which is registered pursuant to section 12, or who is a director or an officer of the issuer of such security, shall file the statements required by this subsection with the Commission (and, if such security is registered on a national securities exchange, also with the exchange).

(2) **Time of filing.**—The statements required by this subsection shall be filed—

(A) at the time of the registration of such security on a national securities exchange or by the effective date of a registration statement filed pursuant to section 12(g);

(B) within 10 days after he or she becomes such beneficial owner, director, or officer;

(C) if there has been a change in such ownership, or if such person shall have purchased or sold a security based swap agreement (as defined in section 206(b) of the Gramm-Leach-Bliley Act (15 U.S.C. 78c note)) involving such equity security, before the end of the second business day following the day on which the subject transaction has been executed, or at such other time as the Commission shall establish, by rule, in any case in which the Commission determines that such 2-day period is not feasible.

(3) **Contents of statements.**—A statement filed—

(A) under subparagraph (A) or (B) of paragraph (2) shall contain a statement of the amount of all equity securities of such issuer of which the filing person is the beneficial owner; and

(B) under subparagraph (C) of such paragraph shall indicate ownership by the filing person at the date of filing, any such changes in such ownership, and such purchases and sales of the security-based swap agreements as have occurred since the most recent such filing under such subparagraph.

(4) Electronic filing and availability.—Beginning not later than 1 year after the date of enactment of the Sarbanes-Oxley Act of 2002—

(A) a statement filed under subparagraph (C) of paragraph (2) shall be filed electronically;

(B) the Commission shall provide each such statement on a publicly accessible Internet site not later than the end of the business day following that filing; and

(C) the issuer (if the issuer maintains a corporate website) shall provide that statement on that corporate website, not later than the end of the business day following that filing.

(b) For the purpose of preventing the unfair use of information which may have been obtained by such beneficial owner, director, or officer by reason of his relationship to the issuer, any profit realized by him from any purchase and sale, or any sale and purchase, of any equity security of such issuer (other than an exempted security)or a security-based swap agreement (as defined in section 206B of the Gramm-Leach-Bliley Act) involving any such equity security within any period of less than six months, unless such security or security-based swap agreement was acquired in good faith in connection with a debt previously contracted, shall inure to and be recoverable by the issuer, irrespective of any intention on the part of such beneficial owner, director, or officer in entering into such transaction of holding the security or security-based swap agreement purchased or of not repurchasing the security or security-based swap agreement sold for a period exceeding six months. Suit to recover such profit may be instituted at law or in equity in any court of competent jurisdiction by the issuer, or by the owner of any security of the issuer in the name and in behalf of the issuer if the issuer shall fail or refuse to bring such suit within sixty days after request or shall fail diligently to prosecute the same thereafter; but no such suit shall be brought more than two years after the date such profit was realized. This subsection shall not be construed to cover any transaction where such beneficial owner was not such both at the time of the purchase and sale, or the sale and purchase, of the security or security-based swap agreement (as defined in section 206B of the Gramm-Leach-Bliley Act) involved, or any transaction or transactions which the Commission by rules and regulations may exempt as not comprehended within the purpose of this subsection.

(c) It shall be unlawful for any such beneficial owner, director, or officer, directly or indirectly, to sell any equity security of such issuer (other than an exempted security), if the person selling the security or his principal

1. does not own the security sold, or

2. if owning the security, does not deliver it against such sale within twenty days thereafter, or does not within five days after such sale deposit it in the mails or other usual channels of transportation; but no person shall be deemed to have violated this subsection if he proves that notwithstanding the exercise of good faith he was unable to make such delivery or deposit within such time, or that to do so would cause undue inconvenience or expense.

(d) The provisions of subsection (b) of this section shall not apply to any purchase and sale, or sale and purchase, and the provisions of subsection (c) of this section shall not apply to any sale, of an equity security not then or theretofore held by him in an investment account, by a dealer in the ordinary course of his business and incident to the establishment or maintenance by him of a primary or secondary market (otherwise than on a national securities exchange or an exchange exempted from registration under Section 5 of this title) for such security. The Commission may, by such rules and regulations as it deems necessary or appropriate in the public interest, define and prescribe terms and conditions with respect to securities held in an investment account and transactions made in the ordinary course of business and incident to the establishment or maintenance of a primary or secondary market.

(e) The provisions of this section shall not apply to foreign or domestic arbitrage transactions unless made in contravention of such rules and regulations as the Commission may adopt in order to carry out the purposes of this section.

(f) Treatment of transactions in security futures products.—The provisions of this section shall apply to ownership of and transactions in security futures products.

(g) The authority of the Commission under this section with respect to security-based swap agreements (as defined in section 206B of the Gramm-Leach-Bliley Act) shall be subject to the restrictions and limitations of section 3A(b) of this title.

SEC Rule 144

(a) *Definitions.* The following definitions shall apply for the purposes of this rule.

(1) An "affiliate" of an issuer is a person that directly, or indirectly through one or more intermediaries, controls, or is controlled by, or is under common control with, such issuer.

(2) The term "person" when used with reference to a person for whose account securities are to be sold in reliance upon this rule includes, in addition to such person, all of the following persons:

(i) Any relative or spouse of such person, or any relative of such spouse, any one of whom has the same home as such person;

(ii) Any trust or estate in which such person or any of the persons specified in paragraph (a)(2)(i) of this section collectively own ten percent or more of the total beneficial interest or of which any of such persons serve as trustee, executor or in any similar capacity; and

(iii) Any corporation or other organization (other than the issuer) in which such person or any of the persons specified in paragraph (a)(2)(i) of this section are the beneficial owners collectively of ten percent or more of any class of equity securities or ten percent or more of the equity interest.

(3) The term "restricted securities" means:

(i) Securities acquired directly or indirectly from the issuer, or from an affiliate of the issuer, in a transaction or chain of transactions not involving any public offering;

(ii) Securities acquired from the issuer that are subject to the resale limitations of 230.502(d) under Regulation D or 230.701(c);

(iii) Securities acquired in a transaction or chain of transactions meeting the requirements of 230.144A;

(iv) Securities acquired from the issuer in a transaction subject to the conditions of Regulation CE (230.1001); and

(v) Equity securities of domestic issuers acquired in a transaction or chain of transactions subject to the conditions of 230.901 or 230.903 under Regulation S (230.901 through 230.905, and Preliminary Notes).

(vi) Securities acquired in a transaction made under §230.801 to the same extent and proportion that the securities held by the security holder of the class with respect to which the rights offering was made were as of the record date for the rights offering "restricted securities" within the meaning of this paragraph (a)(3); and

(vii) Securities acquired in a transaction made under §230.802 to the same extent and proportion that the securities that were tendered or exchanged in the exchange offer or business combination were "restricted securities" within the meaning of this paragraph (a)(3).

(b) *Conditions to be Met.* Any affiliate or other person who sells restricted securities of an issuer for his own account, or any person who sells restricted or any other securities for the account of an affiliate of the issuer of such securities, shall be deemed not to be engaged in a distribution of such securities and therefore not to be an underwriter thereof within the meaning of Section 2(11) of the Act if all of the conditions of this rule are met.

(c) *Current Public Information.* There shall be available adequate current public information with respect to the issuer of the securities. Such information shall be deemed to be available only if either of the following conditions is met:

(1) Filing of Reports. The issuer has securities registered pursuant to Section 12 of the Securities Exchange Act of 1934, has been subject to the reporting requirements of Section 13 of that Act for a period of at least 90 days immediately preceding the sale of the securities and has filed all the reports required to be filed thereunder during the 12 months preceding such sale (or for such shorter period that the issuer was required to file such reports), other than Form 8-K reports (§249.308 of this chapter); or has securities registered pursuant to the Securities Act of 1933, has been subject to the reporting requirements of Section 15(d) of the Securities Exchange Act of 1934 for a period of at least 90 days immediately preceding the sale of the securities and has filed all the reports required to be filed thereunder during the 12 months preceding such sale (or for such shorter period that the issuer was required to file such reports), other than Form 8-K reports (§249.308 of this chapter). The person for whose account the securities are to be sold shall be entitled to rely upon a statement in whichever is the most recent report, quarterly or annual, required to be filed and filed by the issuer that such issuer has filed all reports required to be filed by Section 13 or 15(d) of the Securities Exchange Act of 1934 during the preceding 12 months (or for such shorter period that the issuer was required to file such reports), other than Form 8-K reports (§249.308 of this chapter), and has been subject to such filing requirements for the past 90 days, unless he knows or has reason to believe that the issuer has not complied with such requirements. Such person shall also be entitled to rely upon a written statement from the issuer that it has complied with such reporting requirements unless he knows or has reason to believe that the issuer has not complied with such requirements.

(2) *Other Public Information.* If the issuer is not subject to Section 13 or 15(d) of the Securities Exchange Act of 1934, there is publicly available the information concerning the issuer specified in paragraph (a)(5)(1) to (xiv), inclusive, and paragraph (a)(5)(xvi) of Rule 15c2-11 (§240.15c2-11 of this chapter) under that Act or, if the issuer is an insurance company, the information specified in Section 12(g)(2)(U)(i) of that Act.

(d) *Holding Period for Restricted Securities.* If the securities sold are restricted securities, the following provisions apply:

(1) *General Rule.* A minimum of one year must elapse between the later of the date of the acquisition of the securities from the issuer or from an affiliate of the issuer, and any resale of such securities in reliance on this section for the account of either the acquiror or any

subsequent holder of those securities. If the acquiror takes the securities by purchase, the one-year period shall not begin until the full purchase price or other consideration is paid or given by the person acquiring the securities from the issuer or from an affiliate of the issuer.

(2) *Promissory Notes, Other Obligations or Installment Contracts.* Giving the issuer or affiliate of the issuer from whom the securities were purchased a promissory note or other obligation to pay the purchase price, or entering into an installment purchase contract with such seller, shall not be deemed full payment of the purchase price unless the promissory note, obligation or contract

(i) provides for full recourse against the purchaser of the securities;

(ii) is secured by collateral, other than the securities purchased, having a fair market value at least equal to the purchase price of the securities purchased; and

(iii) shall have been discharged by payment in full prior to the sale of the securities.

(3) *Determination of Holding Period.* The following provisions shall apply for the purpose of determining the period securities have been held:

(i) *Stock Dividends, Splits and Recapitalizations.* Securities acquired from the issuer as a dividend or pursuant to a stock split, reverse split or recapitalization shall be deemed to have been acquired at the same time as the securities on which the dividend or, if more than one, the initial dividend was paid, the securities involved in the split or reverse split, or the securities surrendered in connection with the recapitalization;

(ii) *Conversions.* If the securities sold were acquired from the issuer for a consideration consisting solely of other securities of the same issuer surrendered for conversion, the securities so acquired shall be deemed to have been acquired at the same time as the securities surrendered for conversion;

(iii) *Contingent Issuance of Securities.* Securities acquired as a contingent payment of the purchase price of an equity interest in a business, or the assets of a business, sold to the issuer or an affiliate of the issuer shall be deemed to have been acquired at the time of such sale if the issuer or affiliate was then committed to issue the securities subject only to conditions other than the payment of further consideration for such securities. An agreement entered into in connection with any such purchase to remain in the employment of, or not to compete with, the issuer or affiliate or the rendering of services pursuant to such agreement shall not be deemed to be the payment of further consideration for such securities.

(iv) *Pledged Securities.* Securities which are bona fide pledged by an affiliate of the issuer when sold by the pledgee, or by a purchaser, after a default in the obligation secured by the pledge, shall be deemed to have been acquired when they were acquired by the pledgor, except that if the securities were pledged without recourse they shall be deemed to have been acquired by the pledgee at the time of the pledge or by the purchaser at the time of purchase.

(v) *Gifts of Securities.* Securities acquired from an affiliate of the issuer by gift shall be deemed to have been acquired by the donee when they were acquired by the donor.

(vi) *Trusts.* Where a trust settlor is an affiliate of the issuer, securities acquired from the settlor by the trust, or acquired from the trust by the beneficiaries thereof, shall be deemed to have been acquired when such securities were acquired by the settlor.

(vii) *Estates.* Where a deceased person was an affiliate of the issuer, securities held by the estate of such person or acquired from such estate by the beneficiaries thereof shall be deemed to have been acquired when they were acquired by the deceased person, except that no holding period is required if the estate is not an affiliate of the issuer or if the securities are sold by a beneficiary of the estate who is not such an affiliate.

Note. While there is no holding period or amount limitation for estates and beneficiaries thereof which are not affiliates of the issuer, paragraphs (c), (h) and (i) of the rule apply to securities sold by such persons in reliance upon the rule.

(viii) *Rule 145(a) transactions.* The holding period for securities acquired in a transaction specified in Rule 145(a) shall be deemed to commence on the date the securities were acquired by the purchaser in such transaction. This provision shall not apply, however, to a transaction effected solely for the purpose of forming a holding company.

(e) *Limitation on Amount of Securities Sold.* Except as hereinafter provided, the amount of securities which may be sold in reliance upon this rule shall be determined as follows:

(1) *Sales by affiliates.* If restricted or other securities are sold for the account of an affiliate of the issuer, the amount of securities sold, together with all sales of restricted and other securities of the same class for the account of such person within the preceding three months, shall not exceed the greater of (i)

one percent of the shares or other units of the class outstanding as shown by the most recent report or statement published by the issuer, or (ii) the average weekly reported volume of trading in such securities on all national securities exchanges and/or reported through the automated quotation system of a registered securities association during the four calendar weeks preceding the filing of notice required by paragraph (h), or if no such notice is required the date of receipt of the order to execute the transaction by the broker or the date of execution of the transaction directly with a market maker, or (iii) the average weekly volume of trading in such securities reported through the consolidated transaction reporting system, contemplated by Rule 11Aa3-1 under the Securities Exchange Act of 1934 (§240.11Aa3-1) during the four-week period specified in subdivision (ii) of this paragraph.

(2) *Sales by persons other than affiliates.* The amount of restricted securities sold for the account of any person other than an affiliate of the issuer, together with all other sales of restricted securities of the same class for the account of such person within the preceding three months, shall not exceed the amount specified in paragraphs (e)(1)(i), (1)(ii) or (1)(iii) of this section, whichever is applicable, unless the conditions in paragraph (k) of this rule are satisfied.

(3) *Determination of Amount.* For the purpose of determining the amount of securities specified in paragraphs (e)(1) and (2) of this rule, the following provisions shall apply:

(i) Where both convertible securities and securities of the class into which they are convertible are sold, the amount of convertible securities sold shall be deemed to be the amount of securities of the class into which they are convertible for the purpose of determining the aggregate amount of securities of both classes sold;

(ii) The amount of securities sold for the account of a pledgee thereof, or for the account of a purchaser of the pledged securities, during any period of three months within one year after a default in the obligation secured by the pledge, and the amount of securities sold during the same three-month period for the account of the pledgor shall not exceed, in the aggregate, the amount specified in subparagraph (e)(1) or (2) of this section, whichever is applicable.

(iii) The amount of securities sold for the account of a donee thereof during any period of three months within one year after the donation, and the amount of securities sold during the same three-month period for the account of the donor, shall not exceed, in the aggregate, the amount specified in paragraph (e)(1) or (2) of this section, whichever is applicable;

(iv) Where securities were acquired by a trust from the settlor of the trust, the amount of such securities sold for the account of the trust during any period of three months within one year after the acquisition of the securities by the trust, and the amount of securities sold during the same three-month period for the account of the settlor, shall not exceed, in the aggregate, the amount specified in paragraph (e)(1) or (2) of this section, whichever is applicable;

(v) The amount of securities sold for the account of the estate of a deceased person, or for the account of a beneficiary of such estate, during any period of three months and the amount of securities sold during the same period for the account of the deceased person prior to his death shall not exceed, in the aggregate, the amount specified in paragraph (1) or (2) of this paragraph, whichever is applicable; *Provided,* That no limitation on amount shall apply if the estate or beneficiary thereof is not an affiliate of the issuer;

(vi) When two or more affiliates or other persons agree to act in concert for the purpose of selling securities of an issuer, all securities of the same class sold for the account of all such persons during any period of three months shall be aggregated for the purpose of determining the limitation on the amount of securities sold;

(vii) The following sales of securities need not be included in determining the amount of securities sold in reliance upon this section: securities sold pursuant to an effective registration statement under the Act; securities sold pursuant to an exemption provided by Regulation A (230.251 through 230.263) under the Act; securities sold in a transaction exempt pursuant to Section 4 of the Act (15 U.S.C. 77d) and not involving any public offering; and securities sold offshore pursuant to Regulation S (230.901 through 230.905, and Preliminary Notes) under the Act.

(f) *Manner of sale.* The securities shall be sold in "brokers' transactions" within the meaning of section 4(4) of the Act or in transactions directly with a "market maker," as that term is defined in section 3(a)(38) of the Securities Exchange Act of 1934, and the person selling the securities shall not (1) solicit or arrange for the solicitation of orders to buy the securities in anticipation of or in connection with such transaction, or (2) make any payment in connection with the offer or sale of the securities to any person other than the broker who executes the order to sell the securities. The requirements of this paragraph, however, shall not apply to securities sold for the account of the estate of a deceased person or for the account of a beneficiary of such estate provided the estate or beneficiary thereof is not an affiliate of the issuer; nor shall they apply to securities sold for the account of any person other than an affiliate of the issuer, provided the conditions of paragraph (k) of this rule are satisfied.

(g) *Brokers' Transactions.* The term "brokers' transactions" in Section 4(4) of the Act shall for the purposes of this rule be deemed to include transactions by a broker in which such broker—

(1) does no more than execute the order or orders to sell the securities as agent for the person for whose account the securities are sold; and receives no more than the usual and customary broker's commission;

(2) neither solicits nor arranges for the solicitation of customers' orders to buy the securities in anticipation of or in connection with the transaction; provided, that the foregoing shall not preclude

(*i*) inquiries by the broker of other brokers or dealers who have indicated an interest in the securities within the preceding 60 days,

(*ii*) inquiries by the broker of his customers who have indicated an unsolicited bona fide interest in the securities within the preceding 10 business days; or

(*iii*) the publication by the broker of bid and ask quotations for the security in an inter-dealer quotation system provided that such quotations are incident to the maintenance of a bona fide inter-dealer market for the security for the broker's own account and that the broker has published bona fide bid and ask quotations for the security in an inter-dealer quotation system on each of at least twelve days within the preceding thirty calendar days with no more than four business days in succession without such two-way quotations;

Note to Paragraph g(2)(ii): The broker should obtain and retain in his files written evidence of indications of bona fide unsolicited interest by his customers in the securities at the time such indications are received.

(3) after reasonable inquiry is not aware of circumstances indicating that the person for whose account the securities are sold is an underwriter with respect to the securities or that the transaction is a part of a distribution of securities of the issuer. Without limiting the foregoing, the broker shall be deemed to be aware of any facts or statements contained in the notice required by paragraph (h) below.

Notes:

(i) The broker, for his own protection, should obtain and retain in his files a copy of the notice required by paragraph (h).

(ii) The reasonable inquiry required by paragraph (g)(3) of this section should include, but not necessarily be limited to, inquiry as to the following matters:

(a) The length of time the securities have been held by the person for whose account they are to be sold. If practicable, the inquiry should include physical inspection of the securities;

(b) The nature of the transaction in which the securities were acquired by such person;

(c) The amount of securities of the same class sold during the past three months by all persons whose sales are required to be taken into consideration pursuant to paragraph (e) of this section;

(d) Whether such person intends to sell additional securities of the same class through any other means;

(e) Whether such person has solicited or made any arrangement for the solicitation of buy orders in connection with the proposed sale of securities;

(f) Whether such person has made any payment to any other person in connection with the proposed sale of the securities; and

(g) The number of shares or other units of the class outstanding, or the relevant trading volume.

(h) *Notice of proposed sale.* If the amount of securities to be sold in reliance upon the rule during any period of three months exceeds 500 shares or other units or has an aggregate sale price in excess of $10,000, three copies of a notice on Form 144 shall be filed with the Commission at its principal office in Washington, D.C.; and if such securities are admitted to trading on any national securities exchange, one copy of such notice shall also be transmitted to the principal exchange on which such securities are so admitted. The Form 144 shall be signed by the person for whose account the securities are to be sold and shall be transmitted for filing concurrently with either the placing with a broker of an order to execute a sale of securities in reliance upon this rule or the execution directly with a market maker of such a sale. Neither the filing of such notice nor the failure of the Commission to comment thereon shall be deemed to preclude the Commission from taking any action it deems necessary or appropriate with respect to the sale of the securities referred to in such notice. The requirements of this paragraph, however, shall not apply to securities sold for the account of any person other than an affiliate of the issuer, provided the conditions of paragraph (k) of this rule are satisfied.

(i) *Bona Fide Intention to Sell.* The person filing the notice required by paragraph (h) shall have a bona fide intention to sell the securities referred to therein within a reasonable time after the filing of such notice.

(j) *Non-exclusive rule.* Although this rule provides a means for reselling restricted securities and securities held by affiliates without registration, it is not the exclusive means for reselling such securities in that manner. Therefore, it does not eliminate or otherwise affect the availability of any exemption for resales under the Securities Act that a person or entity may be able to rely upon.

(k) *Termination of certain restrictions on sales of restricted securities by persons other than affiliates.* The requirements of paragraphs (c), (e), (f) and (h) of this section shall not apply to restricted securities sold for the account of a person who is not an affiliate of the issuer at the time of the sale and has not been an affiliate during the preceding three months, provided a period of at least two years has elapsed since the later of the date the securities were acquired from the issuer or from an affiliate of the issuer. The two-year period shall be calculated as described in paragraph (d) of this section.

SEC Rule 701

Exemption for offers and sales of securities pursuant to certain compensatory benefit plans and contracts relating to compensation.

Preliminary Notes

1. This section relates to transactions exempted from the registration requirements of section 5 of the Act (15 U.S.C. 77e). These transactions are not exempt from the antifraud, civil liability, or other provisions of the federal securities laws. Issuers and persons acting on their behalf have an obligation to provide investors with disclosure adequate to satisfy the antifraud provisions of the federal securities laws.

2. In addition to complying with this section, the issuer also must comply with any applicable state law relating to the offer and sale of securities.

3. An issuer that attempts to comply with this section, but fails to do so, may claim any other exemption that is available.

4. This section is available only to the issuer of the securities. Affiliates of the issuer may not use this section to offer or sell securities. This section also does not cover resales of securities by any person. This section provides an exemption only for the transactions in which the securities are offered or sold by the issuer, not for the securities themselves.

5. The purpose of this section is to provide an exemption from the registration requirements of the Act for securities issued in compensatory circum-

stances. This section is not available for plans or schemes to circumvent this purpose, such as to raise capital. This section also is not available to exempt any transaction that is in technical compliance with this section but is part of a plan or scheme to evade the registration provisions of the Act. In any of these cases, registration under the Act is required unless another exemption is available.

(a) Exemption. Offers and sales made in compliance with all of the conditions of this section are exempt from section 5 of the Act (15 U.S.C. 77e).

(b) Issuers eligible to use this section.

(1) General. This section is available to any issuer that is not subject to the reporting requirements of section 13 or 15(d) of the Securities Exchange Act of 1934 (the "Exchange Act") (15 U.S.C. 78m or 78o(d)) and is not an investment company registered or required to be registered under the Investment Company Act of 1940 (15 U.S.C. 80a-1 et seq.).

(2) Issuers that become subject to reporting. If an issuer becomes subject to the reporting requirements of section 13 or 15(d) of the Exchange Act (15 U.S.C. 78m or 78o(d)) after it has made offers complying with this section, the issuer may nevertheless rely on this section to sell the securities previously offered to the persons to whom those offers were made.

(3) Guarantees by reporting companies. An issuer subject to the reporting requirements of section 13 or 15(d) of the Exchange Act (15 U.S.C. 78m, 78o(d)) may rely on this section if it is merely guaranteeing the payment of a subsidiary's securities that are sold under this section.

(c) Transactions exempted by this section. This section exempts offers and sales of securities (including plan interests and guarantees pursuant to paragraph (d)(2)(ii) of this section) under a written compensatory benefit plan (or written compensation contract) established by the issuer, its parents, its majority-owned subsidiaries or majority-owned subsidiaries of the issuer's parent, for the participation of their employees, directors, general partners, trustees (where the issuer is a business trust), officers, or consultants and advisors, and their family members who acquire such securities from such persons through gifts or domestic relations orders. This section exempts offers and sales to former employees, directors, general partners, trustees, officers, consultants and advisors only if such persons were employed by or providing services to the issuer at the time the securities were offered. In addition, the term "employee" includes insurance agents who are exclusive agents of the issuer, its subsidiaries or parents, or derive more than 50% of their annual income from those entities.

(1) Special requirements for consultants and advisors. This section is available to consultants and advisors only if:

(i) They are natural persons;

(ii) They provide bona fide services to the issuer, its parents, its majority-owned subsidiaries or majority-owned subsidiaries of the issuer's parent; and

(iii) The services are not in connection with the offer or sale of securities in a capital-raising transaction, and do not directly or indirectly promote or maintain a market for the issuer's securities.

(2) Definition of "Compensatory Benefit Plan." For purposes of this section, a compensatory benefit plan is any purchase, savings, option, bonus, stock appreciation, profit sharing, thrift, incentive, deferred compensation, pension or similar plan.

(3) Definition of "Family Member." For purposes of this section, family member includes any child, stepchild, grandchild, parent, stepparent, grandparent, spouse, former spouse, sibling, niece, nephew, mother-in-law, father-in-law, son-in-law, daughter-in-law, brother-in-law, or sister-in-law, including adoptive relationships, any person sharing the employee's household (other than a tenant or employee), a trust in which these persons have more than fifty percent of the beneficial interest, a foundation in which these persons (or the employee) control the management of assets, and any other entity in which these persons (or the employee) own more than fifty percent of the voting interests.

(d) Amounts that may be sold.

(1) Offers. Any amount of securities may be offered in reliance on this section. However, for purposes of this section, sales of securities underlying options must be counted as sales on the date of the option grant.

(2) Sales. The aggregate sales price or amount of securities sold in reliance on this section during any consecutive 12-month period must not exceed the greatest of the following:

(i) $1,000,000;

(ii) 15% of the total assets of the issuer (or of the issuer's parent if the issuer is a wholly-owned subsidiary and the securities represent obligations that the parent fully and unconditionally guarantees), measured at the issuer's most recent balance sheet date (if no older than its last fiscal year end); or

(iii) 15% of the outstanding amount of the class of securities being offered and sold in reliance on this section, measured at the issuer's most recent balance sheet date (if no older than its last fiscal year end).

(3) Rules for calculating prices and amounts.

(i) Aggregate sales price. The term aggregate sales price means the sum of all cash, property, notes, cancellation of debt or other consideration received or to be received by the issuer for the sale of the securities. Non-cash consideration must be valued by reference to bona fide sales of that consideration made within a reasonable time or, in the absence of such sales, on the fair value as determined by an accepted standard. The value of services exchanged for securities issued must be measured by reference to the value of the securities issued. Options must be valued based on the exercise price of the option.

(ii) Time of the calculation. With respect to options to purchase securities, the aggregate sales price is determined when an option grant is made (without regard to when the option becomes exercisable). With respect to other securities, the calculation is made on the date of sale. With respect to deferred compensation or similar plans, the calculation is made when the irrevocable election to defer is made.

(iii) Derivative securities. In calculating outstanding securities for purposes of paragraph (d)(2)(iii) of this section, treat the securities underlying all currently exercisable or convertible options, warrants, rights or other securities, other than those issued under this exemption, as outstanding. In calculating the amount of securities sold for other purposes of paragraph (d)(2) of this section, count the amount of securities that would be acquired upon exercise or conversion in connection with sales of options, warrants, rights or other exercisable or convertible securities, including those to be issued under this exemption.

(iv) Other exemptions. Amounts of securities sold in reliance on this section do not affect "aggregate offering prices" in other exemptions, and amounts of securities sold in reliance on other exemptions do not affect the amount that may be sold in reliance on this section.

(e) Disclosure that must be provided. The issuer must deliver to investors a copy of the compensatory benefit plan or the contract, as applicable. In addition, if the aggregate sales price or amount of securities sold during any consecutive 12-month period exceeds $5 million, the issuer must deliver the following disclosure to investors a reasonable period of time before the date of sale:

(1) If the plan is subject to the Employee Retirement Income Security Act of 1974 ("ERISA") (29 U.S.C. 1104 - 1107), a copy of the summary plan description required by ERISA;

(2) If the plan is not subject to ERISA, a summary of the material terms of the plan;

(3) Information about the risks associated with investment in the securities sold pursuant to the compensatory benefit plan or compensation contract; and

(4) Financial statements required to be furnished by Part F/S of Form 1-A (Regulation A Offering Statement) (§239.90 of this chapter) under Regulation A (§§230.251 - 230.263). Foreign private issuers as defined in §230.405 must provide a reconciliation to generally accepted accounting principles in the United States (U. S. GAAP) if their financial statements are not prepared in accordance with U. S. GAAP (Item 17 of Form 20-F (§249.220f of this chapter)). The financial statements required by this section must be as of a date no more than 180 days before the sale of securities in reliance on this exemption.

(5) If the issuer is relying on paragraph (d)(2)(ii) of this section to use its parent's total assets to determine the amount of securities that may be sold, the parent's financial statements must be delivered. If the parent is subject to the reporting requirements of section 13 or 15(d) of the Exchange Act (15 U.S.C. 78m or 78o(d)), the financial statements of the parent required by Rule 10-01 of Regulation S-X (§210.10-01 of this chapter) and Item 310 of Regulation S-B (§228.310 of this chapter), as applicable, must be delivered.

(6) If the sale involves a stock option or other derivative security, the issuer must deliver disclosure a reasonable period of time before the date of exercise or conversion. For deferred compensation or similar plans, the issuer must deliver disclosure to investors a reasonable period of time before the date the irrevocable election to defer is made.

(f) No integration with other offerings. Offers and sales exempt under this section are deemed to be a part of a single, discrete offering and are not subject to integration with any other offers or sales, whether registered under the Act or otherwise exempt from the registration requirements of the Act.

(g) Resale limitations.

(1) Securities issued under this section are deemed to be "restricted securities" as defined in §230.144.

(2) Resales of securities issued pursuant to this section must be in compliance with the registration requirements of the Act or an exemption from those requirements.

(3) Ninety days after the issuer becomes subject to the reporting requirements of section 13 or 15(d) of the Exchange Act (15 U.S.C. 78m or 78o(d)), securities issued under this section may be resold by persons who are not affiliates (as defined in §230.144) in reliance on §230.144 without compliance with paragraphs (c), (d), (e) and (h) of §230.144, and by affiliates without compliance with paragraph (d) of §230.144.

Glossary

Acceleration: With respect to unvested shares, speeding up the vesting schedule (that is, decreasing the period over which vesting restrictions lapse).

Affiliate: Under Rule 144, a person who directly or indirectly controls, is controlled by, or is under common control with the issuer. As a rule, executive officers and directors are deemed to be affiliates. Affiliates are subject to certain limitations as to volume and timing with respect to sale of unregistered (restricted) stock of the issuer.

Alternative Minimum Tax (AMT): Alternative tax system to federal income tax intended to recapture certain tax preference or adjustment items (such as the spread on exercise of an ISO); the tax is assessed on "alternative minimum taxable income" and, to the extent it is greater than regular taxable income, must be paid in the year computed. AMT is treated as a credit against regular income tax and may be carried forward to future years.

APB 25: Accounting Principles Board (APB) Opinion No. 25 ("APB 25"), issued in 1972, sets out the accounting standards for both compensatory and noncompensatory options. While APB 25 is still in existence, its application has been extensively reinterpreted by the FASB since 1999.

Black-Scholes Valuation: A mathematical formula used for valuing stock options that considers such factors as the volatility of returns on the underlying securities, the risk-free interest rate, the expected dividend rate, the relationship of option price to price of underlying securities, and expected option life. Developed in 1973 by two economists, the model was originally created to value options traded on European commodity exchanges.

Blue Sky Laws: State securities laws governing the purchase and sale of securities. The phrase "blue sky" originates from a federal case that described such laws as aimed against "speculative schemes which hold no more basis than so many feet of blue sky."

Board of Directors: Board elected by a corporation's shareholders to set policies and oversee the affairs of the corporation, generally elected on an annual basis.

Cashless Exercise: Form of stock option exercise where the option price for the number of shares of stock being purchased is paid with consideration other than cash. Common cashless exercise methods include stock swaps, the delivery of a promissory note, and broker-assisted same-day-sale transactions.

California Commissioner's Rules: Regulations implementing the California Securities Act of 1968.

Change in Control: A transaction that alters the ownership of a corporation, including a merger, consolidation, stock sale, or asset sale. With respect to options, events that constitute a change in control are generally defined in the plan.

Code: See "Internal Revenue Code (Code)."

Collateral: Property given to secure a promissory note.

Common Stock: Basic ownership interest in a corporation that typically confers on the holder of the security the right to vote, select directors, receive dividends, and share in residual assets upon the dissolution or winding up of the business.

Compensation Expense: *For financial reporting purposes,* the cost recognized by a corporation on its financial statements with respect to the issuance of its securities in connection with stock-based compensation, either pursuant to APB 25 or FAS 123. If pursuant to APB 25, compensation expense is measured based on the intrinsic value of the shares. If pursuant to FAS 123, it is measured based on the fair value of the shares. *For tax purposes,* the amount realized on exercise of an option that is potentially deductible by a corporation on its income tax return as a trade or business expense under Section 162 of the Code (generally limited to the amount included in income by the employee at the time of exercise or disposition).

Discount Option: Option with an exercise price below fair market value on date of grant.

Director: Member of a corporate board of directors. Independent (or outside) directors may not be employed by the corporation.

Disposition: Sale, gift, or other transfer of stock purchased pursuant to an option.

Disqualifying Disposition: For purposes of stock purchased pursuant to a statutory stock option, a disposition made within two years from grant or one year from exercise (pursuant to Section 421 of the Code).

Early Exercise: With respect to stock purchased under an option, a purchase made subject to ongoing vesting restrictions.

EDGAR (Electronic Data Gathering Analysis and Retrieval System): The automated computer system developed and implemented by the SEC for filing of registration statements, periodic reports, and other federal securities law filings.

Employee: An individual who performs services for an employer, subject to the control of the employer as to the type of work and manner of performance.

Employee Stock Purchase Plan (ESPP): Type of stock option plan that provides for ongoing stock purchases by employees pursuant to a subscription agreement. Generally includes a discount from market price, determined either as of the first or last day of the applicable exercise period. May be a tax-qualified statutory option plan under Section 423 of the Code, or may result in nonstatutory option treatment under Section 83. See "Section 423 Plan."

Employment Tax: A general term used to describe taxes imposed under FICA and FUTA.

Exchange Act: See "Securities Exchange Act of 1934 (Exchange Act)."

Exercise: Purchase of stock pursuant to an option.

Exercise Price: The price at which an option may be exercised, stated in the option agreement. Also called the "strike price."

Evergreen Provision: A replenishment features in a stock plan that automatically increases at regular intervals the number of shares reserved under the plan.

Fair Market Value: For tax and accounting purposes, the value of a share of stock on any given date. In a privately held company, fair market value is determined by the corporation's board of directors. In a public company, fair market value is determined with reference to the price posted on the applicable stock market (generally this is closing price, but it depends on how the plan was drawn up).

Fair Value: For accounting purposes, the value of an option determined in accordance with FAS 123, using a pricing model such as Black-Scholes.

FAS 123: Statement of Financial Accounting Standards No. 123, "Accounting for Stock-Based Compensation." FAS 123 requires companies to place a "fair value" on employee stock options not otherwise covered by APB 25 as of the date of grant, and to either reflect such value as a charge to earnings during the service period or disclose the amount that would have been charged in a footnote to the company's financial statements.

FAS 123(R): The Financial Accounting Standards Board's (FASB's) revision of its FAS 123 accounting standard. The new standard follows the International Accounting Standards Board's (IASB) recommendation that member countries revise their general accounting principles so that stock options and awards are treated as an expense to earnings, among other things.

Federal Insurance Contributions Act (FICA): A series of employment taxes imposed on employees and employers with respect to employee wages, including Social Security and Medicare taxes.

Federal Unemployment Tax Act (FUTA): An employment tax imposed on employers with respect to employee wages.

Financial Accounting Standards Board (FASB): A private sector organization recognized by the SEC as the source for GAAP for corporations that offer and sell securities in the U.S.

Fixed Award: Under APB 25, an award for which the measurement date is the date of grant (e.g., an option with service-related vesting only).

GAAP: See "Generally Accepted Accounting Practices (GAAP)."

Generally Accepted Accounting Practices (GAAP): Substantive rules for the practice of accounting as established by the body of opinions and decisions issued by the FASB.

Golden Parachute: Under Section 280G of the Code, a package of compensation-related benefits (including options) awarded to an employee contingent upon a change in control of the employer corporation.

Grant Date: The date upon which an employee stock option is approved by the company's board of directors.

Holding Period: *For tax purposes,* the length of time stock must be held before transfer in order for any gain to be eligible for capital gain treatment. For statutory option purposes, the period is one year from exercise and two years from grant (set out in Section 421 of the Code); for general capital gains purposes, the period is one year from the date of transfer of capital property (Sections 1221–1223 of the Code). The tax holding period begins on the date the property is first transferred (regardless of whether purchased with a note or subject to contractual restrictions). *For Rule 144 purposes,* the length of time unregistered stock must be held before transfer. For affiliates, one year provided Rule 144 is complied with. For nonaffiliates, one year, provided Rule 144 is complied with; after two years, no compliance is necessary. If purchase is with a note, the securities holding period begins only when the note is paid off or fully collateralized with property other than the underlying stock.

IASB: See "International Accounting Standards Board (IASB)."

Incentive Stock Option (ISO): A statutory stock option described in Section 422 of the Code.

Independent Contractor: A service provider who is not an employee.

Insider: A general term referring to persons who, by virtue of their positions within a corporation, have access to confidential information about a corporation. Frequently used to denote directors, officers, 10% shareholders, and persons otherwise subject to the Exchange Act.

Insider Trading: A person's wrongful use or wrongful communication, whether directly or indirectly, of confidential information to purchase or sell securities.

Internal Revenue Code (Code): The Internal Revenue Code of 1986, as amended; the key federal statute providing for taxation of individuals, corporations, and other persons.

Internal Revenue Service (IRS): An agency of the federal government, under the supervision of the Department of the Treasury, that is responsible for administering the federal tax laws.

International Accounting Standards Board (IASB): Voluntary global accounting standards-setting organization whose member nations include the U.S, Australia, Canada, France, Germany, Japan, New Zealand, and the U.K. IASB standards are intended to establish GAAP on an international basis.

In the Money: Term used to describe an employee stock option where the current fair market value of the shares of stock subject to the option is greater than the exercise price.

Intrinsic Value: For accounting purposes, the compensation cost of an option computed in accordance with APB 25; equal to the difference (if any) between the exercise price and the fair market value of a share of the underlying stock on the measurement date.

Lattice Models: Models for determining the fair value of employee stock options that use a decision-tree approach of possible future outcomes, then calculates a value based on all possible future outcomes. There are many different kinds of lattice models including binomial models and, trinomial models, among many others.

Mark to Market: For variable award accounting purposes, a measurement of option expense taken periodically over the life of the option (i.e., from date of grant/modification until the option is either exercised or is no longer outstanding). Under APB 25, variable award expense is measured based on the difference between the exercise price and its fair market value, with subsequent changes to fair market value marked to market. Under FAS 123, variable award expense is measured as the difference between fair value and the amount (if any) paid on date of grant, with subsequent changes to fair value marked to market.

Measurement Date: For accounting purposes, the first date on which both the number and the price of shares subject to an option is known. The measurement date for a fixed award is the date of grant, while the measurement date for a variable award is the date of vesting (or expiration).

Modification: *For purposes of fixed vs. variable award accounting,* such changes as cancellation/reissuances of options, extensions/renewals of option terms, and the addition of accelerated vesting (including acceleration at the company's discretion). The modification of an already outstanding fixed option will change treatment for unexercised shares from fixed to variable. *For purposes of a statutory option,* a beneficial change to the terms of an option (including by way of example, the number of shares, an extension of the term, pricing, or the method of financing). Under Section 424 of the Code, the underlying option will be disqualified from statutory option treatment unless it is treated as a new option as of the date of the modification.

National Association of Securities Dealers (NASD): A self-regulatory organization subject to the Exchange Act, comprised of brokers and dealers in the over-the-counter (OTC) securities market. The NASD was established in the late 1930s to regulate the OTC market.

National Association of Securities Dealers, Inc., Automated Quotations System (NASDAQ): A computerized network showing quotations and transaction information with respect to securities traded in the OTC market which meet the size and trading volume requirements to be quoted on the system.

New York Stock Exchange (NYSE): The oldest organized stock exchange.

No-Action Letter: Interpretive letter issued by the SEC to a specific requestor, indicating the SEC staff's advice regarding the application of specific securities forms or rules; available to the public.

Non-Approved Plan: A stock option plan that has not been approved by the shareholders.

Nonstatutory (or Nonqualified) Stock Options (NSO): Any option other than a statutory stock option; its tax treatment is governed by Section 83 of the Code.

One Million Dollar Cap: Under Section 162(m) of the Code, the maximum amount of compensation paid to "covered employees" that may be deducted by a publicly traded corporation.

Option: A contract right granted to an individual to purchase a certain number of shares of stock at a certain price (and subject to certain conditions) over a defined period of time.

Optionee: An individual who has been granted an option.

Ordinary Income: Income, such as compensation income, taxed at ordinary rather than capital gains rates under the Code.

PLR: See "Private Letter Ruling (PLR)."

Preferred Stock: Equity securities of a corporation that carry certain rights, preferences, and privileges superior to common stock. Preferred stock generally receives an investment return at a specific rate whenever dividends are declared, and has priority to the earnings and assets in the event of a sale or liquidation of the corporation before distributions may be made to common shareholders.

Privately Held Company (Closely Held Company): A company whose stock is not publicly traded.

Private Letter Ruling (PLR): A ruling issued by the IRS to a specific taxpayer, indicating the IRS interpretation of tax law with respect to a stated set of facts. PLRs include private letter rulings and technical advice memoranda, and are available to the public, although they may not be cited as precedent and do not bind the IRS other than as to the taxpayer requesting the ruling. Other forms of non-precedental IRS rulings include field service memoranda and IRS Chief Counsel Advisory memoranda.

Promissory Note: A written promise to pay a specified amount of money at a specified time in the future; may be unsecured or secured with collateral acceptable to the holder of the note; if recourse is not limited specifically to the underlying collateral, holder will be entitled to recourse against all of the assets of the maker.

Public Company: A company whose stock is publicly traded on a recognized stock exchange; subject to the registration, disclosure, and related rules enforced by the SEC.

Public Offering: An offering of securities to the general public under a registration statement prepared and filed with the SEC in accordance with the 1933 Act and any applicable blue sky laws.

Qualifying Disposition: For purposes of stock purchased pursuant to a statutory stock option, a disposition made after a minimum of two years from grant and one year from exercise (pursuant to Section 421 of the Code).

Registration: The formal process for the issuance of securities under federal and/ or state securities laws that permit public sale of securities.

Reload Option: A stock option granted to an individual who has exercised an option (typically by a stock swap) that restores the original number of shares under option; the terms of the option (e.g., the price) need not be the same as those of the swapped option.

Repricing: An amendment to a previously granted stock option that reduces the exercise price.

Restricted Stock: For securities law purposes, shares of stock issued in a transaction that was not registered under the 1933 Act in reliance on an exemption. Resale of such shares is generally subject to Rule 144 (or subsequent registration).

Revenue Procedure: A notice published by the IRS giving administrative guidance on the application of tax laws; intended to be relied upon by taxpayers.

Revenue Ruling: A ruling published by the IRS that states the IRS audit position on the application of the tax law to specific facts; establishes precedent that may be relied upon.

Rule 144: Rule promulgated by the Securities and Exchange Commission as a "safe harbor" for the resale of "restricted securities" (that is, securities that were acquired other than in a public offering) and "control securities" (that is, securities owned by affiliates of the corporation).

SAR: See "Stock Appreciation Right (SAR)."

Section 423 Plan: ESPP that complies with statutory option rules under Section 423 of the Code. See "Employee Stock Purchase Plan."

Securities Act of 1933 (1933 Act): A federal statute governing the offer and sale of securities in interstate commerce; prescribes registration, disclosure and fraud rules.

Securities and Exchange Commission (SEC): An agency of the federal government created under the Exchange Act that administers the federal laws regulating the offer and sale of securities within the U.S.

Securities Exchange Act of 1934 (Exchange Act): A federal statute that requires stock exchanges to register with (or obtain an exemption from) the SEC as a prerequisite to doing business; includes reporting, proxy solicitation, tender offer, and insider trading rules.

Shareholder/Stockholder: A person who owns one or more of the outstanding shares of stock of a corporation.

Shareholder/Stockholder Approval: Authorization by shareholders of a corporate transaction or event.

Spread: For any share purchased under an option, the difference between the option price and the fair market value of a share of stock on the date of exercise.

Statutory Stock Option: An employee option accorded favorable tax treatment under Sections 421–424 of the Code; that is, an ISO or Section 423 ESPP option.

Strike Price: See "Exercise Price."

Stock Appreciation Right (SAR): A contractual right granted to an individual that gives the recipient the right to receive a cash amount equal to the appreciation on a specified number of shares of stock over a specified period of time.

Stock Swap: A transaction in which already owned stock is exchanged in lieu of cash to pay the option price for the exercise of an employee stock option.

Tax Basis: A tax concept representing the actual and constructive cost of property to a taxpayer; for purposes of stock purchased under an option, the tax basis is equal to the amount paid on exercise plus any amount included in ordinary income prior to disposition.

Tax Withholding: The retention of certain amounts from an employee's wages or compensation by a corporation to satisfy income tax and/or employment tax obligations.

Transferable Stock Option: An NSO that permits the optionee to transfer the option to one or more third parties.

Underwater or "Out of the Money": A term used to describe an employee stock option where the current fair market value of the shares of stock subject to the option is less than the exercise price.

Variable Award: Under APB 25, an award for which the measurement date is not the date of grant but instead is dependent on the occurrence of future events (e.g., an SAR).

Vesting: With respect to an option, the process of earning shares of stock over the term of the option; the process by which shares under option become first transferable or not subject to a substantial risk of forfeiture under Section 83(b) of the Code (e.g., by satisfying continuing service or performance-based conditions)

Vesting Period: With respect to an option, period over which shares subject to the option vest.

Wages: Under Section 3401 of the Code, remuneration (in any form) paid to an employee in connection with services rendered to the employer.

Bibliography

Books

Blasi, Joseph, et al. *Stock Options, Corporate Performance, and Organizational Change.* Oakland, CA: NCEO, 2000.

Carberry, Ed., and Scott Rodrick, eds. *Employee Stock Purchase Plans*, rev. ed. Oakland, CA: NCEO, 2001.

Hicks, J. William. *Resales of Restricted Securities.* 2005 ed. Eagan, MN: Thompson West, 2005.

Kafka, Gerald A. *Reasonable Compensation,* Tax Management Portfolio 390-3rd. Washington, D.C.: BNA: 2002.

Kraus, Herbert. *Executive Stock Options and Stock Appreciation Rights.* New York: Law Journal Press, 2004.

Miller, Robert H. et al., *Statutory Stock Options,* Tax Management Portfolio 381-2nd. Washington, D.C.: BNA: 2001.

Nadel, Alan A., Thomas M. Haines, and Gregory M. Kopp, *Accounting for Equity Compensation,* 2nd ed. Oakland, CA: NCEO, 2004.

Rodrick, Scott S., ed. *Beyond Stock Options,* 4th ed. Oakland, CA: NCEO, 2006.

_____, ed. *Equity Compensation in a Post-Expensing World.* Oakland, CA: NCEO, 2003.

_____, ed. *Equity-Based Compensation for Multinational Corporations,* 7th ed. Oakland, CA: NCEO, 2005.

_____, ed. *Model Equity Compensation Plans.* Oakland, CA: NCEO, 2000.

_____, ed. *Selected Issues in Equity Compensation,* 3d edition. Oakland, CA: NCEO, 2006.

Romeo, Peter J., and Alan L. Dye. *Comprehensive Section 16 Outline.* 2005, updated annually each August.

Rosen, Corey. *Ownership Solutions.* Oakland, CA: NCEO, 2004.

Sirkin, Michael S. and Lawrence K. Cagney, *Executive Compensation*. New York: Law Journal Press, 2002.

St. Ville, Thomas J. *Stock Option Litigation Guide.* Silver Spring, MD: Pike & Fischer, 2002.

Weeden, Ryan, Corey Rosen, Ed Carberry, and Scott Rodrick. *Current Practices in Stock Option Plan Design,* 2nd ed. Oakland, CA: NCEO, 2001.

Articles

Baker, Alisa. "Incentive Stock Options Continue to Be a Viable Choice Despite TRA '86." *Journal of Taxation* 68 (1988): 164.

Baker, Alisa J., and Renee R. Deming. "Are Disqualifying Dispositions of Statutory Option Stock Subject to Withholding?" *Journal of Taxation* 72 (1990): 218.

Barron, Robert A. "Some Comments on the Usual Rule 144 Scenario and Related Matters." *Securities Regulation Law Journal* 25 (Winter 1997): 431.

"Broad-Based Stock Options Improve Corporate Performance, Offset Dilution (2000)" (citing Douglas Kruse, Joseph Blasi, Jim Sesil, and Maya Krumova). *Journal of Employee Ownership Law and Finance* 14, no. 1 (2001): 89.

Hevener, Mary. "Golden Parachutes: New Exemptions for Some People and Some Deals But Bigger 'Excess Parachutes.'" *Journal of Taxation* 96 (May 2002): 261.

_____. "Tax Withholding Changes Under Consideration for ISOs and Employee Stock Purchase Plans." *Tax Management Compensation Planning Journal* 18 (1990): 249.

Maldonado, Kirk F. "Rule 701: Its Parameters and Nuances." *The Journal of Employee Ownership Law and Finance* 14, no. 3 (summer 2002): 91.

Melcher, Peter J., and Warren Rosenbloom, "Transferable Options: When They Work, When They Don't." *Practical Tax Lawyer* 15, no. 1 (Fall 2000): 5.

Nuzum, R. "When Will a Change to an ISO Constitute a Modification?" *Journal of Taxation* 61 (1984): 406.

Olup, Linda. "Stock Options and Divorce." In *Stock Options: Beyond the Basics,* 3rd ed. Oakland, CA: NCEO, 2002.

Schneider, Carl. "Broker Non-votes and Abstentions: An Analysis of Legal Issues." Reprinted in *The Corporate Counsel,* May–June 1998.

Sweeney, Paul. "Stock Option Pitfalls and Strategies Du Jour." *Journal of Accountancy Online* 192, no. 4 (October 2001).

Topham, Matthew. "State Securities Law Considerations for Stock Option and

Stock Purchase Plans." In *Stock Options: Beyond the Basics*, 3rd ed. Oakland, CA: NCEO, 2002.

Periodicals

Corporate Counsel and *Corporate Executive* (Executive Press)

Employee Ownership Report (NCEO)

The Journal of Employee Ownership Law and Finance (NCEO)

The Stock Plan Advisor (NASPP)

WorldatWork Journal (formerly *ACA Journal*) (WorldatWork)

Web Sites

www.firstgov.gov (U.S. government Web portal)

www.fwcook.com (Frederic W. Cook & Co.)

www.globalequity.org (Global Equity Organization)

www.mystockoptions.com (myStockOptions.com)

www.naspp.com (National Association of Stock Plan Professionals)

www.nceo.org (National Center for Employee Ownership)

Index

About the Author

Alisa J. Baker is a nationally recognized equity compensation expert who specializes in counseling individuals and companies on the full range of compensation-related matters, including:

- Preparing and negotiating executive employment agreements, severance/separation agreements, consulting agreements, and individual equity arrangements, including representation of founders in merger and acquisition transactions;

- Designing, implementing, and providing counseling for all aspects of employee compensation, including stock option plans, non-equity performance plans, qualified/nonqualified deferred compensation arrangements, and fringe benefit programs;

- Counseling management and boards of directors on executive compensation assessment and compensation committee review procedures; and

- Expert witness and consulting services for equity and stock-option litigation

Alisa's comprehensive book on equity compensation, *The Stock Options Book* (NCEO: 2002–2006) is the core required text for the Santa Clara University/Certified Equity Professional Institute (CEPI) credential program. Her extensive list of published work includes articles in publications ranging from the *Wall Street Journal* to the *Journal of Taxation*. Alisa's speaking engagements include many appearances before industry groups, including the National Association of Stock Plan

Professionals (NASPP), the National Center for Employee Ownership (NCEO), the E*TRADE Business Solutions Group, and the Society for Human Resources Management (SHRM). She is a founding member of the CEPI Board of Advisors and currently serves on the MyStockOptions Board of Advisors, the NCEO Stock Option Advisory Board, and the Review Board for the National Board of Certified Option Advisors. She is a member of the editorial board of the *Journal of Employee Ownership Law and Finance*.

Alisa received her B.A. and M.A. in English with honors, and her M.S. in higher education with distinction, from the University of Pennsylvania in Philadelphia. She earned her J.D. with honors from Georgetown University Law Center in Washington, D.C., where she was an associate editor of the Georgetown Law Journal. She has been a teaching fellow at Stanford Law School and an adjunct lecturer in executive compensation at Golden Gate University.

Before establishing Levine & Baker LLP with partner Richard E. Levine, Alisa was a partner with the Mountain View law firm of GCA Law Partners LLP (formerly General Counsel Associates), and before that practiced with the employee benefits group at Wilson Sonsini Goodrich & Rosati and the tax group at Fenwick & West. During 2000-2001, she served as executive vice president/general counsel of Snapfish.com Corporation in San Francisco.

Alisa may be contacted by telephone at 415-391-3510 or by email at *abaker@levinebakerlaw.com*.

About the NCEO and Its Publications

The National Center for Employee Ownership (NCEO) is widely considered to be the leading authority in employee ownership in the U.S. and the world. Established in 1981 as a nonprofit information and membership organization, it now has over 2,500 members, including companies, professionals, unions, government officials, academics, and interested individuals. It is funded entirely through the work it does.

The NCEO's mission is to provide the most objective, reliable information possible about employee ownership at the most affordable price possible. As part of the NCEO's commitment to providing objective information, it does not lobby or provide ongoing consulting services. The NCEO publishes a variety of materials on employee ownership and participation, holds dozens of seminars, Webinars, and conferences on employee ownership annually, and offers a variety of online courses. The NCEO's work includes extensive contacts with the media, both through articles written for trade and professional publications and through interviews with reporters. It has written or edited five books for outside publishers during the past two decades. Finally, the NCEO maintains an extensive Web site at *www.nceo.org*.

See the following page for information on membership benefits and fees. To join, see the order form at the end of this section, visit our Web site at *www.nceo.org,* or telephone us at 510-208-1300.

Membership Benefits

NCEO members receive the following benefits:

- The bimonthly newsletter, *Employee Ownership Report*, which covers ESOPs, stock options, and employee participation.

- Access to the members-only area of the NCEO's Web site, which includes a searchable database of well over 200 NCEO members who are service providers in this field, plus many other resources..

- Substantial discounts on publications and events produced by the NCEO (such as this book).

- The right to telephone the NCEO for answers to general or specific questions regarding employee ownership.

An introductory NCEO membership costs $80 for one year ($90 outside the U.S.) and covers an entire company at all locations, a single professional offering services in this field, or a single individual with a business interest in employee ownership. Full-time students and faculty members who are not employed in the business sector may join at the academic rate of $35 for one year ($45 outside the U.S.).

Selected NCEO Publications

The NCEO offers a variety of publications on all aspects of employee ownership and participation. Following are descriptions of our main publications.

We publish new books and revise old ones on a yearly basis. To obtain the most current information on what we have available, visit our extensive Web site at *www.nceo.org* or call us at 510-208-1300.

Stock Options and Related Plans

- This book, *The Stock Options Book*, is a straightforward, comprehensive overview covering the legal, accounting, regulatory, and design issues involved in implementing a stock option or stock purchase plan, including "broad-based" plans covering most or all employees. It is our main book on the subject and possibly the most popular book in the field.

$25 for NCEO members, $35 for nonmembers

- *Selected Issues in Equity Compensation* (formerly titled *Stock Options: Beyond the Basics* and then *Selected Issues in Stock Options*) is more detailed and specialized than *The Stock Options Book*, with chapters on issues such as repricing, securities issues, and evergreen options.

  $25 for NCEO members, $35 for nonmembers

- *Beyond Stock Options* is a complete guide, including annotated model plans, to phantom stock, restricted stock, stock appreciation rights, performance awards, and more. Includes a CD with plan documents.

  $35 for NCEO members, $50 for nonmembers

- *The Stock Administration Book* is a comprehensive guide to administering stock options and other equity compensation plans. It includes a CD with templates for immediate use.

  $50 for NCEO members, $75 for nonmembers

- *Equity Compensation in a Post-Expensing World* is a collection of essays on strategies for choosing and structuring equity compensation plans when expensing is required.

  $25 for NCEO members, $35 for nonmembers

- *The Employee's Guide to Stock Options* is a guide for the everyday employee that explains in an easy-to-understand format what stock is and how stock options work.

  $25 for both NCEO members and nonmembers

- *Tax and Securities Sources for Equity Compensation* is a compilation of statutory and regulatory material relevant to the study of equity compensation.

  $35 for NCEO members, $50 for nonmembers

- *Model Equity Compensation Plans* provides examples of incentive stock option, nonqualified stock option, and stock purchase plans, together with brief explanations of the main documents. A disk is included with copies of the plan documents in formats any word processing program can open.

  $50 for NCEO members, $75 for nonmembers

- *Current Practices in Stock Option Plan Design* is a highly detailed report on our survey of companies with broad-based stock option plans conducted in 2000. It includes a detailed examination of plan design, use, and experience broken down by industry, size, and other categories.

  $25 for NCEO members, $35 for nonmembers

- *Communicating Stock Options* offers practical ideas and information about how to explain stock options to a broad group of employees. It includes the views of experienced practitioners as well as detailed examples of how companies communicate tax consequences, financial information, and other matters to employees.

  $35 for NCEO members, $50 for nonmembers

- *Employee Stock Purchase Plans* covers how ESPPs work, tax and legal issues, administration, accounting, communicating the plan to employees, and research on what companies are doing with their plans. The book includes sample plan documents.

  $25 for NCEO members, $35 for nonmembers

- *Stock Options, Corporate Performance, and Organizational Change* presents the first serious research to examine the relationship between broadly granted stock options and company performance, and the extent of employee involvement in broad option companies.

  $15 for NCEO members, $25 for nonmembers

- *Equity-Based Compensation for Multinational Corporations* describes how companies can use stock options and other equity-based programs across the world to reward a global work force. It includes a country-by-country summary of tax and legal issues as well as a detailed case study.

$25 for NCEO members, $35 for nonmembers

- *Incentive Compensation and Employee Ownership* takes a broad look at how companies can use incentives, ranging from stock plans to cash bonuses to gainsharing, to motivate and reward employees. It includes both technical discussions and case studies.

  $25 for NCEO members, $35 for nonmembers

- *Tax and Securities Sources for Equity Compensation* is a compilation of statutory and regulatory material relevant to the study of equity compensation.

  $35 for NCEO members, $50 for nonmembers

Employee Stock Ownership Plans (ESOPs)

- *The ESOP Reader* is an overview of the issues involved in establishing and operating an ESOP. It covers the basics of ESOP rules, feasibility, valuation, and other matters, and then discusses managing an ESOP company, including brief case studies. The book is intended for those with a general interest in ESOPs and employee participation.

  $25 for NCEO members, $35 for nonmembers

- *Selling to an ESOP* is a guide for owners, managers, and advisors of closely held businesses. It explains how ESOPs work and then offers a comprehensive look at legal structures, valuation, financing, and other matters, especially the tax-deferred section 1042 "rollover" that allows owners to indefinitely defer capital gains taxation on the sale proceeds.

  $25 for NCEO members, $35 for nonmembers

- *Leveraged ESOPs and Employee Buyouts* discusses how ESOPs borrow money to buy out entire companies, purchase shares from a retiring owner, or finance new capital. Beginning with a primer on leveraged ESOPs and their uses, it then discusses contribution limits, valuation, accounting, feasibility studies, financing sources, and more.

$25 for NCEO members, $35 for nonmembers

- The *Model ESOP* contains a sample ESOP plan, with alternative provisions given to tailor the plan to individual needs. It also includes a section-by-section explanation of the plan and other supporting materials.

$50 for NCEO members, $75 for nonmembers

- *ESOP Valuation* brings together and updates where needed the best articles on ESOP valuation that we have published in our *Journal of Employee Ownership Law and Finance,* described below.

$25 for NCEO members, $35 for nonmembers

- *How ESOP Companies Handle the Repurchase Obligation* includes both essays and research on the subject.

$25 for NCEO members, $35 for nonmembers

- The *ESOP Committee Guide* describes the different types of ESOP committees, the range of goals they can address, alternative structures, member selection criteria, training, committee life cycle concerns, and other issues.

$25 for NCEO members, $35 for nonmembers

- *Wealth and Income Consequences of Employee Ownership* is a detailed report on a comparative study of ESOP companies in Washington State that found ESOP companies pay more and provided better benefits than other companies.

$10 for NCEO members, $15 for nonmembers

- *ESOPs and Corporate Governance* covers everything from shareholder rights to the impact of Sarbanes-Oxley to choosing a fiduciary.

$25 for NCEO members, $35 for nonmembers

- The *ESOP Communications Sourcebook* provides ideas for and examples of communicating an ESOP to employees and customers. It includes a CD with communications materials, including many documents that readers can customize for their own companies.

  $35 for NCEO members, $50 for nonmembers

- *Executive Compensation in ESOP Companies* discusses executive compensation issues, special ESOP considerations, and the first-ever survey of executive compensation in ESOP companies.

  $25 for NCEO members, $35 for nonmembers

- *S Corporation ESOPs* introduces the reader to how ESOPs work and then discusses the legal, valuation, administrative, and other issues associated with S corporation ESOPs.

  $25 for NCEO members, $35 for nonmembers

Employee Involvement and Management

- *Ownership Management* draws upon the experience of the NCEO and of leading employee ownership companies to discuss how to build a culture of lasting innovation by combining employee ownership with employee involvement programs. It includes specific ideas and examples of how to do this.

  $25 for NCEO members, $35 for nonmembers

- *Front Line Finance Facilitator's Manual* gives step-by-step instructions for teaching business literacy, emphasizing ESOPs.

  $50 for NCEO members, $75 for nonmembers

- *Front Line Finance Diskette* contains the workbook for participants in electronic form (so a copy can be printed out for everyone) in the *Front Line Finance* course.

  $50 for NCEO members, $75 for nonmembers

Other

- *Section 401(k) Plans and Employee Ownership* focuses on how company stock is used in 401(k) plans, both in stand-alone 401(k) plans and combination 401(k)–ESOP plans ("KSOPs").

  $25 for NCEO members, $35 for nonmembers

- *Employee Ownership Concepts in Nonprofits and Government* discusses how nonprofits and governmental units, despite their lack of stock, can implement employee ownership concepts and build a more productive and satisfying ownership culture in the workplace.

  $25 for NCEO members, $35 for nonmembers

- *Employee Ownership and Corporate Performance* reviews the research that has been done on the link between company stock plans and various aspects of corporate performance.

  $25 for NCEO members, $35 for nonmembers

- *Ownership Solutions* is a booklet that discusses the various ways in which a company can share equity with its employees.

  $10 for NCEO members, $15 for nonmembers

- *The Journal of Employee Ownership Law and Finance* is the only professional journal solely devoted to employee ownership. Articles are written by leading experts and cover ESOPs, stock options, and related subjects in depth.

  One-year subscription (four issues):
  $75 for NCEO members, $100 for nonmembers

To join the NCEO as a member or to order any of the publications listed on the preceding pages, use the order form on the following page, use the secure ordering system on our Web site at www.nceo.org, or call us at 510-208-1300. If you join at the same time you order publications, you will receive the members-only publication discounts.

Order Form

To order, fill out this form and mail it with your credit card information or check to the NCEO at 1736 Franklin St., 8th Flr., Oakland, CA 94612; fax it with your credit card information to the NCEO at 510-272-9510; telephone us at 510-208-1300 with your credit card in hand; or order at our Web site, *www.nceo.org.* If you are not already a member, you can join now to receive member discounts on any publications you order.

Name

Organization

Address

City, State, Zip (Country)

Telephone   Fax   E-mail

Method of Payment: ❏ Check (payable to "NCEO")   ❏ Visa   ❏ M/C   ❏ AMEX

Credit Card Number

Signature   Exp. Date

Checks are accepted only for orders from the U.S. and must be in U.S. currency.

Title	Qty.	Price	Total

Tax: California residents add 8.75% sales tax (on publications only, not membership or Journal subscriptions)

Shipping: In the U.S., first publication $5, each add'l $1; elsewhere, we charge exact shipping costs to your credit card, plus a $10 handling surcharge; no shipping charges for membership or Journal subscriptions

Introductory NCEO Membership: $80 for one year ($90 outside the U.S.)

Subtotal	$
Sales Tax	$
Shipping	$
Membership	$
TOTAL DUE	$

Quantity Purchase Discounts

If your company would like to buy this book in quantity (10 or more) for its employees, a client company's employees, or others, we can sell it to you at a discount below the $25 members/$35 nonmembers price given above if you are an NCEO member or if you buy a high quantity. Contact us by e-mail at *nceo@nceo.org* or by phone at 510-208-1300 to work out the details.